Working with Families

Barbara F. Okun
Louis J. Rappaport

Department of Counselor Education
Northeastern University

Working with Families

An Introduction to Family Therapy

Okun/Rappaport/WORKING WITH FAMILIES

Brooks/Cole Publishing Company
A Division of Wadsworth, Inc.

Printed in the United States of America
10   9   '8   7   6   5   4

Library of Congress Cataloging in Publication Data

Okun, Barbara F.
  Working with families.

  Includes bibliographies and index.
  1. Family psychotherapy.   I. Rappaport, Louis J., 1941-
joint author.   II. Title.
RC488.5.039   616.8'915   79-16138

ISBN 0-8787-2234-3

Editor: Sarah Evans
Interior Design: Joanna Prudden Snyder
Cover Design: Elizabeth Rotchford
Illustrations: Jean Dorion Kauper

To our families, who have taught us at times more than we wanted to know about family systems but who have provided us with the love to enable us to learn and grow.

Sherman, Marcia, Jeffrey, and Douglas Okun

Maurice, Sonia, Bernard Rappaport, Linda Bennett
Adrienne Rappaport, Jason Bennett, Adam Rappaport

Contents

Preface

Over the years, we have seen an increasing need for a comprehensive introductory text in the area of family therapy theory and practice. The existing texts appear either to promulgate a single viewpoint or to introduce a variety of viewpoints, but with little attempt to integrate them into a conceptually sound framework. Thus students and instructors are dependent on time-consuming search for materials to help synthesize differing schools of thought. The idea for this book came from the suggestions of students in our family therapy courses, who shared our frustrations about the lack of an appropriate text.

Our purpose in writing this text and the accompanying manual has been to provide a comprehensive overview of the theories and major techniques of family therapy. The text is intended to introduce human service trainees and experienced practitioners alike to the growing specialized branch that is generally known as "family therapy"; the manual is intended to help readers integrate didactic and experiential learning.

As authors, we share an eclectic view of family therapy theory and practice that stems principally from an integration of systems theory and developmental theory. This integration has influenced our teaching, research, and clinical practice. Consequently, in this text we subsume communication theory and structural theory under family systems theory and attempt to combine their implications with those of developmental family theory. In this way, we arrive at a holistic position that uses communication, structural, and developmental theory in the assessment and treatment of family dysfunction.

A fundamental assumption of this text is that it is impossible to understand clients by separating them from their past and present contexts. Whether the client is an individual, a couple, a small group of family members, or an entire family, we believe that the client's behavior has full meaning only when viewed within the following: (1) its antecedents in the "distant" past of the family or origin; (2) its antecedents in the more immediate developmental history of the present family system; (3) its current sustaining variables within, as well as its implications for, the structures and communication styles of the present family system; and (4) its appropriateness as a response to the developmental challenges currently facing the family system and the individuals within it.

We strongly believe in a tripartite model of education: (1) didactic presentation of theoretical material; (2) structured activities that help one to experience the implications of the theoretical material, as well as to increase one's self-knowledge; and (3) case study providing an opportunity to integrate the first two types of learning. We have tried to implement at least two of the components of our tripartite model in this text by presenting the work of the major family therapy theorists and by including comprehensive references and stimulating case examples. Although there is obviously no substitute for actual experience, the exercises and activities in the manual attempt to implement the third component: through simulation of a variety of therapeutic situations and issues, they focus on promoting experiential learning, on integrating that learning with theoretical material, and on increasing self-awareness. This emphasis on self-awareness reflects our belief that to be effective family therapists, we must first recognize and deal with our own attitudes, values, and beliefs about families, marriage, parenting, and other family issues. We trust that this text and the training manual that accompanies it reflect our convictions.

We certainly do not intend to produce trained family therapists with the study of this material. Nor do we claim to cover all the schools of thought associated with family therapy. But we do hope to stimulate your interest, whether as novice or seasoned practitioner, and to encourage you to continue your study of what we believe is a most exciting, dynamic approach to helping people.

We wish to thank all the people who have encouraged and helped us. Our editor, Ed Murphy, has been enthusiastically supportive of the book and manual since their inception and has continuously responded to our needs in developing and completing them. Sarah Evans, our copy editor, has earned our unreserved gratitude and respect for her meticulous and sensitive editing of the manuscript. Our departmental colleagues and students have been continuously encouraging of our efforts and direction. In particular, Dr. Salvatore Rizzo has reviewed parts of the manuscript and has frequently supported us in our belief in the need for this text.

Our spouses, Sherman Okun and Linda Bennett, and our children Marcia, Jeffrey, and Douglas Okun, Adrienne Rappaport, Jason Bennett, and Adam Rappaport, have been incredibly patient and tolerant of our preoccupation with this project over the past two years. Needless to say, developing *Working with Families* at times took our energies away from our families in a way that perhaps only devoted families can understand.

Our thanks also go to Dr. Ann Cain, University of Maryland, Baltimore, and Dr. Linda White, Arizona State University, Tempe, who reviewed our initial outline and prospectus. We are especially grateful to Dr. Robert Phillip, University of Maryland, College Park, and Dr. Leslie Strong, University of Connecticut, Storrs, for their painstaking reviews of the final manuscript. We found their suggestions for the inclusion and organization of content invaluable.

Last, but not least, if each of us were writing this preface separately, each of us would want special mention made of the development of our relationship as coauthors, colleagues, and friends. Our experience has confirmed again that systems do work, that two people can work better than one and can challenge and learn from each other and still have fun in the process.

Barbara F. Okun, Ph.D.
Louis J. Rappaport, Ph.D.

Introduction

The evolution of family therapy theory and practice is currently at a stage where the integration of systems theory and developmental theory is not only possible, but is also a requisite for beginning to understand the subtleties of today's theory and practice. Although we base our view of family therapy theory and practice on this synthesis of systems theory and developmental theory, we also include in this text more generally known therapeutic strategies (such as those stemming from social learning theory and client-centered theory). However, we subsume these strategies as tactics under the rubric of our larger framework.

To facilitate our presentation and the integration of family systems theory with developmental family theory, we have organized the text into four major sections.

Section I presents the underlying conceptual framework for our approach to the theory and treatment of the family. Chapter 1 contains an overview of systems theory and developmental theory, while chapter 2 provides an overview of the historical antecedents of family therapy and its current status.

Section II presents a classification model of family theory along with six major theoretical viewpoints within a family systems approach. In chapter 3 we delineate the rationale for our classification scheme. Our intention is to highlight the subtle differences between and among communication and structural theorists rather than to present them as having separate, divergent viewpoints. In chapter 4 we explore the work of three major communication theorists—Don Jackson, Virginia Satir, and Jay Haley. In chapter 5 we turn our attention to the contributions of three major structural theorists—Murray Bowen, David Kantor, and Salvador Minuchin.

Section III integrates family systems theory with developmental family theory in three ways. It introduces the contention that family crisis may be the result of normal family development or of an idiosyncratic nondevelopmental dysfunction; in either case, family crisis is seen as the critical ingredient in facilitating substantial family change. Chapters 6 and 7 focus on the marital dyad as the key to the transformation of family structures and communication styles in the majority of developmental crises. Chapter 6 focuses on the couple as spouses, while chapter 7 focuses on the couple as parents. Finally, chapter 8 considers those family crises that are not developmental in nature. It integrates structural and communication theory to present a rationale for dividing nondevelopmental family crises into those that are induced by family members and those that are thrust upon a family system with no choice involved.

Section IV assesses the future directions in the field of family therapy. Chapter 9 reviews the current state of research in family therapy theory and practice, while chapter 10 examines a variety of professional issues currently facing the practitioner.

The manual is designed to be used simultaneously with the text. This design reflects our strong belief in the value of integrating experiential and didactic learning. Whereas the text contains the didactic theory and practice presentation, the manual contains lists of media, lists of training organizations, suggested readings that supplement the references in the text, case examples, individual and group exercises, activities, and annotated bibliographies.

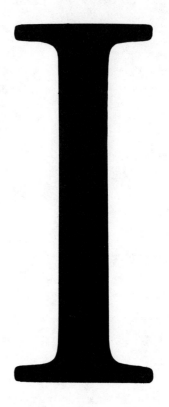

Overview:
Family Theory
and Therapy

The family is the primary unit of our society and serves as the social environment through which we are first introduced to the world. Our family of origin thus has a most significant impact on our psychological development.

In this section, we begin to define and view the family group as a system of interrelated members. Chapter 1 shows how this view is derived from systems theory and introduces you to the basic concepts and characteristics of systems theory. It also lays out a scheme for considering the developmental stages within the family life cycle. In doing so, it reviews the implications of individual developmental theory. Thus, chapter 1 depicts the family unit as a *system* that passes through a series of orderly *developmental* stages.

Family therapy is defined in chapter 2, where we begin to develop a philosophical orientation to viewing individual dysfunction in relation to the family system. After defining family therapy, we show how it emerged as a psychotherapeutic specialty in the past few decades by tracing its origins and development from a field of research into a growing field of practice. This overview of the "zeitgeist" of the mental health profession in the first half of this century gives us a better appreciation of the full impact of family therapy today. Chapter 2 concludes with an examination of the current status of family therapy and a discussion of the indications and contraindications for its use.

The Family Unit

Chapter

1

All animal species provide for some type of organizational structure during the time that an infant is too young to satisfy its own needs for food, shelter, and safety. The time involved may be a few years, as with lion cubs, or it may extend to two or more decades, as has become the norm for human beings in our culture.

This organizational structure forms a relatively brief portion of the entire life cycle of the individual in most species. Because the animal infant grows quickly, it is soon able to leave its parents and begin an independent life of its own, which results in the disbandment of the organizational structure. We may refer to this short-lived structure as a "family," but certainly not in the sense that we have come to know it in our species.

The human infant, whose development is slower and more complex than that of other animal species, not only has a "family" to provide for its early needs, but also remains connected with that family, in a variety of ways, for all of its life. As the human infant develops into childhood, and eventually into adulthood, the family to which it belongs grows and remains with it, rather than disbanding as in other species. In fact, the uniquely human capacity to conceptualize relationships allows one to "belong" to a family even when one has no actual contact. Indeed, long after an entire family has been lost, an individual may continue to "be" with them. Remember Hamlet who, when asked where he "saw" his deceased father, replied, "In my mind's eye, Horatio."

We will examine the family in two ways. The first is as an organizational structure that at any time in its existence has specific goals (one goal, for example, may be raising an infant), as well as strategies for working toward those goals. This is the family as a *system*. The second way we may understand the family is by examining it as an ongoing process of changing relationships among its members. These relationships evolve through a cycle that has predictable stages of development. This is the *developmental life cycle* of the family. Let us look at each of these views of family.

The Family Unit as a System

The notion of the family as a "system" has its roots in the general systems theory that was pioneered by Ludwig von Bertalanffy (Bertalanffy 1934). Bertalanffy's early formulations, based on his work in the biological sciences, saw the essential phenomena of life as individual entities called "organisms." An organism was defined as a form of life "composed of mutually dependent parts and processes standing in mutual interaction" (Bertalanffy 1968, p. 33). The organism was seen to have self-regulative capacities and to be intrinsically active. While it interacted with its surrounding environment, taking in matter and energy and sending out matter and energy in exchange, its primary motivation for behavior was in the autonomous activity resting *within* the organism itself.

Bertalanffy's work allowed social scientists to see that the formulation and derivation of interaction principles from biological, economic, and engineering sciences are valid for all systems, including systems of human interaction—that is, all systems, regardless of their content or functions, share the same general principles of organization and operation.

The Family and General Systems Theory

An *organizational structure* is defined as a system composed of a set of interdependent parts. A change in one part of the system will effect change in other parts of the system. The system itself has basic needs to adapt, survive, and maintain itself, and it therefore takes action and behaves. When conflict between the needs of the component parts and the goals of the system arises, system behavior attempts to regulate and control the behavior of the component parts. Control of the system is maintained by its structures and by its cybernetic principles of communication and feedback, which we will define shortly. Let us look at the characteristics and functions of a system by using the family system as an example.

One might begin defining a family system by paraphrasing Bertalanffy and defining it as "a dynamic order of *people* (along with their intellectual, emotional, and behavioral processes) standing in mutual interaction." This system would have a multitude of ways and styles of exchanging matter and energy with its environment, including the distinctive human capacity for imagining that an exchange has taken place even when it hasn't. It would have self-regulating capacities (moral, political, social, religious, economic, and idiosyncratic values and constraints). In addition, it would be intrinsically active—that is, one would not have to look outside the family system to understand a sudden shift in family dynamics.

Family Subsystems.   The family system consists of special functional units called *subsystems*. A subsystem may be a piece of a larger structure and at the same time also be a complete structure in itself. Let us illustrate this by looking at a family consisting of grandmother, father, mother, and two children. Together they comprise a family system with five members standing in mutual interaction with each other.

Within the system there are a myriad of smaller "combinations." The father-daughter-son unit, for example, is only a part of the five-person system. It is a subsystem of the larger structure. Yet, at the same time, it may have a life of its own, such as a special weekend project involving just the three members of this unit. In that sense, it is a system with even smaller units within it. The brother-sister unit is an example of a subsystem that may be active within the father-daughter-son unit.

The particularly human faculty of perspective may frequently complicate the exact description of what constitutes system or subsystem membership. As an example, let us look at one small subsystem within this family, the father-daughter unit. The only adult male in this family and the only female child in the family may certainly view this as a "father-daughter" subsystem. However, grandmother may view it with equal facility as a "son-granddaughter" subsystem, mother may see a "husband-daughter" subsystem, and son may view it as "father-sister." With each of these views come expectations for behavior, and, in this case, the adult male in the family is expected to behave simultaneously as "father," "son," and "husband." How he behaves may be interpreted differently by the members of the different subsystems to which he belongs. One's idea of "what's going on" in this family will obviously be filtered by one's perspective of the subsystem in which the "going on" is taking place. It is easy to see how a family system may be bursting not only with conflicting expectations for behavior, not all of which may be met simultaneously, but also with the disappointments that understandably but unfortunately ensue. Figure 1–1 maps out how this particular family system and its subsystems view the father-daughter relationships.

Other Family System Properties.   In addition to the larger concept of subsystems and their interaction with the larger family system, there are four general system properties that may be illustrated within the family system. These properties are *wholeness, feedback, homeostasis, equifinality.*

   Wholeness refers to the relationship between the total system and its parts. The system is an integrated, coherent entity that is more than the mere composite of independent elements. This wholeness transcends the sum of the system's component elements. A family consisting of Mother, Father, Sally, Johnny, and David Brown is viewed as a total interactional process that characterizes them as "the Browns"; it is not viewed as the sum of Mr. Brown, Mrs. Brown, Sally Brown, Johnny Brown, and David Brown. If Sally is away at college and you are going to visit the family, you are still going to visit "the Browns," not "the Browns minus Sally."

   Despite this wholeness, a change in one part of the system may cause a change in many parts (subsystems) of the larger system and in the larger system itself. Suppose that Mr. Brown comes for treatment because he is having difficulties with alcoholism and that he is cured of his alcoholism. This cure may have an impact on every subsystem within his family and on the total family system itself. For example, the subsystem of Mrs. Brown and her daughter Sally may be affected. Mrs. Brown may have to transfer her anger to Sally, since Mr. Brown will no

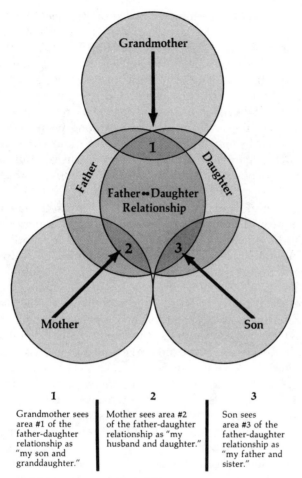

1	2	3
Grandmother sees area #1 of the father-daughter relationship as "my son and granddaughter."	Mother sees area #2 of the father-daughter relationship as "my husband and daughter."	Son sees area #3 of the father-daughter relationship as "my father and sister."

Figure 1–1   *Family Systems and Subsystems*

longer be a feasible target. Sally, in turn, may act more aggressively toward her younger brothers, Johnny and David. David may begin to suck his thumb and whimper because of Sally's aggression, and Mr. Brown himself may express resentment that his family is not behaving appreciatively toward his giving up drinking. All members of the Brown family may change their characteristics, as well as their ways of relating, because of one person's change in behavior. And the *whole* family system may be changed in a way that is greater than the sum of its individual changes. Thus, the system cannot be fully comprehended or represented by *summing* its subsystems. This principle is called *nonsummativity* by the systems theorists.

Feedback refers to the interactional process *among* the parts of the system. Feedback refers to *how* the elements within a system relate to each other. This process of feedback maintains the system's functioning. Feedback is not seen as linear cause and effect, wherein one event influences another event, which has consequences for a third event, which has an impact on a fourth event, and so on, never coming back to the original event. Feedback is instead seen as a circular or simultaneous process, wherein one event influences a second event, which in turn influences a third event, which may impact upon either the second or first event, triggering off a new cycle of responses. Thus, a response to a stimulus becomes a stimulus to further responses, which may immediately, or in time, affect the initial stimulus.

As an example, imagine the feedback system in the heating unit of a house. A drop in temperature in the room (A) is perceived by the thermostat (B), which turns on the furnace (C), which sends heat to the radiator (D), which raises the temperature in the room (A), whereupon the feedback process has returned to the initial stimulus.

This feedback system has the function of maintaining the temperature at a certain preselected level. The maintenance is called *homeostasis,* a concept referring to the dynamic balance of the system. In our example of the Brown family, the feedback (the family's behavioral responses to Mr. Brown's abstinence from drinking) eventually returns to Mr. Brown (which triggers his resentment at his family's behavior), and in consequence he may return to drinking, thereby maintaining the homeostatic balance, or stability, of the tension in the family. We will return to this concept of homeostasis in section II.

Equifinality refers to the results of the interactions among the parts of the system. These results may spring from different origins, but no matter where one begins, the same results are likely to occur. For example, a family who is scapegoating one of its members would probably blame that member for causing a family crisis regardless of who actually precipitated the crisis. Therefore, interactions are more significant than initial causal conditions, if such entities as causal conditions can be considered even to exist. Thus, to understand a family, one usually does not need to get a complete history of each member of the family, as the family pattern will be apparent from studying the current interactions of the family members. It is the nature of the organization of the system, the *interactional process*, that determines the *results* of the system.

All these system parts and processes—the systems and subsystems within the family and the properties of wholeness, feedback, homeostatic maintenance, and equifinality that regulate family transactions

—operate within the framework of two major system characteristics: family structures and family communications.

Family Structures and Communications. Structures and communication patterns within a family are not really separable. In fact, they define each other in many ways, and in many situations it is futile to attempt to assess which determined which.

By family *structures,* we mean not only the relationship of the subsystems to each other and to the whole system, but also the rules and regulations for control and maintenance of the family system. By family *communications,* we mean the process and manner in which the rules and regulations are implemented. As an example, consider a family in which one structure is an unwritten rule that says: "When Dad comes down in the morning and finds that daughter's dog has messed on the rug, he will communicate this observation to Mom, his wife, who will then see that daughter cleans up the mess." Imagine also that this family has the following communication pattern: Dad is ambivalent about his parenting prerogatives and so is not comfortable communicating directly with his daughter. Thus, when he does communicate, the tone of his voice carries this message: "Although I have asked you to do something [practically ordered you to], I do not really expect that you will do it [without creating a fuss that makes it really not worthwhile to have asked you]."

In this family, it is possible that the structure (Dad must ask Mom in order to get daughter to clean up) created the communication style (nonassertive message that assumes lack of compliance); or it could be that Dad's habitually communicating in a nonassertive way created the structure of Mom as the middle person. Clearly, this particular structure and communication style make each other possible. Numbers upon numbers of these structures and communication styles evolve and grow together to form the complex organization that we call the family system.

We will discuss these internal structures and styles of communication more fully in section II when we discuss the major theorists in the field of family therapy. Many of the more salient contributions of these theorists are based on the significance of structures and communication styles within the family system. However, since these structures and communication styles *evolve within the family system,* let us now consider the process that allows for their evolution, the developmental life cycle of the family.

Developmental Life Cycles

The increasing complexity of life in the last quarter of the twentieth century, the current variety of lifestyles, and the multiplicity of opportunities for social and institutional involvements are among the variables that make it difficult to generalize about the "normal" development of even one individual, let alone about the development of an entire family system. However, despite the many exceptions, people still do marry, have children, raise them, launch them toward their own careers and families, and then grow old with their partners. This sequence of events comprises the developmental life cycle of the family. The events themselves—marrying, child raising, launching of children, and so forth—may be viewed as "stages" in the ongoing evolution of the family system.

Before looking at what are currently accepted as the developmental stages in the family life cycle, let us examine the concept of the individual life cycle, which provides the conceptual framework underlying the notion of the developmental life cycle of the family.

Individual Life Cycle

The riddle "What walks on four legs in the morning, two legs in the afternoon, and three legs in the evening?" is as old as antiquity. It is a rather poetic encapsulation of the life cycle of the individual, who crawls in infancy, walks independently in maturity, and hobbles with a cane in old age. Shakespeare's perception was less complimentary:

> Life's but a walking shadow, a poor player
> That struts and frets his hour upon the stage
> And then is heard no more. It is a tale
> Told by an idiot, full of sound and fury,
> Signifying nothing.
>
> (*Macbeth*, Act V, Scene V)

Throughout the centuries and across cultures, literature is replete with descriptions of and assumptions about the life cycle. However, it has only been in this century that the serious study of human development has added substantially to the contributions of the early philosophers and poets.

Notable among those who pioneered the clinical notion of the individual life cycle are Carl Jung, Charlotte Buhler, and Erik Erikson. Let us briefly review their key contributions to the concept of normal individual development before we turn to the concept of the developmental life cycle of the family.

Stages of Development. Carl Gustav Jung, through his clinical studies and careful observations of his own pattern of development, was perhaps the first social scientist to delineate a theory of human development that emphasized adult development (Jung 1971). Jung paid little attention to childhood, arguing that while children may be a problem, they rarely have problems that are truly their own. Whatever problems they have are the creations of their parents, educators, or physicians. (It is striking to see, half a century later, how many family therapists and theoreticians agree that childhood behavior problems and symptomatology have their etiology in a larger parental system.)

Jung saw "youth," which extended from puberty into the thirties, as the prelude to the real work of life: adulthood and the process of individuation. For Jung, adulthood and individuation involved the integration of the various intrapsychic forces within the individual. Jung believed that through such integration the individual gains a sense of autonomy and self-sufficiency.

Jung postulated an *expansion-contraction* type of adult development. During the first half of adulthood, the thirties and forties, one expands one's life experiences by focusing on the development of family and career. During the latter half of adult life, a contraction occurs. This contraction involves a "turning inward," where the individual may find personal meaning and wholeness in life and the ability to move toward and accept death.

Charlotte Buhler and her students studied biographies and autobiographies collected in the 1930s in Vienna. From their sifting and sorting, an orderly progression of "phases" seemed to emerge and delineate individual development more fully than Jung's presentations. Buhler (1968) grouped the experiences, attitudes, and accomplishments of the individual into five *biological* phases: (1) progressive growth—up to age 15; (2) continued growth augmented by the ability to reproduce sexually—age 15–25; (3) stability of growth—age 25–45; (4) loss of sexual reproductive ability—age 45–65; and (5) regressive growth and biological decline—age 65 on.

The following five *developmental* life stages, which parallel the five biological phases, emerged:

Age	Phase
0–15	Child at home; prior to self-determination of goals
15–25	Preparatory expansion and experimental self-determination of goals
25–45	Culmination: definite and specific self-determination of goals
45–65	Self-assessment of the results of striving for these goals
65 up	"Experience of fulfillment or failure, with the remaining years spent in either continuance of previous activities or a return to the need-satisfying orientations of childhood"*

Of course, there is considerable individual variation in any such scheme. Ages are understood to reflect societal events and broad ranges. For example, "age 65 up" is an approximation of "retirement."

In more recent work, Buhler has emphasized the process of *goal setting* within these various phases. Goals may be personal, familial, and occupational. They are set within the first two phases, fulfilled during the third and fourth phases, and then reevaluated and reaffirmed, consolidated, or abandoned during the later years.

We see then that for both Jung and Buhler, individual development is an orderly process; its general stages include growth, consolidation, and contraction. There is a definite trend towards expansion and achievement in the early adult years, with more attention paid to reflection and introspection in the later years.

Erikson's theory of individual development is based on his own clinical experiences and shares the general expansion-contraction format. However, his theory is much more comprehensive than either Jung's or Buhler's. Incorporating much of his own Freudian orientation toward human development, Erikson (1963, 1968) postulated eight stages (ages) of individual development. They are each *critical transition points* in a developmental scheme from birth through death.

Each of Erikson's stages, which are depicted in table 1–1, presents a different developmental challenge. The alternative outcomes to how the individual meets the challenge are described by a pair of concepts. One concept indicates the positive growth that is inherent in successfully meeting the developmental challenge; the other indicates the consequence of an unsuccessful resolution of the challenge. The last

---

Table 1-1 Erikson's Eight Stages of Psychological Development

Stage	Age	Positive Growth		Unsuccessful Resolution	Radius of Significant Relationships
1	Infancy: birth–1 year	Basic trust	vs.	Basic mistrust	Maternal person
2	Early childhood: 1–3 years	Autonomy	vs.	Shame and doubt	Parental persons
3	Childhood: 3–6 years	Initiative (ego ideal)	vs.	Guilt (conscience)	Nuclear family
4	School age: 6–12 years	Industry	vs.	Inferiority	Neighborhood and school
5	Adolescence and youth: 13–22 years	Identity	vs.	Identity confusion	Peer groups (same sex); leaders and heroes
6	Young adult: 22–30 years	Intimacy	vs.	Isolation	Partners in friendship, sex, competition, cooperation (opposite sex)
7	Adulthood: 30–50 years	Generativity	vs.	Stagnation and self-absorption	Care for a new generation; regeneration of society
8	Mature age: 50–death	Integrity	vs.	Despair	Mankind; family of man

column of table 1–1 indicates the people who might be involved in significant relationships at each stage of development.

Erikson's first four stages follow the Freudian scheme of child development. The last four stages have more relevance to Buhler's and Jung's concepts of adult development and are less well formulated than the first four stages.

Stage five, "identity versus identity confusion," begins as one enters adolescence and faces the challenges that academic and/or vocational training, occupational choice, and mate selection pose. The individual who successfully completes this stage is prepared to meet the challenge of the next stage.

Stage six, "intimacy versus isolation," implies more than the sexual intimacy of which the adolescent is capable. Erikson had in mind a deeper relationship, which, while it might include sexuality, is founded upon the capacity for a mature psychosocial relationship with another individual, for a full sharing of one's "self" with another.

Stage seven, "generativity versus stagnation," speaks to the years during which the individual produces his or her life's work. *Generativity* refers to the contribution that outlives the individual. Although the individual may accomplish this generative work within the span of a few years, the period usually extends from young adulthood through old age. Many individuals attempt to meet the challenge of this stage through parenthood and/or career achievements.

The last stage, "integrity versus despair," is truly the fruition of the first seven stages in the sense that it builds upon the successful resolution of the challenges that each of the earlier stages poses. This last stage is the time for the final assessment and review, the time to determine whether one's life has made a meaningful contribution to human life. This stage may be triggered by mandated retirement, serious illness, or impending death. It involves an acceptance of old age and death and requires that the individual come to terms with the future as well as the past.

In the last few years, many researchers have begun to build upon the work of Jung, Buhler, and Erikson. More recent studies (Levenson 1978; Gould 1972; Lowenthal, Thurner, and Chiriboga 1975; Neugarten 1976) have paved the way for more specific delineation within the developmental stages of these models. These studies have paid particular attention to mid-life development, the developmental cycles of men and of women, mid-life career change, and so forth.

For our purposes, we need to recognize some very general but significant developmental assumptions that can be made from the contributions of Jung, Buhler, and Erikson, as well as from the theory developed by the more recent researchers. The first assumption is that although childhood and adolescence may be past, the individual does not simply and finally become an adult. Adulthood is a continuous "becoming" in itself. Development does not stop with adolescence; the life of an individual is a process of passing through a normal series of developmental stages from birth until death. The second assumption is that the movement from one stage to the next is facilitated by the successful management of the critical challenge posed during the preceding stage. Thus, one cannot be fully prepared to meet the challenge of a later stage without having mastered the developmental tasks of the previous stage. Perhaps implicit in the first two assumptions is the third, that each stage is different from, and no less important than, any other in the developmental scheme.

Let us remember that not all individuals pass through all the developmental stages in the same way or at the same pace. Some may have difficulty at an early stage, and this early difficulty may thwart individual development and be the cause of dysfunction in the family system. Also, as we shall see in chapter 6, dysfunction in a couple system often emerges from the irregular individual development of each partner.

Let us now turn to the concept of the life cycle of the family to see whether the developmental principles of the individual life cycle are applicable to the family unit.

Family Life Cycle

The family album, chock-full of photographs and perhaps supplemented with audio and videotape, documents the "milestones" of early life. We see when baby had the first bath, took the first steps, and so on. The milestones of later life are not always recorded for posterity with such conscientiousness as the early milestones, but they are nevertheless equally important in an individual's life. These later milestones include one's first job, one's first "real" departure from home, one's first marriage, perhaps even one's first divorce—and not necessarily in that order.

The later milestones, which involve moving the individual out of a family of origin and into the development of a family of his or her own, form a bridge between one system and another and imply different changes for each family. For the family of origin, these later milestones are another step in the completion of a cycle. For the family into which the individual moves, they mark the beginning of an entirely new cycle.

Let us consider the cycle of family life by examining the stages of a general model that has evolved over the last three decades.

Eight-Stage Model. Early work by Duvall and Hill (1948) and subsequent refinements of that work by Rodgers (1964), Hill and Rodgers (1964), and Duvall (1971) have established the validity of considering the family life cycle from a developmental point of view. Duvall postulated a cycle of eight stages through which the family passes in the normal cycle of its development. These stages are:

1. Beginning family
2. Infant family
3. Preschool family
4. School-age family
5. Adolescent family
6. Launching family
7. Postparental family
8. Aging family

Kimmel (1974) suggests a slight refinement of these stages to include a ninth stage that precedes the other eight. This ninth stage is called "premarriage." In premarriage, Kimmel details the complexity of personal and cultural factors that must be integrated in order for each member of the couple to date, love, and decide to marry. Let us, however, look more carefully at each of the eight major stages.

Stage 1. *Beginning Family*: The first stage of the family life cycle begins with marriage and continues until the first child is born. The major work of this stage involves the marriage partners' learning how to function as a new dyad, a couple system. This initial stage presents all sorts of boundary issues—for example, our dyad versus your parents and mine; our dyad versus your siblings and mine; our dyad versus your friends and mine; our dyad versus your professional colleagues and obligations and mine. The negotiation and renegotiation of new boundaries, the sorting and resorting of "pecking orders" and priorities, and the establishment of new rules (spoken or unspoken) about who speaks for whom are some of the immediate major challenges to be met.

On a more mundane level, there are the "profound" issues, such as: Will the toilet seat be left up or down? Who puts the dishes away and who takes out the trash? Should we have one checking account or two? And what could be more relevant to communication theory than the subtleties involved in deciding by whose names the newly marrieds will be known in the world?

The resolution of the major and minor issues of this initial stage in the family life cycle may establish major patterns that will endure over the entire life cycle of the family. These issues include: How do we deal with conflict? How will control and feelings be handled in this family? In what ways will we regulate our boundaries with the outside world? Who is responsible for whom in this family, and under what conditions?

It is in this initial stage that the communication styles, power dynamics, and boundary and relationship structures—keys in the theories we will cover in section II—begin to be formulated and developed.

The couple may arrive at their first major family crisis because of failure and frustration in resolving the early challenges. Failure and frustration can result from unrealistic fantasies of the "ideal marriage," from the individual's experiences in his or her family of origin, and from different styles of communication and negotiation. When a couple faces a major crisis, they may successfully resolve it alone or through the intervention of friends, counseling, or therapy. Regardless of how they resolve it, their need in the midst of the crisis is for change and growth. If they are able to resolve the conflict, they move toward growth. An alternative solution to successful resolution may be a divorce, the incidence of which, as we know, rises to a peak during the early years of marriage. However, there are other alternatives; one common method of moving the dyad to "change" is to make it become a triad—that is, to have a child. This is not to imply that the vast majority of couples have their first child in an attempt to resolve the difficult challenges of the marital dyad. We wish only to indicate that for some couples "triangling in" a third party may be a superficial style of conflict resolution.

In the case of the child conceived to "save the marriage," the style of conflict resolution is unfortunate, for it usually creates the illusion of change in the system when, in all probability, the failures to establish styles of conflict resolution, rules for boundary regulation, and so forth, are merely submerged during the excitement of the pregnancy and the new baby and will simply emerge at some later time. In a similar vein, couples who could not successfully communicate and negotiate needs for "special time" together before the arrival of a child have little hope of expressing needs more effectively once the baby arrives and becomes the focus of attention. Couples who have not renegotiated power and control issues with families of origin, who have not redrawn boundaries between themselves and their parents before the arrival of the new baby, have little hope of more successfully drawing those lines once the new grandparents appear. Thus, the critical importance of successfully negotiating the challenges of this first stage in the family life cycle cannot be overestimated. Couples who manage these initial challenges may then look forward to the next stage in their family life cycle by planning for children.

Stage 2. *Infant Family*: This stage begins with the first pregnancy and the birth of the first child and continues until that child becomes a "preschooler," usually between ages three and five.

As carefully as the young couple may have planned for all the changes in communications and structures that a three-person system implies, the reality of it is usually quite something else. The husband may feel that his wife devotes proportionately too much time to the new member of the system. The wife may feel suddenly restricted to one member of the family and "tied" down to the borders of the family, while her husband sails "free" in the outside world. Even couples who have not romanticized marriage and who have successfully met the challenges of the first stage (the beginning family) may still have unrealistic notions of what parenthood entails. Thus, the utility of communication patterns and styles of structure regulation may be severely tested.

During this stage the couple must make some major decisions. Couples who submerged earlier failures and even those who were successful in the first stage must answer some awesome questions (unfortunately seldom put so explicitly), such as: How will our family system share power and affect? How and why will we fight? What mechanisms are needed here for all of us—each in our own way—to implement our personal and family goals? After this stage, divorce rates decline progressively.

Thus, the infant family is a crucial turning point in the life of the family. Persons who had the single role of spouse must now assume the double role of spouse/parent. Responsibility as providers for each other becomes responsibility as provider for "all of us." One of the major steps to adulthood has been taken.

Stage 3. *Preschool Family*: This stage occurs when the oldest child in the family is between the ages of three and five. In several parts of the country, children may actually begin school full time at age five or earlier. With the fuller implementation of Federal Public Law 94–142, which mandates special educational programs for physically and/or emotionally handicapped children who are between the ages of three and twenty-one, more and more three-year olds may no longer be considered "preschoolers." Nevertheless, this family stage begins after the couple and their child have adjusted to the initial challenges of the new triad and ends when that youngster attends school full time.

This stage presents the couple with many parenting challenges. Psychoanalytic theory and many other theories of development see this stage in the child's life as one of tremendous, significant emotional growth, setting the stage for what occurs in later life. From our systems theory perspective, we would argue not only that the child passes through and attempts to resolve certain psychosexual stages of development, but also that the parents relive and perhaps finally come to terms with some of their own psychosexual development in the process. In other words, the child's development has a cybernetic effect on the parents' unresolved issues with each person's responses to the challenges of this stage having a further impact on other members of the family system.

Similarly, at the same time that the parents are socializing the child (and anyone remotely connected with raising children knows this), the child is quite effectively "socializing" the parents. We will speak more specifically about the dimensions of parenting in chapter 7. It is sufficient to acknowledge at this point that this third stage is one in which *everyone* grows up a little.

Stage 4. *School-Age Family*: This fourth stage begins with the child entering school full time and ends when that child reaches puberty. This may be a time of considerable system adjustment, for as the child is no longer in the home full time, the mother has the opportunity to "escape" the mother-housewife syndrome. She may return to work, go back to school, and/or pursue avocational interests. Although during stage three many parents place their children in day care or some other type of caretaking situation so that both parents may work, it is really in stage four that the majority of families make this system shift.

During this stage the family system becomes vulnerable to feedback from outside systems, namely, the school and the neighborhood. Within the family, more sharing, a "renegotiation" of boundaries and responsibilities, becomes a critical adjustment. For example, Dad may share some of his "breadwinning" prowess with Mom. In turn, as her time becomes budgeted more tightly, Mom may wish to share many of her "housewifing" chores with Dad. Both of them must share whatever "guilt" they experience when their youngster can't just "come home after school" or has difficulty accommodating to a new, different system—that of the school. How the couple communicates and how they renegotiate their boundaries within the context of these new stresses are the critical tasks of this stage. The dividends to be reaped from the sharing of the financial, social-parenting responsibilities may help to cement substantial bonds between the members of the couple as their relationship blossoms into full maturity.

As we will see in chapter 7, couples who attempt to avoid these tasks by communicating and negotiating through their children are merely postponing the tasks, *not* avoiding them. Eventually they will be forced to come to terms one way or another with the conflict that results from unsuccessful resolution.

Stage 5. *Adolescent Family*: Between the time that the first child reaches puberty and the time that he or she leaves home, the family system is usually at its largest size. Family concerns increasingly focus on the outside world as the adolescent brings home "what's happening" for the edification of the older generation. The adolescent's interests may range widely: selection of a college or a vocational training program; sexuality; steady intimate relationships; alcohol and other substance use and abuse problems.

During this stage the adolescent challenges and tests the family's rules and regulations concerning privacy, control, and responsibility. Many changes, sometimes as resolutions to crises, begin to transform the established system. Again, the way in which the critical tasks of communication and boundary negotiation have been resolved in past stages will affect the resolution of the challenges of this stage. In chapters 6 and 7 we will discuss another factor that affects the family system at this stage—that is, the parents' ways of coping with their own mid-life transitions during this period.

Depending upon whom you study, the "generation gap" does or does not appear. Bengston (1971) found that young people tend to perceive greater differences between themselves and their parents and that parents, and especially grandparents, have a "developmental" stake in minimizing these differences. However, even with the tendency of young people to see greater differences, a national poll of young adults aged eighteen to twenty-four, taken in 1968 during the stress of the Vietnam War protests, revealed that fewer than one-fourth of those polled felt there was a substantial difference between their values and those of their parents (Bengston 1971).

Stage 6. *Launching Family*: This stage is the time of "letting go." The degree of differentiation of self the young adult has achieved, the complexities of triangulation, the double binds and enmeshments—all come to the forefront as parents and children prepare to leave each other. The interactional patterns that the young adult has learned within the family system will determine the types of interactions he or she can achieve with people outside of the family system.

The way in which the "family cutoff" (Minuchin 1974) is made determines whether the young adult takes a responsive (choosing) position or a reactive (obligated) position in relation to the family he or she has left. Given an appropriate and effective "launching," the young adult may return to visit without the anger that accompanies a feeling of "having to be there." On the other hand, with an equally effective launching, the young adult may not interact very much with the family of origin at all and yet avoid the guilt attached to the obligated feeling of "but I really should." Effective launchings enable young adults to see that although they might be able to help a troubled family system, it is clearly not their role in the situation.

During this stage both members of the couple subsystem face the prospect of being alone together again for the first time in twenty to twenty-five years. Other potential sources of stress and crises are the physical and emotional strains that the woman encounters in renegotiating her time. This may involve launching a new career, resuming an old one, or finding new avocational activities. Another source of stress may be the man's involvement in putting the "finishing touches" on his own career expectations.

We will see in chapter 6 how sexuality takes on a new dimension for the couple at this time. Many women report an increased interest in sexuality, possibly related to genuine but unfounded fears of losing sexual satisfaction during menopause, or possibly related to their no longer fearing pregnancy. On the other hand, many men report a decreased interest in sexual activity, which may be related to their investing substantial energy in vocational or avocational pursuits. To the extent that impotence becomes a primary problem in itself, it is likely to be related to other primary problems, such as a monotonous sexual relationship, the type of energy drain we have just described, or anxiety about personal adequacy occasioned by the unaccustomed lack of parental responsibilities.

Stage 7. *Postparental Family*: In the folk myth of our culture, this stage is characterized by the "empty-nest syndrome." The implication is that members of the couple, now alone and childless, experience substantial dissatisfaction with each other and the relationship. The research in the field actually indicates the contrary. Glenn (1975) found that only 6 percent of the wives who were polled, and none of the husbands, clearly considered the quality of their lives to be worse after the children left home. In six national surveys middle-aged women whose children had left home reported somewhat greater happiness and enjoyment of life, as well as considerably greater marital happiness, than did women of a similar age with a child or children living at home (Glenn 1975). (Single parents, widows, and widowers may not handle the transition into the postparental role with the same facility as two-parent families; more study of the difficulties encountered by these special parents is needed.)

Thus, for the average two-parent family, the challenges of the postparental stage, although they may be numerous, do not seem to be of the "empty-nest" variety. In fact, many couples at this stage report that the relief they experience from not having turbulent adolescents and young adults living at home, financial burdens, and so on, far outweighs the loneliness or bereavement they experience at the loss of the major function of parenting.

Moreover, mean standard scores on marital satisfaction at each stage of an eight-stage family life cycle, measured by no fewer than three reputable inventories of marital satisfaction (Rollins and Cannon 1974), indicate an increase in marital satisfaction for men and for women as they move from the adolescent family stage to the launching stage, and another increase in marital satisfaction—again for both men and women—as they move from the launching stage to the postparental stage.

The challenges of the postparental stage include two major role changes. At about this time the couple's own parents are usually old enough to require care. Therefore, just as the couple step out of the child-care role, they may find themselves stepping into a parent-care role. And eventually the couple will have to deal with the death and loss of their parents, which at any age constitutes one of the major steps into adulthood.

The other major role change facing the couple in the postparental stage involves the probability that they will become grandparents. Having renegotiated the boundaries between themselves and their children when the children left home, they must now negotiate new boundaries in order to enter the new and different systems of their children's families. How they negotiate these new boundaries will be affected by the history of their relationship with their children and by the manner in which they passed through the previous stages of the family life cycle.

Neugarten and Weinstein (1964) pioneered a reconceptualization of this stage. They identified five different styles of grandparenting. These involve: (1) the "formal" grandparent, who leaves parenting to the parent, but has the prerogative of special times or favors with the grandchildren; (2) the "surrogate parent," more often the grandmother, who is allowed parental responsibility for the child by the parents; (3) the "reservoir of family wisdom," who is still in a position of authority, dispensing special "wisdom" or skills; (4) the "funseeker," frequently in his or her late forties or early fifties, not "old" by our current standards, who actively joins with the grandchildren in play; and (5) the "distant figure," absent on most occasions, who has sporadic and peripheral contact with the grandchildren. The first three types of grandparenting roles are of a more traditional variety that is associated with past generations. The last two are increasingly found in current family systems.

Stage 8. *Aging Family*: This last stage begins with retirement and ends when the original couple ends, with the death of a spouse. Retirement, like parenthood and grandparenthood, precipitates a major role change—this time an economic one. In our culture, the definition of who one *is* is too often determined by what one *does*. Gratuitous and tacit assumptions about character, values, and so forth, are made on the basis of occupation, be it plumber, securities analyst, or nurse.

When both members of the couple are no longer gainfully employed and rely on income from savings, pensions, the government, or family, they confront two issues: (1) What is our personal relationship to be like now that some of our roles are different? (2) What is the relationship between us as a couple and the outside world to be like? Financial dependence on family, change in lifestyle as income declines, more frequent and more serious illnesses—all pose major emotional and economic challenges to the integrity of the couple in their last years together.

On the other hand, increased longevity may mean new and varied family relationships. A decade ago, 40 percent of people over age sixty-five had great-grandchildren (Riley and Foner 1968). Thus many couples in this last stage of the family life cycle find themselves as the heads of four-generation families, alive with excitement and love. Increased longevity also offers many people opportunities for second careers after retirement and new and different lifestyles.

Other Models.   Our intent in sketching the eight stages of a family life cycle has been to indicate that the life of a family can be viewed developmentally as a sequence of stages. Although we have concentrated on the typical challenges facing family members as they pass through these eight stages (and we will elaborate upon these in following chapters), we want to acknowledge that there are exceptions to the general scheme we have presented—other varieties of lifestyles, determined in part by different socioeconomic conditions and ethnic backgrounds and traditions (see Allen 1978). We have focused on the general developmental pattern because, as Kimmel (1974) points out, it is probably the "pervasive stereotype in our society that influences these other family styles."

Other developmental models are as relevant as the eight-stage model, and several add refinements. For example, Feldman and Feldman (1975) argue for a concept of *family careers*, which may run through several of the stages of the family life cycle in sequence or, at times, simultaneously. The concept of the family career is developmental. Its intent is to describe the individual's participation in the family during his or her lifetime. The four careers that Feldman and Feldman postulate are: (1) the *sex-experience* career—beginning with early sexual development long before marriage and extending possibly into one's eighties; (2) the *marital* career—subsuming all the stages of the eight-stage model; (3) the *parent-child* career—stages two through six; and (4) the *adult-parent* career—beginning with the assumption of various caretaking responsibilities for one's own or one's spouse's parents and ending with the death of the parents.

These careers then become the units of analysis in studying the family life cycle. They have utility for our systems perspective because of their special characteristics: (1) they are usually dyadic and are at the least interpersonal in nature, thereby identifying a system with which to work; (2) they may be differentiated from other nonfamily "careers," such as one's occupation or one's personal leisure time; and (3) they ignore geographical distance or proximity while permitting a focus on system relationships. For example, Feldman and Feldman's "adult-parent career" model makes it possible to explore an individual's boundaries and communication patterns with parents throughout several stages without citing as a primary variable whether the individual has left home or returned.

Moving further away from our general eight-stage model, Yorburg (1975) points to the conceptual confusion inherent in generalizations about the stereotype of the nuclear family. She argues for a typology of family structures that provides at least four possible conceptualizations of the "family": (1) *nuclear* family—complete self-sufficiency and family autonomy, no kin network influence, minimal contact outside of parents and children; (2) *modified nuclear* family—substantial self-sufficiency, occasional help in emergencies, weak but potential kin network with regular, but not daily, contact; (3) *modified extended* family—independent economic resources within the nuclear family units, but daily exchange of goods and services, strong kin network with daily influence, daily contact, and geographic proximity; and (4) *extended* family—complete economic interdependence, common ownership of economic resources, powerful kin network providing almost all socialization, emotional support, and protection, and arbitrary, linear, intergenerational authority with daily contact. Considering such a four-family typology complicates the developmental model presented in this chapter. But that is precisely the reality of the study of the family unit: specificity dramatically highlights its complexity.

In sections II and III, we will look more closely at the contributions of other theorists to family development theory. What is important for us at this point is not to endorse a specific developmental model, but to recognize the importance of developmental stages within a generalized systems framework.

Integration of Systems and Developmental Perspectives

We may now integrate the two major points of emphasis in this chapter: (1) the family unit as a system, and (2) the family as an ongoing developmental process.

Recall the family in which Dad, Mom, and daughter (and the dog) had created a structure and communication style around who cleans up the rug and how. We saw that the structure (Dad and daughter use Mom as the middle person) and the communication style (nonassertiveness due to lack of certainty of prerogatives) simultaneously reinforced each other. Although somewhat oversimplified, this situation is a microcosm of the dynamics of the structure-communication interaction of the family as a system.

However, viewing the issue of the rug just from the perspective of the family as a system leaves us with incomplete data; knowledge of the family's current developmental stage adds a salient dimension. Let us illustrate this by viewing this family at each of two developmental stages, first in stage three (the family with the preschool child) and second in stage five (the family with an adolescent).

You will recall that at stage three the couple faces many parenting challenges. What a three-year-old child may or must do is certainly open to negotiation. Few would argue that a three-year-old should clean up the dog's mess or be a party to the final resolution of the question; the middle-person structure and the lack of assertiveness as styles of parenting are not congruent with the usual patterns for that developmental stage. We may therefore assume that this family's structure (Mom as the middle person) and communication style (Dad's nonassertiveness) quite probably have evolved out of complications within the dynamics of the couple system and not out of normal family development. Much of the lack of clarity within this family may have in fact preceded this developmental stage. Moreover, failure to transform the structure and the communication style into more effective and appropriate interactions may seriously delay the family's negotiation of the tasks of this stage of development and may delay individual development as well. Change in this family's interactions might require some type of intervention in the couple system.

At stage five, the couple again faces many parenting challenges. What a thirteen-year-old may or must do is also open to negotiation. However, in this particular stage it is more likely that the structure (Mom as middle person) and communication style (Dad's nonassertiveness) evolve out of predictable complications of the developmental stage

itself, rather than the dynamics of the couple system. These complications include new rules concerning privacy, control, and responsibility,
and the consequent realignment of family power when a child enters
adolescence. While the middle-person structure and nonassertive
communication are not congruent with patterns of the preschool stage,
they are typical of usual parenting dilemmas of the adolescent stage in
the family life cycle. Nevertheless, as in stage three, failure to transform
the structure and communication style at stage five into more effective
and more congruent interactions may seriously delay individual and
family development. However, the intervention in this case might not
be in the form of therapy within a dysfunctional couple system. Rather,
it more probably would take the form of consultation, encouraging the
family as a three-person system to see its problem as the quite
understandable and temporary confusion that arises when a healthy
family attempts to meet a developmental challenge by transforming its
structures and communication styles.

Thus, a knowledge of systems theory as it applies to the interplay
of a family's structures and communication styles, combined with a
knowledge of specific family developmental stages, gives us a more
complete view of a particular family dilemma or crisis. Such a perspective allows us to differentiate between predictable developmental crises and disabling and dysfunctional strategies that lead to chronic
crisis and stagnation. Although developmental crises also need resolution, their generation and resolution weave the very rich fabric of
fulfilling family life.

Summary

In this chapter, we presented our two
key concepts for studying the family unit. The first concept involves
viewing the family unit as an organizational system at any time and
place in its growth and development. The second views the family unit
as an evolutionary process that has a developmental life cycle of its own.

The concept of the family as a system has its historical antecedents
in general systems theory. This theory involves a conceptual framework
of systems, subsystems, and their regulation mechanisms. Systems
theory is as easily applicable to the family unit as it is to other interactional systems; it views the family as a group of individuals who
interact through a matrix of regulating structures and communication
mechanisms.

The perception of the family unit as an evolutionary process with a developmental life cycle of its own has its roots in the conceptual framework of the individual life cycle. Developmental theory postulates a series of stages of growth, each of which the organism must successfully negotiate in order to avoid stagnation and chronic crisis.

The structures and communication styles of the family unit will determine the family's success in negotiating the various developmental stages. At the same time, the nature of the particular developmental stage through which the family is passing will affect its structures and communication styles. Transition from one stage to another inevitably transforms family structures and communications; transformations in family structures and communications are requisites for successful developmental stage negotiation. They are inseparable.

The ability to conceptualize the interrelationship between the family system's present structure-communication functions and its longitudinal developmental challenges is the key to choosing effective and appropriate intervention strategies.

In chapter 1 in the manual you will find exercises designed to help you integrate your understanding of the family system and its developmental stages. These exercises will also help you become more aware of how your own family system influences you.

We will now look at the development of family therapy theory and practice, themselves the result of an evolutionary process, and see how they have emerged as the approach that attempts to resolve family dysfunction.

References

Allen, Walter R. 1978. "The Search for Applicable Theories of Black Family Life." *Journal of Marriage and the Family* 40 (1):117–29.

Bengston, Vern L. 1971. "Interage Perceptions and the Generation Gap." *Gerontologist* 11 (4), part 2.

Bertalanffy, Ludwig von. 1934. *Modern Theories of Development: An Introduction to Theoretical Biology.* London: Oxford University Press.

———. 1968. *General Systems Theory.* New York: George Braziller.

Buhler, Charlotte. 1968. "The Developmental Structure of Goal Setting in Group and Individual Studies." In Charlotte Buhler and Fred Massarik, eds., *The Course of Human Life: A Study of Goals in the Humanistic Perspective.* New York: Springer.

Duvall, Evelyn M. 1971. *Family Development.* Philadelphia: J.B. Lippincott.

Duvall, Evelyn M., and Reuben Hill. 1948. "Report of the Committee for the Dynamics of Family Interaction." Prepared at the request of the National Conference on Family Life. Mimeographed.

Erikson, Erik H. 1963. *Childhood and Society.* New York: Norton.

———. 1968. Identity: Youth and Crisis. New York: Norton.

Feldman, Harold, and Margaret Feldman. 1975. "The Family Life Cycle: Some Suggestions for Recycling." *Journal of Marriage and the Family* 37 (2):277–84.

Glenn, Norvald, D. 1975. "Psychological Well-Being in the Post-Parental Stage: Some Evidence from National Surveys." *Journal of Marriage and the Family* 1.

Gould, Robert. 1972. "The Phases of Adult Life: A Study in Developmental Psychology." *American Journal of Psychiatry* 129 (5).

Hill, Reuben, and Roy H. Rodgers. 1964. "The Developmental Approach." In Harold T. Christensen, ed., *Handbook of Marriage and the Family.* Chicago: Rand McNally.

Jung, Carl Gustav. 1971. "The Stages of Life." In Joseph Campbell, ed., *The Portable Jung.* New York: Viking Press.

Kimmel, Douglas C. 1974. *Adulthood and Aging.* New York: Wiley.

Levenson, Daniel. 1978. *The Seasons of a Man's Life.* New York: Knopf.

Lowenthal, Marjorie F., Majda Thurner, and David Chiriboga. 1975. *Four Stages of Life.* San Francisco: Jossey-Bass.

Minuchin, Salvador. 1974. *Families and Family Therapy.* Cambridge, Mass.: Harvard University Press.

Neugarten, Bernice L. 1976. "Adaptation and the Life Cycle." *The Counseling Psychologist* 6 (1).

Neugarten, Bernice L., and Karol K. Weinstein. 1964. "The Changing American Grandparent." *Journal of Marriage and the Family* 26 (2).

Riley, M.W., and A. Foner. 1968. "Aging and Society." *Volume One: An Inventory of Research Findings.* New York: Russell Sage Foundation.

Rodgers, Roy H. 1964. "Toward a Theory of Family Development." *Journal of Marriage and the Family* 26.

Rollins, Boyd C., and Kenneth Z. Cannon. 1974. "Marital Satisfaction over the Family Life Cycle: A Reevaluation." *Journal of Marriage and the Family* 36 (2).

Yorburg, Betty. 1975. "The Nuclear and the Extended Family: An Area of Conceptual Confusion." *Journal of Contemporary Family Studies* 6 (1).

What Is Family Therapy?

Chapter

2

It is only within the past few decades that family therapy has emerged as a psychotherapeutic specialty. In this chapter, we will examine family therapy as a treatment modality, trace its origins and development from individual psychodynamic psychotherapy, review the current status of the field, and discuss the indications and contraindications for its use.

The Family Therapy Perspective

At its simplest and its most complex moments, family therapy is a point of view. It is a point of view that finds its focus primarily in work with family systems. It regards problems and dysfunction as emanating from the family system rather than from the intrapsychic problems of any one individual. Individual symptoms are seen as reflections of stress arising within a larger family system (or other social system). This stress may occur when the family is unable to negotiate a developmental passage or when a nondevelopmental crisis occurs.

The mental health worker who has been trained in the family therapy perspective sees human beings as "belonging to something." The "thing" to which they belong is invariably a larger group of people—one that, in many stages of life, is called a family. The family therapy perspective maintains that the individual cannot be considered as separate from the social context in which he or she lives.

Case Example

Theoretically, as well as in clinical practice, the family therapy point of view may differ substantially from more traditional perspectives on human behavior. Let us take, for example, a catatonic adolescent female. The traditional view of her catatonic condition is presented in figure 2–1. Here we see only the girl and her catatonic symptoms. No other people or object relationships appear; the girl appears to be isolated by her symptoms. The mental health worker who shares this point of view usually confines treatment to the adolescent and her problem only. This type of treatment, with its single focus on intrapsychic phenomena, frequently occurs in a hospital setting.

Figure 2–1   *Traditional View of a Catatonic Adolescent*

Figure 2–2 *A Somewhat More Open View of a Catatonic Adolescent*

Figure 2–2 presents a more open, yet still fairly traditional view of the catatonic adolescent. Here the focus is still on the girl and her symptoms. However, in the distant borders, other people appear. In most cases, these are people important to the young girl, possibly family members. Nonetheless, they are considered only peripherally related to the "problem." The major focus remains on the girl, and treatment consists of work with her and her symptoms. In neither of these two early perspectives has it been considered an integral part of treatment to ask, "To whom does this person belong, and what role might they have in this problem?"

Figure 2–3, on the other hand, shows a dramatic shift in point of view on the part of the adolescent and on the part of the mental health worker. Here we find the adolescent's catatonic symptoms placed within the context of her family. It is acknowledged that this problem has more

Figure 2–3   *A Beginning Family Systems View of a Catatonic Adolescent*

than a peripheral effect on the adolescent's significant others. It is the beginning of a family therapy point of view in that it not only recognizes that the adolescent "belongs" to something, but also defines what that "thing" is, in this case, her family. The mental health worker who adopts this point of view may begin to work with the family members, as well as with the adolescent, but the focus continues to be on the adolescent and "how we can all help *her*." Family members still define themselves in terms of one person and one problem. They see themselves as "father of catatonic adolescent," "mother of catatonic adolescent," and "sisters and brothers of the adolescent," and although they acknowledge that they are in various ways related to and affected by the problem, it is still clearly *her* problem.

Figure 2–4 represents the true family therapy point of view. The work may be with the entire family, as in figure 2–3, or with smaller groups of family members. In fact, the therapy may be with the adolescent herself. What differentiates this perspective from the others is that the adolescent is now entitled to a broader perspective. She is still a disturbed youngster; however, she is also a girl who has a variety of roles, such as student, daughter, sister, friend. This shift in emphasis, away from her symptoms and bringing into view a multiplicity of her other behaviors, requires a comparable shift in our perspective and emphasis on other family members. We now view other members of the family in the multiplicity of *their* roles, such as husband, father of daughter, father of son, family provider, and so forth.

This change in perspective, this different point of view, allows both the family and the family therapist to begin to place the ad-

Figure 2–4 *True Family Systems View of a Catatonic Adolescent*

olescent's symptoms in the larger context of the varied, subtle, and complex interactions of the family. With this perspective, they begin to examine the different roles that people play, as well as the styles of communication and interaction within the family system.

This focus allows questions that go beyond the question of "how can *we* help *her* with her problems that cause her catatonic symptoms?" Using the family therapy perspective, the family and the family therapist may now consider the following: (1) what meaning the catatonic symptoms may have for the other family members; (2) what other behaviors are of concern to family members; (3) what developmental stage the family system was in at the onset of the symptoms and what issues emerged at that time; (4) whether the girl's catatonic behavior is the actual "problem" or whether it is her way of responding to a more fundamental problem within the family system itself. In other words, is the catatonia a reflection of individual stress or family stress? What functions do these symptoms serve within the family? Perhaps the girl's illness will keep her dependent and under the control of her parents so that they will not have to deal with the separation issues that arise when a family system has an adolescent about to finish high school and go off into the world. Thus, the symptoms could be viewed as the "solution" to another problem. The girl's disorder may also serve as a bridge between the parents, who now have something in common to worry about and discuss, or it may take some of the pressure and attention off other youngsters within the family, granting them some freedom to pursue their own interests. Whatever the case, the family therapy perspective is that the symptom must be viewed as serving multiple functions.

Obviously a catatonic episode in adolescence is a symptom that may be viewed and treated from any one of the four points of view that we have described. Numerous complaints may be seen as having their etiology, consequences, and "cure" within the intrapsychic life of the individual (figure 2–1). On the other hand, they may be viewed as chiefly intrapsychic, but with some marginal relation to significant others on the periphery of the individual's introspective focus (figure 2–2). They may also be viewed as having substantial antecedents and consequences within the family system—although the "problem" is still seen as the specific complaint or behavior, and the "patient" is still seen as the individual (figure 2–3).

What characterizes the family therapy point of view (figure 2–4) is a position that holds that: (1) the individual with the symptom belongs to a larger system; (2) regardless of the eventual treatment modality, that larger system is an essential diagnostic focus in assessing the etiology of the complaint; and (3) the treatment plan, regardless of the specific unit, must include strategies aimed at modifying or altering the behaviors and structure of the entire family system.

Therefore, once an appropriate diagnosis has been made, the actual family treatment involves intervention with all or some of the family members. Remember from our discussion of the family system in chapter 1 that a change in one or more units of the system will effect change in the entire system. Thus, all members of the family system do not need to participate in treatment in order for change in the family system to occur. Individual treatment of a family member can be a useful alternative or concurrent treatment strategy to family therapy. In certain cases, group treatment for an individual, couple, or larger family subsystem can be the most effective way of intervening in a dysfunctional family system.

Comparison with Other Therapies

To recapitulate, family therapy is a point of view that regards the problem as the problem of a family system, not as the problem of an individual family member. Even if only one member of the family is seen in treatment, the treatment can be considered family therapy as long as its focus is on the family system.

The difference between individual and family therapy lies in this point of view. Most individual therapies deal with the transference relationship between the patient and the therapist and ignore the actual interactional processes between the patient and the social environment, namely, the family. Thus, individual therapy focuses on insight, fantasies, history, and the client-therapist relationship. In contrast, family therapy focuses upon the communication processes, power balances and imbalances, influence processes, structures for conflict resolution, and the current functioning of the family system as a system. The goal of family therapy is not simply to effect change in an individual within the family, but rather to effect change in the structure of the family and the sequences of behavior among its members.

Group therapy shares some of the techniques of conjoint family therapy. In both types of treatment, the therapist meets with the entire group (or family) simultaneously and focuses on its interactional patterns. Both treatment modalities develop and focus on group norms, as well as emphasize action and decision making. Conjoint family therapy differs from group therapy in that members of a group are not related and do not have the history or the emotional investment of a family group. Therefore, the way in which a group made up of strangers competes for group time and individual focus differs from that of a family group.

A review of the historical antecedents and the development of the family therapy point of view will help place the current theory and practice of family therapy in perspective.

Origins of Family Therapy

Family therapy has evolved from the traditions of individual psychotherapy and has been influenced by the work of anthropologists and sociologists. The early work of Freud, Adler, and Sullivan exemplifies the ways in which the pioneers of individual psychotherapy regarded the relationship between the individual and the family. It was in reaction to and as development of these seminal ideas that later work with families began leading to what is now called family therapy.

Precursors of Family Therapy

Sigmund Freud, the founder of psychotherapy, postulated that unresolved conflicts from one of the psychosexual stages of childhood were responsible for individual pathology. Two of his concepts had a particular influence on the later work of Nathan Ackerman, the "grandfather" of family therapy. These concepts are: (1) personality is "developed" in stages, and (2) the impact of family members during an individual's early life can have profound implications for that development. For example, unsuccessful resolution of the oedipal conflict can adversely affect adult heterosexual relationships; similarly, unresolved castration anxiety from early childhood can hinder adult sexual relationships.

Freud believed that it was more effective to work directly with a patient and his or her problems, with minimal contact with the patient's family. The actual family was considered background; the patient's ideation of the family was the real therapeutic material. Family problems could be worked through in the transference between the patient and the therapist. Freud did, however, report several cases in which families either took the patient out of treatment when the patient began to improve or else subtly undermined the treatment. Thus, while Freud did not like to include the family in therapy, he was often frustrated by the family's power over the patient and its ability to sabotage treatment.

It is interesting to note that the closest Freud (1964) ever came to family treatment was with his famous patient "little Hans." In 1908 Freud was consulted by the father of a five-year-old boy, called little Hans, who had a severe phobia in regard to horses and who was constantly fantasizing about penises. Hans's father was a physician, and Freud encouraged him to handle the psychoanalytic treatment of his son under Freud's supervision. In an attempt to uncover the child's fears, Freud met with the father regularly to interpret the material that the father brought him. Much of the analysis of the phobia dealt with the fear that the horse would castrate little Hans, and Freud was able to explain to the father that the boy unconsciously equated the horse with the father. Hans feared his father might castrate him because of the hostility he felt toward his father. As a result of this treatment, Hans was relieved of his phobic symptoms.

We see from this example that change in one member of the family was effected through modification of the behaviors of another member of the family, a significant other to the targeted patient. Freud's psychoanalytical concepts served as the basis for the later Ackerman school of family therapists who, as we shall see, view themselves as incorporating the Freudian constructs with rudimentary family systems concepts.

Alfred Adler differed from Freud in that he regarded biological stresses and instinctual strivings as less significant in the etiology of pathology than the individual's social roles. For Adler, personality development depended on one's experiences and feelings about one's social roles and the relationships among those roles. In the Adlerian scheme, power and status motives claim more attention that Freud's instinctual sexual drives. Adler argued that character traits, symptoms, and dreams could be understood as the means by which an individual, attempting to compensate for a lack of self-esteem, strives for power and a sense of self-adequacy and belonging. Moreover, since the family is the first social environment, family experiences, as well as perceptions of one's place in the family, are seen as crucial to personality development and behavior.

Although Adler himself did not see families together, his view of the therapeutic relationship was more open and active than Freud's.

Adler's therapeutic outlook, combined with his theory of personality development, set the stage for an active, involved family therapeutic role that was realized by his followers, among them Dreikurs and Dinkmeyer, half a century later. Today, Adlerian family counseling centers throughout the country focus primarily on parenting strategies and family councils for airing and improving communications.

Influenced by Adler, Harry Stack Sullivan emphasized the role of interpersonal relationships in the development of personality. He considered mental illness to consist of, as well as to stem from, disturbed interpersonal relationships. Whereas Freud defined psychosis as a conflict between the person and the external world leading to intrapsychic disturbances between the id, ego, and superego, Sullivan believed that the basic conflict is between the individual and the human environment that comprises the external world.

According to Sullivan's interpersonal theory, each person with whom a particular individual interacts has a different understanding of that individual. Thus, one can be fully understood only within the context of one's family, friendships, and broader social and cultural groups. For Sullivan, there are two basic goals of human behavior: (1) physical satisfactions (food, drink, rest, sex), and (2) security in social relationships. As one passes through childhood, there is often conflict between these two goals, resulting in anxiety and tension. Parental approval and disapproval characterize the interpersonal relationships within the family that are crucial for understanding personality development. Sullivan was particularly interested in the pathology that can emerge from mother-child relationships. He believed that warm, affectionate therapeutic relationships are necessary to help the patient work through earlier distant, faulty family relationships and to develop self-esteem and confidence.

Sullivan's interpersonal theory had a critical impact on psychotherapy theory and practice. It heavily influenced the thinking and work of the early family therapists who further developed the notion of the importance of the family system context for the individual.

The work of anthropologists and sociologists also contributed to the development of family therapy. At the beginning of this century, these social scientists were beginning to focus attention on cultural influences on personality. Early work on the sociology of the family (by Lynch, Parsons, and Bales) stressed observations and descriptions of role structure and organizational functions of the family. The anthropologists (Mead, Malinowski, and Benedict) added data showing how cultural and ethnic systems, as well as nuclear and extended family systems, affect an individual's development and behavior.

Emergence of Family Therapy: The 1950s

In the late 1940s and early 1950s, some therapists found themselves increasingly frustrated as they attempted to apply conventional psychiatric principles to their work with schizophrenics and their families and to their work with delinquent children. In hospitals and other institutions, therapists completed work with patients, sent them home to their families, only to have them return as patients or inmates within a few weeks or months. It became apparent to psychiatric workers that something was amiss, that individual treatment in an office or hospital was not always achieving the desired outcomes. How could an individual who had been a "model" individual patient regress so much once he or she returned to the world outside the institution? Why weren't the conventional techniques working? Was it the nature of the illness? Was it the institution?

It is important to remember that during the 1940s and early 1950s the psychodynamic view of Freud and his followers dominated the mental health profession. There were strong taboos within the entire psychiatric profession against a therapist's having contact with a patient's relatives or straying from conventional practices. It was felt that any contact (other than cursory) with a patient's relatives would contaminate the patient's transference with the therapist and would, therefore, retard treatment. The therapist used the patient's perception of what went on in the family as the patient's reality. It was felt that if the patient got better, the family situation would naturally improve.

Guidance clinics at that time preferred (and many still do) to have separate therapists for different family members. Although these separate therapists sometimes consult with each other, the consultation is often superficial and results in each therapist's becoming the advocate of his or her patient.

Because of the strong taboos against involvement with the patient's family, psychiatric workers were reluctant to admit to practicing family therapy. Thus, the early family work in the 1950s centered around research, which was the legitimate way of looking at the effects of therapy on families. The schizophrenic population was the target population of this early research. Schizophrenia is the most common of the psychotic reactions and occurs in approximately 1 percent of the total population (Coleman 1964). Because of its complexity, relatively long duration, and high rate of incidence, this illness has proved to be one of the most serious and baffling of all the psychopathological syndromes. It is for these reasons that the early researchers chose to focus on the families of schizophrenics.

Early Family Research in the United States. We will now take a look at four early groups of researchers. While we do not claim to include all the early family researchers, we do believe that these four groups are representative of the major research of the 1950s: (1) the Bateson group in California; (2) the Lidz group at Johns Hopkins and later at Yale; (3) the Bowen group at the Menninger Clinic; and (4) the Wynne group in Washington, D.C. These groups began their work independently and somewhat surreptitiously. It was not until the late 1950s that they became aware of each other's activities.

1. *Bateson Group*: This group consisted of Gregory Bateson, John Weakland, Jay Haley, and Don Jackson. In 1952 Bateson, an English anthropologist, received a Rockefeller Foundation grant to study the paradoxical communication styles of animals and humans. Bateson was the prime mover in laying the groundwork for the application of systems thinking to human behavior. In 1953 Bateson hired Haley, then a graduate student, and Weakland, a cultural anthropologist and former chemical engineer, as research assistants. Haley, Weakland, et al. found that animal and human communications included paradoxical levels of abstraction, a message and a message about the message. The different levels of communication may simultaneously contradict each other. In 1954, the Bateson group, which now included Don Jackson as the psychiatric member, received a grant to study the communication styles of schizophrenic patients in a California Veterans Administration hospital.

A major concept to evolve from the Bateson group's work with schizophrenics is the notion of the *double bind*. Although the expression has crept into "coffee-table clinical vocabulary," it connotes a very special set of conditions within a relationship. For a double bind to occur, the relationship must include (1) two or more members; (2) a repeated experience; (3) a primary negative injunction; (4) a secondary injunction conflicting with the first, and, like the first, enforced by punishments or signals that threaten survival; and (5) a tertiary negative injunction prohibiting the victim from escaping from the field.

Let us illustrate the five conditions of the double bind. (1) A family consists of a young girl and her mother and father. (2) The girl is constantly given the message that she does not "show enough consideration" for her parents. (3) When she "approaches" them to "show consideration," she is told, "You are crowding us; don't interrupt our privacy!" (4) When she "retreats" to show consideration for their "privacy," she is told, "You don't care about us; stop ignoring us!" (5) She is ten years old and does not have the permission to leave the family system.

Given this situation, a "schizophrenic" break *does* provide the youngster with a solution, albeit an unsatisfactory one: in her development of a mental "illness," in her retreat from reality, she can leave the family system and not be held responsible for her behavior in doing so.

Negative injunctions may be expressed in the affective quality of statements, may be implicit in the situation of interaction, and may also be expressed directly in the verbal content of the message. It is important to consider the different levels of communication, which operate simultaneously. The verbal and nonverbal levels include specific words, the grammatical placement and positioning of these words, the punctuation that is used, the tone and quality of the voice, the affect that is or is not expressed. Each message has a literal aspect, as well as a connotative aspect; the latter tells us more about the former than does the former itself. Thus, the messages communicated to the youngster in the double-bind message may or may not be verbal.

Another important concept to emerge from this group was Jackson's idea of family *homeostasis*. This concept "implies the relative constancy of the internal environment, a constancy, however, which is maintained by a continuous interplay of dynamic forces" (Jackson 1968, p. 2). Jackson was talking about the equilibrium of the family system, the way family members maintain stability in their communication with each other by developing rules governing who says what to whom and when and in what contexts. Each family has its own dynamic force that maintains the status quo of the family and that strongly resists any change. For example, when a schizophrenic patient returns home, the patient's symptom may cause an imbalance in the family's status quo, and the symptom itself may worsen in response to the upset in the homeostatic balance of the family system. The family may not regain its customary balance until the symptom worsens to the point that the patient must return to the hospital.

The Bateson group's early work on distorted communication between sick patients and their families and on family homeostasis resulted in a classic paper entitled "Toward A Theory of Schizophrenia," which was published in 1956 (Bateson et al. 1956). This paper was a preliminary report on research about the nature of the communicational theory of the origin and nature of schizophrenia. In this paper, the Bateson group described how they deductively developed their communicational theory by first analyzing the nature of schizophrenic communication and then arriving at a set of conditions in a family situation that led to this form of communication and resulted in pathology. The notion that the schizophrenic's bizarre symptoms (confused thinking and communication patterns) resulted from fam-

ily interaction patterns rather than from intrapsychic disturbance
was indeed radical and a definite departure from conventional psychiatric thinking.

The Bateson group continued to develop their beliefs that schizophrenia was a response of the patient to his or her family and that change
in the entire family must occur if the schizophrenia is to be cured.
In late 1958 the Bateson group received funds to study the process
of family therapy with schizophrenic patients. Thus, an early study
of communication evolved into a clinical study of family therapy.

Out of this later research came Jackson and Haley's development
and refinement of active, directive family therapy strategies. They had
learned that the techniques of individual therapy—increasing insight
and interpreting underlying dynamics—simply did not work with
families and that new techniques were needed. Because lasting change
did not result from an understanding of past and current motivations
and behavior, Jackson and Haley began to explore power and conflict
struggles by analyzing and intervening in the processes of communication among family members. They became active members of the family
system, rather than detached observers providing interpretations of the
process. In section II we will discuss the revolutionary technique that
emerged from this research.

2. *Lidz Group*: The members of this group were Theodore Lidz,
Stephen Fleck, Alice Cornelison, and Dorothy Terry. In the mid-1950s,
unaware of the work of the Bateson group, they too began to research the relationship between schizophrenia and the family. Using
psychoanalytic concepts, they conducted diagnostic and therapeutic
interviews with a sample of hospitalized schizophrenic patients and
their families.

The Lidz group discovered some general difficulties that seemed to
appear over and over again in the relationship between the schizophrenic and his or her family. These difficulties were related to (1) the
family's structure of age roles and sex roles; (2) the family's ability to
teach the patient cultural values and appropriate ways of behaving;
and (3) the parents' ability to provide adequate nurturance and
appropriate models for sex roles.

This group developed important concepts concerning the child's
identity formation. They found that in schizophrenic families, there
often was a blurring of age and generation boundaries and that the
parents provided inappropriate role models. Thus, the patient learned
inappropriate behaviors from the inappropriate behaviors of his or her
parents. These factors resulted in the patient's identity distortion, which
in turn became the psychological basis for schizophrenia. As a child can

only learn appropriate sex roles if his or her parents have a clear-cut, consistent understanding of their own sex roles, it became evident that the early family learning context set the stage for later development.

Lidz distinguished between two types of schizophrenic families: *skewed* and *schismatic*. The basis for this distinction was the type of disturbance found in the parents' marital relationship. In the "skewed" family, the marital relationship is characterized by one strong and one weak partner. Lidz found that the strong parent is usually the mother; the weak partner allows this domination and does not attempt to resist it. In the "schismatic" family, the relationship is characterized by chronic hostility and mutual withdrawal. In this family, the marriage has never jelled and there is no common purpose or role reciprocity. One or both parents are excessively attached to their own parents. The tension and confusion within these marital relationships result in the child's identity confusion and can lead to pathology.

Lidz found that schizophrenic girls are more likely to come from a schismatic background, where each parent seeks the support of the daughter, and that schizophrenic boys are more likely to come from skewed backgrounds with dominant mothers and passive fathers. For the Lidz group, *role reciprocity*, which refers to fluid, flexible roles as opposed to rigid, stereotyped roles, is a requisite for a successful marriage. A lack of role reciprocity is characteristic of a skewed or schismatic marital relationship. Such a lack can lead to distortions in role-appropriate behaviors for the different age-sex groups within the family.

The major contributions of Lidz's research stem from his group's focus on the dramatic quality of family relationships and their influence on a schizophrenic breakdown. A schizophrenic breakdown does not happen in isolation. It develops in a pathological family system and is nurtured by the disturbed communication patterns within this family system. Lidz's highlighting of the role of the mother and the father encouraged further research on the effects of disturbed marital systems on offspring.

3. *Bowen Group*: The Bowen group, which included Murray Bowen, Robert Dysinger, Betty Basamania, and Warren Brady, began their research on schizophrenics and their families in the early 1950s at the Menninger Clinic in Topeka, Kansas. Although Bowen began by focusing on the mother-child symbiosis, he did include some fathers in the research. By the mid-1950s, this group had moved to the National Institute of Mental Health (NIMH) in Washington, D.C., where Bowen began to hospitalize whole families of schizophrenics for observation and research.

These families lived in the hospital from six months to between two and five years. Their most notable characteristics were (1) their restrictive relationships; (2) their rigid, stereotyped roles; and (3) their selective use of external variables only insofar as they validated their inner projections.

The original Bowen research focused on the mother-child symbiosis. Bowen's hypothesis was that emotional illness in the child was a product of a less severe problem in the mother. He found that many of his subject families had overadequate mothers and distant, withdrawn fathers. When it became apparent that the mother-child relationship was only a dependent part of the larger family unit, fathers and normal siblings were brought into the research. After all, if the mother-child relationship was the cause of this schizophrenic illness, how could one explain the health of the patient's siblings, all with the same mother? This study helped Bowen move from the psychoanalytic intrapsychic approach toward a systems analysis. Later, he even added grandparents to his family system.

The Bowen group's early research showed that although the parents of schizophrenic patients may appear on the surface to function well, they have difficulty distinguishing between the subjective feeling process and the more objective thinking process. In other words, they are unable to separate their feelings from their thoughts. The research demonstrated variation in the degree of *fusion* or differentiation of feelings and intellect. People with the greatest fusion between feeling and thinking seemed to have the most difficulty in their everyday functioning. Those with the greater ability to distinguish between feeling and thinking appeared to have more effective, adaptive, flexible coping skills.

Another finding of the Bowen group's research was that the parents of schizophrenic children have weak, tense marriages. This poor marital relationship is characterized by emotional distance between the marital partners, which leads to *triangulation* when a child is born into the system. Briefly, Bowen's concept of triangulation refers to a situation in which two people are unable to relate to each other and so use a third person, in this case the child, to reestablish contact and some kind of homeostatic balance. It is as if the third person is needed to maintain a relationship between the first and second persons.

The major conclusion that Bowen drew from his work was that the schizophrenia of the identified patient is merely a symptom of a faulty family system; to understand the patient's pathology, it is necessary to examine the emotional system of the entire family system.

Bowen's early work described his concepts of the nuclear family's emotional system and the family projection process. He discovered facts about emotional functioning—the "how" and "what" rather than the "why"—that helped him to distinguish between functional facts and subjective thought in emotional systems. This work led him to view schizophrenia, neuroses, and normality on a quantitative continuum, rather than as being qualitatively different. For Bowen, the family is a number of systems and subsystems. The same factors operate, to different degrees, in all types of families. Thus, Bowen was a forerunner in applying his findings to families beyond those of the schizophrenic population. This was indeed a new way of looking at pathology and at families.

4. *Wynne Group*: The Wynne group, which included Margaret Singer, Christopher Beels, Irving Ryckoff, Juliana Day, and Stanley Hirsch, took over the family section at NIMH from Bowen in the mid-1950s. The Wynne group's ideology was more traditional than Bowen's in that it emphasized the social-psychological concepts of an individual's identity as the link between persons and their cultures.

This group, which observed families in family therapy situations, was searching for a psychodynamic interpretation of schizophrenia that would incorporate the social organization of the family as a whole. Thus, the Wynne group postulated *two continuously conflicting needs* of an individual: (1) the need to develop a sense of personal identity and (2) the need to relate intimately to significant others. The first need seems to propel one out of the family, while the second need seems to drive one back into the family. The issue of separation can become critical if the conflict between these two needs is not worked through successfully.

The Wynne group developed the concept of *family boundaries.* "Family boundaries" refers to the individual's identity within the family, in relation to self and to other family members, and to the family's identity as a unit unto itself and in relation to a larger social system. This group's research demonstrated that the schizophrenic patient is confused about family boundaries and personal identity as he or she struggles with the conflict between the need to develop personal identity and the need to relate to significant others. The families of schizophrenics aid and abet this confusion with roles that are either too rigidly or too ambiguously structured. To achieve a successful personal identity, one has to be able to experiment with a variety of roles as one is growing up. In schizophrenogenic families, the patient is unable to do so.

The Wynne group found that one has three possible options in terms of fulfilling one's need for self-identity and one's need to relate to significant others. These options are (1) *mutuality*, where there are a divergence of self-interests and a balance between the individual's and family's interests; (2) *nonmutuality*, where there are only the most superficial relationships among family members and no common interests between the individual and the family; and (3) *pseudomutuality*, where there is pressure from the family on the individual to maintain a facade of intimacy within the family at the expense of individual identity. This last option, pseudomutuality, is a characteristic of schizophrenic families. Another possibility is *pseudohostility*, where alienation among family members exists to cover up the need for intimacy among family members.

The Wynne group noted that schizophrenic families display a sameness of role structure, along with an insistence on the desirability and appropriateness of this role structure. In addition, these families put pressure on the individual to remain dependent on this rigid role structure. In such families, there is usually a lack of spontaneity, humor, and zest for living. The boundaries are rigid and stretch only to incorporate those people or things that are complementary and do not pose any threat to the existing family structure; the Wynne group referred to this concept as the *rubber fence*.

Thus, the schizophrenic has problems of identity, perception, and communication because of the *role structure* of his or her family system. The Wynne group was primarily concerned with the quality and structure, rather than with the content, of family role relationships. This group observed that the sicker the family, the more rigid the roles within the family. The individual is not the sole repository of pathology; the pathology resides in the entire family system and is evidenced in the way that family members interact.

Thus, the early research on families in the United States resulted in a new conceptualization of schizophrenia as a symptomatic reaction to stress in the family system. Although the different groups of researchers emphasized different forces within the family system, they all focused on the relationship patterns of the family members.

Early Family Research in Britain.   At about the same time that the early researchers in the United States were developing their theories about schizophrenic families, Ronald Laing was arriving at similar conclusions about schizophrenic families in England. Laing's conclusions about the importance of interactions and communications of family systems are important, not because of their similarity to the American findings, but because of their cross-cultural implications for family study.

More heavily influenced by existentialism and phenomenology than the American researchers, Laing reported on his studies of eleven schizophrenic families in *Sanity, Madness and the Family*, which appeared in 1958. Laing focused on the interpersonal relationships within schizophrenic families, as did the American researchers. In another similarity to the American researchers, Laing stated that behavior has no meaning if considered apart from the action and interaction of the people relating.

Laing described *confirmation* of the self as a process through which individuals are recognized, acknowledged, or validated by others. *Mystification* occurs when one person attempts to manipulate some change in another person, to the benefit and security of the manipulator and the confusion, or "mystification" of the person being manipulated. This concept is similar to the "double bind," but Laing focuses more on the stressful experience of the person being mystified. Laing found that mystification occurs frequently in schizophrenic family life. It is a controlling mechanism aimed at maintaining the status quo. When one experiences mystification frequently, one suffers from a severe anxiety that is symptomatic of a deep, existential insecurity.

Another figure in family research during the 1950s in England was John Howells, one of the pioneers of family psychiatry in Britain. Like the American researchers, Howells focused upon the family system as the patient, rather than upon the individual who was identified as the patient. His interventions involved manipulating the strength and/or direction of emotional forces within the patient's environment. Howells's work was further developed in the 1960s.

Expanding Perspective of Family Research. Because the focus of early family research was on schizophrenia, it was initially thought that the research findings pertained only to families with schizophrenic members. In later studies of normal families, it was recognized that the same patterns that were observed in schizophrenic families were present in all families, although to varying degrees.

The career of Nathan Ackerman, who is often referred to as the "grandfather" of family therapy (Framo 1972), represents the transition between research and the actual practice of family therapy. Ackerman was a psychoanalyst and a child psychiatrist who was also influenced by social psychology. His interest in the family movement stemmed from his experience as a practitioner. He is considered by many today as the bridge between the intrapsychically oriented therapist, who is only peripherally concerned with families insofar as they shed light on the patient, and the systems analyst, who views the family system as the client.

As early as 1938, Ackerman wrote a paper, entitled "The Family as a Social and Emotional Unit," in which he observed that the family is a dynamic psychological and social unit in itself (Ackerman 1938). The family unit responds to internal and external pressures and serves as a medium for the exchange of love and material goods. Ackerman's therapy focused on the continuously interchanging role relationships between the individual, his family, and society.

In the 1940s and 1950s, Ackerman's treatment of individual patients and their families provided empirical evidence for his beliefs about the importance of social roles and the resolution of role conflicts. Ackerman was interested in both the content and the process of communication, and he conceptualized the family unit as seeking *dynamic* homeostasis, which allows for change within the system. He declared that pathology occurs within a family when this homeostasis is thwarted or unbalanced. This pathology will appear in the symptomatic behavior of an individual within the family, reflecting the family's emotional distortion.

Ackerman continued to embrace both the analytical and systems approach to working with families. He refused to choose one over the other and was determined to find a way to utilize the theory from both approaches. As one of the first practicing family therapists to have impeccable psychoanalytic credentials as well, he did much to bring the family movement into the legitimate bailiwick of psychoanalysis and psychiatry in this country. When Ackerman pointed out that the classic one-to-one relationship of traditional psychotherapy tends to isolate the individual without considering the roles the patient plays in his family and that the therapist therefore has no chance of learning the important methods of communication within the family, he commanded the respectful attention of his colleagues.

The family therapy movement surfaced in March 1957 at the annual meeting of the American Orthopsychiatric Association in Chicago, when psychiatrist John Spiegel organized the first professional panel on family research. The panel, which included John Spiegel, Murray Bowen, Theodore Lidz, and David Mendel, presented its findings to a small audience of professionals. This meeting introduced a heretofore unknown area in mental health and generated considerable excitement and interest.

In May 1957 the annual convention of the American Psychiatric Association (APA), also held in Chicago, contained a panel on family work with Nathan Ackerman as the secretary and Jackson, Bowen, and Lidz as panelists. Attendance and excitement at this meeting were much higher than at the earlier American Orthopsychiatric meeting. The family therapy movement was off and running. This 1957 APA meeting resulted in Don Jackson's publishing his well-known book *The Etiology of Schizophrenia* (Jackson 1960), which outlined the family's involvement with this disorder.

It is important to understand how revolutionary the idea of family therapy was, given the "zeitgeist" of the mental health movement at this time. The ground swell of interest that resulted from the 1957 meetings was evidenced by the content of the major 1958 psychiatric conventions, at which a large number of therapists eagerly described their family therapy experiences of the past year. These therapists quickly began to develop their own empirical methods and techniques of family therapy. However, their methods and techniques were not based on the research of the family movement, but rather on the psychoanalytical theory of individual and group psychotherapy.

Thus, the 1950s were marked by an orientation to research and theory and led to the birth of a national network of family-oriented theorists. Most of these theorists had been traditionally trained to focus on the individual who was the identified patient. When they began to look at the entire family system as the patient, they discovered a need to develop new concepts and terminology to describe the family process. Out of this need there developed the concepts of double bind, pseudomutuality, schism, skew, and mystification. Practitioners were gradually incorporated into this national network of family theorists, with some of the theorists themselves becoming leaders in practice.

Family Therapy in the 1960s

A "healthy, unstructured state of chaos" (Bowen 1976, p. 55) is how Bowen described the rush into the practice of family therapy in the early 1960s. This family therapy practice was not based on any of the theoretical research of the 1950s, but on the application of existing psychodynamic techniques and concepts to family situations. It was as if the research groups of the 1950s had given practicing therapists permission to begin treating entire families; these therapists merely adapted their regular techniques to families.

Throughout the 1960s the Bateson and Bowen groups continued to develop their systems theories. Although the Bateson group officially disbanded in 1962 when Bateson went off to the Oceanic Institute in Hawaii, Haley and Jackson further developed their own communication theories and techniques for understanding and working with families. We will discuss their theoretical contributions in detail in chapter 4. At this point, it is sufficient to say that Haley departed from Bateson by developing his own notion that all communications denote a power struggle for control of the nature of the relationship, and that Jackson developed his own ideas about cognition in communications.

In 1960 Ackerman founded the Family Institute in New York City to further his work and to train family therapists. The Ackerman Family Institute quickly grew into one of the leading training institutes of its time. Throughout the 1960s Ackerman continued to develop his theory about an individual's psychological identity within the family system and a family's stability of behavior, which allows a family to keep a sense of self in the midst of conflict and still allows for growth and change. Thus, a healthy family will have flexible roles, stable behavior, and a sense of shared identity, while a sick family will have rigid roles or disagreement, unstable behavior, and a lack of shared identity. Healthy role adaptation is the optimal balance between continuity of the old and an openness to new experience.

As Ackerman developed his theory, he also developed his format for training family therapy practitioners. Ackerman believed that the therapist should act as a medium through which change can occur. The therapist plays a number of different roles—activator, challenger, supporter, confronter, interpreter, and reintegrator. The therapist's goal is to shift the balance within the family so that family members can learn to relate to each other in new ways and, if appropriate, to modify their value system. It is important to remember that Ackerman was concerned with the interaction between the person, the family, and society and that he refused to emphasize one of these variables over another. This insistence allowed him to give equal weight to the intrapsychic process and the systems process; it also separated from the other systems practitioners, whose ideas of family systems theory were continuing to gain popularity.

The 1960s spawned new professional publications as family therapy became a popular topic at national meetings and conventions. In 1964 there was the Zuk and Nagy conference on family systems and psychopathology, and in 1967 Framo's conference of family researchers, theorists, and therapists took place (Boszormenyi-Nagy and Framo 1965; Framo 1972). Theorists and practitioners from such diverse disciplines as psychology, sociology, anthropology, ethology, theology, and nursing began to contribute to the field of family therapy. The field was now attracting practitioners from the ranks of counseling, psychology, psychiatry, social work, nursing, the ministry, and teaching.

This decade also saw change in the geographical loci of family therapy research, as well as change in the ranks of the researchers and theorists themselves. When the Bateson project officially ended in 1962, Jackson and Haley opened the Mental Research Institute (MRI) in California. They were joined there by Virginia Satir, a psychiatric social worker who, before moving to California, had worked and taught at the Chicago Psychiatric Institute. Satir quickly became a pivotal force in the field of family therapy, more as a practitioner with exceptional skills than as an innovative theorist. In the mid-1960s Satir left MRI and joined the personal growth movement at the Esalen Institute, also in California. Haley too left MRI in the 1960s, subsequently going to Philadelphia where he continued to develop his ideas about family systems. The tragic, untimely death of Jackson in 1968 dealt the final blow to the original Bateson group. However, this group's concepts and ideas have been the cornerstone of the family therapy movement and continue today to wield a heavy influence on family systems thinking.

During the 1960s Philadelphia became the locus of significant family therapy work. It was during these years that the Philadelphia Family Institute was founded. This institute developed the network therapy of Ross Speck and Carolyn Attneave, which, by treating families in their homes was able to include members of the identified patient's extended family and social network in the therapy.

In 1965 Salvador Minuchin founded the Philadelphia Child Guidance Clinic. Minuchin, who invited Jay Haley to join him, added his own brand of structural systems theory to the original findings of the Bateson and Bowen groups and demonstrated considerable clinical artistry in his treatment of families. It was at the Philadelphia Child Guidance Clinic that Minuchin and Haley, along with Carter Umbarger, Jerome Ford, Marianne Walters, and Rae Weiner, attempted to apply family therapy constructs to working-class families and to develop cross-cultural family systems interventions.

Minuchin came to the United States from Argentina (via Israel) after World War II to train as a child psychiatrist. While working with delinquent youths at the Wiltwyck School for Boys, Minuchin familiarized himself with the work of Jackson and Satir. Subsequently he decided to see if the principles developed by Ackerman, Satir, and Jackson, who worked primarily with middle-class families, could be applied to working-class families. Minuchin's group developed their own concepts and techniques as they worked with ghetto families of the inner city. We will discuss Minuchin's concepts and techniques in detail in chapter 5.

As the 1960s progressed, an increasing amount of therapy was being done with families of neurotic patients. However, the bulk of family therapy was still conducted with the families of institutionalized psychotic patients and delinquent children since the control that was possible within the institutional settings facilitated research and supervision. As the research continued, more attention was given to systems theory.

By the end of the 1960s, there were, in addition to the institutes founded by Ackerman and Minuchin and Haley, several new family institutes. Chief among these were the Family Studies Section at Bronx State Hospital in New York (affiliated with Albert Einstein College of Medicine) and the Chicago Family Institute. While an antitheory, practitioner trend was developing, an ideological conflict was also intensifying between the proponents of the psychoanalytic approach to family therapy and advocates of the systems approach. This conflict centered around certain psychoanalytic concepts that are at variance with systems concepts, such as homeostasis. The psychoanalytic view holds that the patient's intrapsychic conflicts disturb family relationships, whereas the systems view sees these same conflicts as developing in order to maintain the homeostatic balance of the family. The psychoanalytic view sees the symptoms as divisive, while the systems view sees them as holding the family together. The different family institutes reflected the different orientations to this ideological conflict. The ramifications of this conflict are still felt today, even though Ackerman's death in 1971 left the family therapy movement largely in the hands of the systems proponents.

Thus the 1960s were characterized by conflict between analysts and systems theorists, between clinicians and researchers, between whether clinical observation does or does not constitute "systematic" research. While certainly not new, the issue of whether psychotherapy is a science or an art, and a hard or a soft science if it is a science at all, continues to be a critical one for family therapy.

Family Therapy Today

The 1970s saw such a proliferation of family therapy that at times it seemed to be considered a panacea for all of society's ills. While family therapy has as many schools and views today as any other form of therapy, there is a definite leaning toward the systems view. On the other hand, some recent and fascinating conceptual innovations have drawn their inspiration from psychoanalytic theory.

In 1970 the Group for the Advancement of Psychiatry (GAP 1970) published the results of a survey in which the group's members had been asked to name the most important theorists in the field of family therapy. Although the data were collected in 1967, the survey is representative of the thinking within the mental health profession during the late 1960s and early 1970s. Not too surprisingly, the family theorists at the top of the list were Virginia Satir, Nathan Ackerman, Don Jackson, Jay Haley, and Murray Bowen. Foley (1974), who conducted a similar study in 1970, received the same results.

Recent theorists and practitioners have contributed their own styles of theoretical interpretation and application of therapeutic technique. Among the major new figures in family therapy are Carl Whitaker, James Framo, Phil Guerin, Donald Bloch, David Kantor, Thomas Fogarty, John Bell, Peggy Papp, Ivan Boszormenyi-Nagy, and Norman Paul.

The pioneers of the 1950s are, however, still considered the "masters" of the family therapy movement. Many of them are affiliated with well-established schools and training institutions throughout the country. In short-term workshops and training conferences at these institutions, they meet to disseminate their viewpoints and skills.

Neither the 1960s nor the 1970s led to a single accepted approach to family therapy. There is still conflict between the intrapsychic viewpoint and the systems concept, as well as between the theorists and the practitioners. The influence of systems theory has been predominant, certainly since the death of Nathan Ackerman. However, there does seem to be a trend toward "balancing" a systems approach with an integration of clinical knowledge of individual psychodynamics. In other words, as practitioners have gained experience, they have seemed more willing to include in their "family practice" strategies that had previously been reserved for the intrapsychic difficulties of the individual. For example, it is not uncommon today for a co-therapy team to work at times with a couple and at other times for each member of the team to work individually with the members of the couple. Similarly, in a family situation, the therapy team or an individual therapist may work individually with a child or with all of the children. While interactional difficulties can certainly be the source of intrapsychic symptoms, intrapsychic difficulties can also be the source of interactional problems. In the latter case, individual treatment may be necessary before conjoint family therapy is possible.

Along these same lines, practitioners are now more aware than ever that family therapy research has given little consideration to cultural factors. We do not yet know whether cultural differences in family roles and values have significance for treatment interventions —that is, whether families from different ethnic and sociocultural groups should be approached and treated in the same ways.

Current Settings

Family therapy today is most prevalent in metropolitan areas, where medical schools and affiliated universities frequently contain family therapy units. Many urban and suburban psychiatrists and social workers are currently seeking supervision and training so that they can incorporate the family therapy viewpoint into their existing practice. Although referrals for family therapy are common in these areas, there are pockets of resistance both within and without the metropolitan areas. Many traditional guidance clinics still adamantly separate therapists for different family members and frown upon the idea of conjoint treatment of family members.

Family therapy is a useful treatment modality in many settings. In addition to its application in public and private clinics, it is also practiced in school systems. School social workers may work with the families of school age populations either in home visits or within the school setting itself. School psychologists and counselors also work with the families of school age populations, but these two groups are increasingly coming to view the actual classroom environment as a "family" itself and have found family therapy concepts and intervention strategies to be applicable and effective there as well. For example, the position of the teacher in relation to a student or a group of students is very often like that of the parent to the child in the home environment. The psychologist or counselor who can diagnose the "classroom double bind," the communication problem, or the role distortion in the classroom system may frequently be able to intervene and help the student, the teacher, and the system itself to change and grow, just as a clinician might do with a family outside of the school environment.

Other environments in which family therapy concepts can claim efficacy range far and wide. These include the courtroom, where the judge may view the public offender's behavior as symptomatic of a more fundamental family problem and thus recommend family treatment; the divorce lawyer's office, where the attorney may view the spouse's "indiscretions" as an indication of some real need within the family relationships rather than as simply a matter of infidelity; the pediatrician's office, where the physician may view the child's sudden formation of allergies as reactive to substantial role changes within the child's family environment. The organizational concepts upon which family therapy is based are similar to those used by industrial psychologists involved in organizational development. Thus, with increasing frequency, family therapists and industrial psychologists are finding that they have much to learn from and to contribute to each other.

Current Theoretical Approaches

The major theoretical approaches to family therapy today are (1) the psychodynamic approach (2) the communication approach, and (3) the structural approach.

The psychodynamic approach to family therapy focuses on the intrapsychic conflicts of each member of the family unit. This approach applies the techniques and strategies of individual psychotherapy to family situations. Its major treatment goal is insight; it is believed that the behaviors and feelings of family members will change as each member gains insight about himself or herself and about other family members. Some of the developmental concepts about individuals and family systems that we will discuss in section III are derived from this approach. The communication and structural approaches are subsumed under the rubric of systems theory and practice, which is the subject of section II.

These three approaches to family therapy are not necessarily discrete. Many therapists pride themselves on their attempts to integrate different viewpoints and to draw from whichever perspective appears to be most relevant to a particular family.

Although there are other approaches to family work—for example, behavioral family therapy and "strategic" family therapy—we have chosen not to include separate discussions of them in this text for two reasons. The first reason is that despite the great effectiveness of some of these approaches in specific interventions, they do not advance new theories about family dynamics, but are better understood as *tactics* rather than points of view. The second reason for not including them, perhaps the more important, is that in most instances, although their "tactics" are new, their focuses are nevertheless the actual structures and communication styles within the family system and, as a result, they are subsumed under those theories.

When Is Family Therapy Indicated?

If one accepts the point of view that family therapy is not *always* the answer to a client's problems, the question becomes: When is it the treatment of choice? The answer will, of course, depend on the therapist's orientation and background, but in general it would seem that family therapy is appropriate when (1) the individual referred for treatment is living at home with a family or is working through unfinished business with a family even though not living at home; (2) when the presenting problems are affected by or themselves affect the family system; and (3) when both the therapist and client agree that family therapy is the appropriate modality. Remember, it is not necessary to have the entire family present in order to apply the family therapy point of view.

Consider the following example: Fourteen-year-old Janie, a bright ninth-grade student, with an IQ of 127, is the eldest daughter in a family consisting of forty-year-old Dad, an electrical engineer; Mom, a substitute teacher, who is thirty-six years of age; Martin, aged twelve; and Jerry, aged five. Janie's grades have slipped drastically, and she is currently failing three out of five subjects; she has become moody, withdrawn, and generally uncommunicative. The school counselor has a conference with the parents who express concern about Janie's behavior at home. She stays in her room all the time, resents "helping out with Jerry," and has been picked up for shoplifting within the past month. The parents are eager for help and accept the school counselor's referral to a community mental health clinic.

The clinic requests an initial interview with the parents and a separate interview with Janie by the same social worker. In the interview with the parents, the social worker learns that Jerry requires a great deal of supervision and care because of some learning and emotional disabilities; that Dad is very cognitive in his interactions and has high, perfectionistic standards and expectations for his wife and children; that Mom feels caught between Dad and the children and works very hard to be a "good mother." When talking to Janie, the social worker learns that Janie is very angry at her father, whom she perceives as being impatient and hostile with Jerry; angry at her mother for being "weak" and "unable to stand up to Dad"; and feels forced into therapy, which she is determined to resist. After these two interviews, the social worker arranges for a meeting of the entire family to observe at firsthand the family's communicational and interactional processes.

It was after this session that the social worker suggested a contract for six family therapy sessions. The social worker felt that the problem lay within the family system, not just within Janie, who seemed to be exhibiting the acting-out symptoms of a disturbed family system. Once Janie realized that she did not have to submit to the "identified patient role," she lowered her resistance to therapy. The parents, because of their genuine concern, were perfectly willing to be a part of the therapy. The two boys participated in the therapy sessions without any apparent concern. After six sessions, the family reported better understanding and a more balanced power system. Janie's symptoms disappeared, and she expressed higher satisfaction with her role in this family system.

Obviously, Janie could have been referred for individual therapy. It is highly possible that the same results would eventually have occurred. However, in this case, the whole family system benefited from being involved in the treatment, which initiated new patterns of relating and problem solving.

Let us now look at a case in which family therapy was not recommended: Joe K., aged 12, is referred by the courts to a local community mental health agency after being charged with truancy and vandalism. He is also suspected of being involved with a gang that has broken into neighborhood stores. Joe has not seen his father since his parents' divorce eight years ago. An only child, Joe lives in an upper duplex with his mother, who is a waitress. Mrs. K. is an alcoholic, who alternates between extreme dependency and rage toward Joe. She brings a succession of male friends into their home and leaves Joe to his own devices most of the day and evening. In elementary school, Joe had been an above-average student with above-average peer relationships. He has been slow entering puberty and expressed concern about "being small" as he entered junior high school.

In three individual sessions, the clinic's intake psychologist found Joe cooperative, frightened about his anger and lack of impulse control, and seeking attention and affiliation however possible. Joe verbalized bitterness about his family situation and his eagerness to do well in school so that he could graduate and be able to leave home. The intake psychologist felt that because of Mrs. K.'s instability, family therapy would be futile in this case; she instead referred Joe to a male therapist for individual therapy, hoping that a supportive, modeling relationship would help Joe gain insight into his developmental difficulties and teach him new ways of coping with his environment. A nine-month follow-up found that Joe had improved his school work, had developed new friendships, and had incorporated some coping techniques for dealing with his mother and his own conflicts.

Ideally, in this case, Mrs. K. would have participated in the therapy sessions with Joe. However, in reality, Mrs. K. exhibited no interest or desire to participate, and Joe therefore had to be the sole focus of treatment. Motivation, availability, goals, and accessibility are only some of the variables in determining the therapeutic modality.

Thus, there are no fixed guidelines that can make the choice of family therapy mandatory. It is often useful as a supplement to individual and group therapies. Assessment and diagnosis are always the crucial steps in determining the appropriate treatment modality, and some treatment cases are clearer than others. But in all cases, the *family therapy viewpoint is crucial to diagnosis and assessment,* regardless of the actual treatment unit and intervention that is ultimately chosen.

Summary

In this chapter, we described the family therapy perspective as one that regards problems and dysfunction as emanating from the family system rather than from the intrapsychic problems of any one individual. We used a case example of a catatonic adolescent to show how the identified patient's symptoms can be viewed both as a response to stress within the family system and as a factor that is necessary in maintaining the balance of the family system. To round out our description of what family therapy actually is, we compared family therapy with individual and group therapies.

To provide a context for understanding the family therapy viewpoint, we sketched the development of individual psychotherapy, out of whose traditions family therapy evolved. We noted that the impetus for the family therapy movement was the frustration that therapists experienced in applying individual psychotherapeutic strategies and techniques to hospitalized schizophrenic and delinquent populations. From early work on communications came the notion that the symptom could not be considered as separate from the system in which the symptom carrier lived; how communications and structures contribute to symptom formation and maintenance became a primary research focus of the early family therapy theorists.

We then pointed out that while there appears to be a current trend to approach family therapy from a systems viewpoint, many family therapists are attempting to integrate the theory and psychotherapeutic strategies of individual psychodynamics in their practice. We also discussed how family therapy has become a legitimate psychotherapeutic specialty today, one that is practiced within the fields of psychology, counseling, psychiatry, social work, pediatrics, nursing, and teaching. Intervention strategies—initially innovative in their progression in focus from the individual to the dyad, from the dyad to the triad, and then to the "nuclear family"—have now leaped outward to include extended families, network therapy, and larger ecological systems.

Our viewpoint is that the family therapy perspective is critical in terms of diagnosis. We also believe that although it is often desirable to treat the entire family unit directly, treatment of an individual or subsystem can be effective as long as one considers the desirability of effecting change within the family system. There are no clear guidelines to indicate when family therapy is a "must"; nonetheless the family therapy perspective is essential to a full assessment of the client's problems and an appropriate determination of treatment unit and modality.

We refer you to chapter 2 in the manual for exercises designed to help you integrate the concepts that emerged as family therapy developed and to understand the status of family therapy today. There you will also find listings of media that document the variety of modalities currently employed by family therapists.

References

Ackerman, N. 1938. "The Family as a Social and Emotional Unit." *Archives of Pediatrics* 55.

Bateson, G., et al. 1956. "Toward a Theory of Schizophrenia." *Behavioral Science* 1 (4):251–64.

Boszormenyi-Nagy, I., and J. Framo, eds. 1965. *Intensive Family Therapy.* New York: Goeber.

Bowen, M. 1976. "Theory in the Practice of Psychotherapy." In P. J. Guerin, Jr., ed., *Family Therapy.* New York: Gardner Press.

Coleman, J. C. 1964. *Abnormal Psychology and Modern Life,* 3rd ed. Glenview, Ill.: Scott, Foresman.

Foley, V. 1974. *An Introduction to Family Therapy.* New York: Grune & Stratton.

Framo, J., ed. 1972. *Family Interaction: A Dialogue between Family Researchers and Family Therapists.* New York: Springer.

Freud, S. 1964. "Analysis of Phobia in a Five-Year-Old Boy." In J. Strachey, ed., *The Complete Works of Sigmund Freud.* London: Hogarth Press.

Group for the Advancement of Psychiatry (GAP). 1970. *The Field of Family Therapy,* 7, no. 78. New York: Science House.

Jackson, D., ed. 1960. *The Etiology of Schizophrenia*. New York: Basic Books.
————, ed. 1968. *Communications, Family and Marriage*, vol. 1. Palo Alto, Calif.: Science & Behavior Books.

Suggested Readings

Ackerman, N. *The Psychodynamics of Family Life*. New York: Basic Books, 1958.
————. *Treating the Troubled Family*. New York: Basic Books, 1966.
Adler, A. *The Practice and Theory of Individual Psychology*. New York: Humanities Press, 1952.
Bloch, D., ed. *Techniques of Family Therapy, A Primer*. New York: Grune & Stratton, 1973.
Boszormenyi-Nagy, I., and G. Spark. *Invisible Loyalties*. New York: Harper & Row, 1973.
Bowen, M. "Family Psychotherapy." *American Journal of Orthopsychiatry* 31 (1961):40–60.
————. "The Use of Family Theory in Clinical Practice." *Comprehensive Psychiatry* 7 (1966):345–74.
Christensen, O. "Family Counseling: An Adlerian Orientation." In G. Gazda, ed., *Proceedings of a Symposium on Family Counseling and Therapy*. Athens: University of Georgia Press, 1971.
Ferber, A., M. Mendelsohn, and A. Napier. *The Book of Family Therapy*. Boston: Houghton Mifflin, 1973.
Haley, J., ed. *Changing Families*. New York: Grune & Stratton, 1971.
Haley, J., and L. Hoffman, eds. *Techniques of Family Therapy*. New York: Basic Books, 1967.
Howells, J. *Family Psychiatry*. Springfield, Ill.: Thomas, 1963.
————. *Theory and Practice of Family Psychiatry*. New York: Brunner/Mazel, 1971.
Laing, R. *The Divided Self*, Pelican Edition. Baltimore: Penguin Books, 1965.
————. "Mystification, Confusion, and Conflict." In I. Boszormenyi-Nagy and J. Framo, eds., *Intensive Family Therapy*. New York: Harper & Row, 1965.
————. *The Politics of Experience*. New York: Ballantine Books, 1967.
Laing, R., and A. Esterson. *Sanity, Madness and the Family*. Baltimore: Penguin Books, 1964.
Lidz, T. *The Family and Human Adaptation*. New York: International University Press, 1963.
Lidz, T., S. Fleck, and A. Cornelison. "The Intrafamilial Environment of Schizophrenic Patients: Marital Schism and Marital Skew." *American Journal of Psychiatry* 28 (1958):764–76.

————, eds. *Schizophrenia and the Family.* New York: International University Press, 1965.

MacGregor, R., et al. *Multiple Impact Therapy with Families.* New York: McGraw-Hill, 1964.

Minuchin, S., et al. *Families of the Slums.* New York: Basic Books, 1967.

Napier, A., with C. Whitaker. *The Family Crucible.* New York: Harper & Row, 1978.

Satir, V. *Conjoint Family Therapy,* 2nd ed. Palo Alto, Calif.: Science & Behavior Books, 1967.

Speck, R., and C. Attneave. *Family Networks.* New York: Pantheon Books, 1973.

Spiegel, J. *Transactions—The Interplay Between Individual, Family and Society.* New York: Science House, 1971.

Sullivan, H.S. *The Interpersonal Theory of Psychiatry.* New York: Norton, 1953.

Watzlawick, P., J. Beavin, and D. Jackson. *Pragmatics of Human Communication.* New York: Norton, 1967.

Watzlawick, P., J. Weakland, and R. Fisch. *Change.* New York: Norton, 1974.

Wynne, L.C. "Communication Disorders and the Quest for Relatedness in Families of Schizophrenics." In C. Sager and H.S. Kaplan, eds., *Progress in Group and Family Therapy.* New York: Brunner/Mazel, 1972.

Wynne, L.C., et al. "Pseudomutuality in the Family Relations of Schizophrenics." *Psychiatry* 21 (1958):205–20.

Zuk, G. *Family Therapy: A Triadic Based Approach.* New York: Behavioral Publications, 1971.

Zuk, G., and I. Boszormenyi-Nagy, eds. *Family Therapy and Disturbed Families.* Palo Alto, Calif.: Science & Behavior Books, 1967.

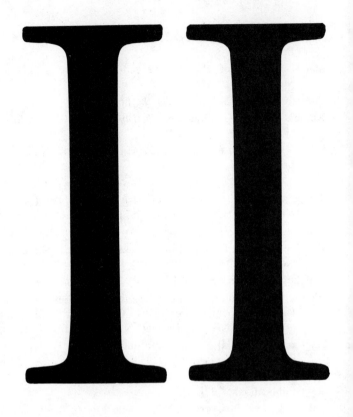

II

Systems Theory
and Practice

In chapter 3 we begin our study of major theoretical viewpoints by presenting a classification system of family therapy theories. Our classification system is based upon emphasis, upon what the theorist considers to be of primary importance. Chapter 3 also presents our rationale for classifying major family therapy theorists as communication theorists or as structural theorists.

Needless to say, our presentation of theorists in chapters 4 and 5 is selective. It is based on two premises: (1) the belief that an introductory work can only include a few major theoretical viewpoints and cannot be a survey of every conceivable theorist; and (2) the belief that the six theorists whom we do present have been the most original and significant contributors to the field of family therapy to date. These beliefs are based on a thorough review of the current literature of family therapy theory and practice, as well as on numerous dialogues with family therapy trainers and practitioners.

In chapter 4, we present Don Jackson, Virginia Satir, and Jay Haley as communication theorists, and in chapter 5, we present Murray Bowen, David Kantor, and Salvador Minuchin as structural theorists.

Classification of Family Therapy Theories

Chapter 3

Until recently one might have been able to define family therapy simply by distinguishing it from other psychotherapies. However, because of the steady, substantial, and sometimes divergent growth that family therapy has experienced during the last two decades, the label of "family therapy" today gives only a very general indication of conceptual framework and little clue as to the therapist's specific point of view or choice of strategies and tactics.

As we have seen in chapters 1 and 2, the complexity of the evolution of family therapy theory has paralleled the evolution of a family system. What began as an individual concept and then evolved into a dyad has become a network of theories and therapists that is itself not unlike an extended family system. The task of conceptualizing and classifying the major points of view is complicated not so much by major differences as it is by subtle distinctions concerning emphasis in theory or practice.

In this chapter we will first present some of the traditional ways of conceptualizing and classifying family therapy theory and practice. We will then present a classification scheme that not only includes the major theories, but also allows for a clearer understanding of their similarities and differences.

Three Traditional Classifications

Olson (1970) attempted a classification of family therapy theories in terms of the focus of the actual treatment. He proposed a variety of treatment focuses, ranging from emphasis on psychodynamically oriented techniques on the one hand, to emphasis on systemwide transactional techniques on the other. Within this spectrum, Olson proposed five categories: (1) intrapersonal, in which the individual is treated with a focus on intrapsychic processes; (2) interpersonal, in which related individuals work on interpersonal relations; (3) quasi-interactional, in which the individual works on interactional skills or relationship issues, not with the other person in the relationship, but by work (role play, for example) with the therapist; (4) interactional, in which an ad hoc group of unrelated or related individuals works on self-improvement and on relating with each other; and (5) transactional, in which a marital or family system works on improving family interrelations. In each case, the emphasis is clearly on the *modality* of therapy. Using Olson's conceptual scheme, the family theorists whom we will study in this section would fall, by virtue of their focus of treatment, into both the interactional and transactional frameworks.

Ferber, Mendelsohn, and Napier (1973) offer an alternative conceptual scheme in which they categorize family therapy theorists by the *role* of the therapist. Therapists may function as "conductors" or as "reactors." Conductors are active leaders and organizers of the therapy session. Reactors are less controlling, less directive therapists who allow the family more freedom of movement. Reactors are further divided into subgroups: the "analysts" who concern themselves with the internal, psychodynamic processes of the individuals within the family, and the "system purists" who are concerned with the communication processes within the family system. Using Ferber's conceptual scheme, we might classify the family theorists studied in this section according to these two categories: the "conductors" might include Bowen, Minuchin, Kantor, and Satir, while the "reactors-system purists" might include Haley and Jackson.

A third model for classifying and categorizing family therapy theorists is that of the Group for the Advancement of Psychiatry (GAP 1970), which offers a conceptual scheme that focuses on the *goal* of treatment. This model's two major goals may be seen as (1) alteration of behavior (behavioral), and (2) alteration of subjective feelings (phenomenological). All the therapists studied in this section fall somewhere on a continuum between these two extremes, with some emphasizing behavioral strategies and others emphasizing phenomenological strategies. In practice, most therapists demonstrate a judicious balance between the two extremes, using both interpersonal behavioral techniques and exploration and clarification of feeling and perceptual states.

Thus, we see that Olson's focus is on the *unit* of treatment, Ferber's is on the *role* of the therapist, and the GAP's is on the *goal* of treatment. We believe that each of these classification schemes pays insufficient attention to theoretical assumptions about the nature of the family. Their emphasis on the therapist and treatment rather than on underlying family theory is perhaps the result of the distances that emerged between family therapy theory and practice during the early 1960s when everyone rushed out to practice family therapy. In any case, we propose a scheme for the classification of family therapy theorists that considers each contributor's theoretical assumptions and notions about the nature of the family and family interaction.

An Alternative Classification

The classification scheme that we offer here is derived from a framework suggested by Ritterman (1976). It builds on the basic distinctions between the Newtonian and Einsteinian world views. Let us look at these distinctions and then integrate the major family therapy theories into the framework derived from them.

Newtonian and Einsteinian World Views

Before the twentieth century, Newtonian physics served as the basis for the Western world's major scientific view. Newtonian physics provided a *mechanistic* outlook, a *reductionistic* view of people and their world. All interactions and bodies were thought to be composed of basic building blocks, or "matter." The world was an assembly of moving parts performing in completely functional motion. Its blocks of matter could be broken down through analysis into smaller and smaller "bits and pieces"; ultimate reality was to be found in objectively observable, causal relationships among the bits and pieces of any situation.

This viewpoint postulated that change took place as a consequence of previous interaction. If one looked carefully enough and if one had sufficiently powerful analytic tools, one could find: (1) the antecedents of any behavior, (2) the consequences of such behavior, and (3) how that consequence became the antecedent for new behavior. In other words, given situation C, one may not only determine its evolution from situation B (which originated from situation A), but also predict situation C's consequences for situation D (which will cause situation E). This view pervaded the physical sciences and ultimately was incorporated into the social sciences and into the development of psycho-analytic theory itself.

It is quite consistent with the Newtonian point of view that Sigmund Freud should have postulated a psychology that held that (1) if one can trace a client's early childhood experiences (the antecedents of behavior), and (2) if one can "analyze" these experiences (break them down into their bits and pieces), then (3) one can correctly diagnose and treat the problem at hand.

With the emergence of Einstein's notions of the physical world, the major scientific perspective of the Western world shifted to a more "organismic" outlook. By *organismic* we mean that the character of the whole system, the overriding structures, determined the system's properties and functions. This was a more *holistic* view, as opposed to the reductionistic view of the Newtonian model.

Its philosophy was that parts or part processes, below a certain point, are nondecomposable units that relate to and derive their meaning from a larger organized "whole." It is the energy and the structure of the organism that determine the relationship of its parts, rather than the parts being preeminent, as in the Newtonian model. Change and growth are interactive processes that have to do with the *current* structure and function of the organism, as it is presently active, not as it developed from its past or from its basic elements.

Therefore, it would be quite consistent with the Einsteinian viewpoint for a clinician (1) to examine the present context and structures within which the symptom manifests itself (for example, an apparently socially disabled twenty-seven-year-old male still living at home as the last of three children to leave), (2) to look for the etiology and the sustaining dynamics of the particular problem within the present active functioning of the organism (the "child's" guilt about leaving and the parents' anxiety about having "no one" at home), and (3) to diagnose and treat the problem on the basis of these "holistic" observations.

Table 3–1 outlines the major differences between the Newtonian and Einsteinian world views. Let us see now how these differences underlie two separate points of emphasis in systems theory and how these emphases distinguish the two major positions in family therapy theory today.

Communication and Structural Theorists: Different Emphases in the Application of Systems Theory

An ever-larger portion of the theory of family therapy today has as its underlying conceptual framework an integration of systems theory and developmental theory. Each of the theorists presented in the next two chapters recognizes the necessity for individuals and for families to negotiate developmental challenges. Their differences lie not in developmental theory, but rather in their points of *emphasis* within *systems theory* itself.

In our review of systems theory in chapter 1, we noted that a system is composed of (1) structures (systems, subsystems, and rules for their function), and (2) parts and interactions (the bits and pieces of actual communication). The different emphases in the Newtonian and Einsteinian world views are precisely those that underlie a belief in "structure," vis-à-vis a belief in "parts and interactions," as being basic to understanding a system. The Newtonian, mechanistic position sees the bits and pieces, the parts and interactions, as the key in systems theory. The Einsteinian, organismic position sees the dynamic order and structure as the key. The former is a "microview"; the latter, a "macroview." In looking at a system, each position concedes partial validity to the other point of view, but considers its own particular emphasis as the key to understanding the system. Thus, proponents of the Newtonian view concede that a system may have an overriding "dynamic order," but they argue that the actual interactions among the bits and pieces within the system are critical in understanding the development of the system, its functions, and strategies for change. Proponents of the Einsteinian view, on the other hand, concede that a

Table 3–1 *Newtonian and Einsteinian World Views*

	Newtonian	*Einsteinian*
Conceptual Model	Mechanistic	Organismic
Function of Organism	Reactive	Active
Physical Model	The inert machine	The living biological system
Basic Building Resource	Matter	Energy
Notion of Causality	Antecedent-consequent	Structure-function (simultaneous)
Object of Analysis	Elementary particles	Structure of the active whole
View of Reality	Objective reality sought in observable, causal relationships between elementary components in any field	Reality inferred because structures cannot be observed or completely predicted; objective reality replaced by analysis of the relationship between the observed and observer

system contains "bits and pieces," but they argue that the dynamic structure within which those interactions take place is the primary factor in understanding system development, function, and change.

Based on these distinctions, we are proposing a classification scheme that attempts to group family therapy theorists into two camps. Our scheme is based *not* on therapist role, goal of treatment, or treatment unit, but on the relative importance that the theorist assigns to "bits and pieces" versus "dynamic order and structure."

Family therapy theorists who emphasize specific interactions, the bits and pieces of actual communication among family members, as the key to understanding family function and dysfunction clearly derive their rationale from a Newtonian framework. And, because their emphasis is primarily upon the cognitive and affective communications among family members, we classify them as *communication theorists*.

On the other hand, family therapy theorists who emphasize the dynamic order of the system, the overriding structure, as the key to understanding family function and dysfunction clearly derive their rationale from the Einsteinian framework. Because their emphasis is primarily upon the system's dynamic structure, we classify them as *structural theorists*.

However, just as the evolution of scientific thought has increasingly bridged the gap between the Newtonian and Einsteinian world views (a gap that may ultimately be seen as a false dichotomy), the direction in family therapy theory and practice seems to be toward a synthesis of communication theory and structural theory. In actual practice, when contending with the overwhelming complexity of one family in crisis, few clinicians can afford to ignore either the family's "bits and pieces" or its "dynamic order and structure." Many family therapists move easily among all the theorists as they add to and borrow from each "camp."

Although communication theory and structural theory may be moving closer together, a classification of theorists based on their positions in relation to communication and structure is nonetheless useful in facilitating an understanding of the theorists' points of view.

Chapter 4 presents the work of Don Jackson and Virginia Satir, family therapy theorists who championed communication theory and whose treatment therefore focused on the bits and pieces of the family system. Chapter 4 also presents the work of Jay Haley, whose initial emphasis was upon communication. More recently, however, Haley has argued more for structural intervention; thus his work forms a bridge between the communication theorists of chapter 4 and the structural theorists of chapter 5.

Chapter 5 presents the work of Murray Bowen, David Kantor, and Salvador Minuchin. Each of these theorists is concerned with the dynamic structure of the family system, and each has made a substantial contribution to structural family therapy.

Summary

In this chapter, we briefly reviewed three traditional classification schemes for family therapy theory. We concluded the chapter by presenting our rationale for classifying the major family therapy theorists as communication theorists or as structural theorists.

In the process of explaining our rationale, we considered the divergent Newtonian and Einsteinian world views: the former, a microview that sees the organism as mechanistic, reactive, and having observable and analyzable interaction; the latter, a macroview that sees the organism as holistic, active, and having a dynamic structure that allows inferences, but that cannot be completely observed or analyzed.

The differences in these two world views were seen to parallel the different emphases of the major family therapy theorists as they apply general systems theory to the study of family systems. Communication theorists, because of a Newtonian orientation, tend to emphasize the bits and pieces of communication when viewing a family system. Structural theorists, on the other hand, have an Einsteinian orientation, which leads them to emphasize the overriding dynamic structure within a family system.

We acknowledged that this classification scheme is useful in facilitating an initial presentation of the therapists' theories, but that in fact theorists from each "camp" acknowledge some validity in the position of the other "camp" and that neither viewpoint by itself presents a wholly adequate explanation of family systems. Moreover, most practitioners invariably feel compelled to consider both points of view when actually contending with the overwhelming complexity of treating a family in crisis.

In chapter 3 in the manual you will find exercises that illustrate how the communication and structural theorists emphasize different points within a systems theory framework. These exercises will also help you to articulate your own personal theories of families and change.

References

Ferber, A., M. Mendelsohn, and A. Napier. 1973. *The Book of Family Therapy.* Boston: Houghton Mifflin.

Group for the Advancement of Psychiatry (GAP). 1970. *The Field of Family Therapy,* 7, no. 78. New York: Science House.

Olson, D. 1970. "Marital and Family Therapy: Integrative Review and Critique." *Journal of Marriage and the Family* 32 (4):501–37.

Ritterman, M.K. 1976. "Paradigmatic Classification of Family Therapy Theories." *Family Process* 14 (6):29–46.

Suggested Readings

Broderick, C.B. "Beyond the Five Conceptual Frameworks." *A Decade of Development in Family Therapy, 1960–1970.* National Council of Family Relations, 1970.

Klein, D. M., J. D. Schvaneveldt, and B. C. Miller. "The Attitudes and Activities of Contemporary Family Theorists." *Journal of Comparative Family Studies* 8, no. 1 (Spring 1977):5–28.

Communication Theorists

Chapter

4

In this chapter, we will deal with those family therapy theorists and practitioners who focus on the "how" of the interactional process. The "how" of family therapy theory refers to the styles of communication between family members. The theorists whom we will discuss in this chapter, Don Jackson, Virginia Satir, and Jay Haley, share an orientation toward communication theory, but are distinguished from each other by their respective emphases on cognition, feelings, and power. Let us look at their common theoretical orientation before discussing their individual theoretical contributions, styles, and approaches.

Conceptual Framework

The general communicational orientation of family therapy was developed by the Bateson and Mental

Research Institute (MRI) groups during the 1950s (see chapter 2). At various times, these groups included Gregory Bateson, Jay Haley, Don Jackson, Paul Watzlawick, and John Weakland. (You will find the principal works of these theorists listed under "Suggested Readings" at the end of this chapter.)

Communication theorists assume that you can learn about the family system by studying communication, both verbal and nonverbal. Their focus is therefore on observable, current interactions (relationships) within the family system, not on a historical analysis of the individual family members. Human interaction is seen as analogous to a chess game, where emphasis is on the relationship of the pieces at present, the rules that govern the players, and the next move. The following are the axioms of the communication theorists:

1. *All behavior is communicative.* It is impossible *not* to communicate, since even silence or withdrawal indicates something about the relationship between two people.

2. *Every communication has a content/report and a relationship/command aspect.* The latter classifies the former and is, therefore, a *metacommunication.* The metacommunication is the nonverbal message about the verbal message. It is that aspect of the message that places a demand on the recipient. For example, if someone tells you that "the roads are slippery," it means that driving conditions are poor, but depending upon the tone of voice and the inflections, the person might be asking for a ride someplace, expressing concern about your ability to drive in these conditions, letting you know that he or she is not going to go someplace, and so forth.

3. *Relationships are defined by the command messages and are dependent upon the punctuation of the communicational sequences between the communications.* It is this command part of the message that is sometimes unclear. Misunderstanding can result when communicators are unaware of the commands they are giving, receiving, or obeying. The punctuational sequence between communicators refers to the flow of communication-response patterns. To return to the example of "the roads are slippery," if the command aspect of this message is a wish for you to drive this person someplace and you do not respond appropriately, the sender of the message may feel resentful and hurt by your lack of response, and you may feel upset because you have no idea why this person is acting hurt, since you never perceived the sender's command message—that is, the punctuational sequence has been ineffective.

4. *Human beings communicate both digitally (verbally) and analogically (nonverbally).* The verbal communication deals with the content/report of the message, while the nonverbal communication deals with the relationship/command aspect, which, as we noted above, is often

unclear and ambiguous. Thus, we are not just concerned with the meaning of the message, but also with what it says about the relationship between the communicators.

5. *All communicational interchanges are either symmetrical (equal and parallel where either can lead) or complementary (where one leads and the other follows).* Thus, interactions are based on equality or on differences and enable us to learn about the nature of the relationship between the communicators. If the relationship is equal and symmetrical, the punctuational sequence is even, and the power wielded by the demands of the metacommunication is equally distributed between the two communicators. If the relationship is complementary, one person usually dominates by demanding of the partner and by the partner's acceding to these demands. Thus, the complementary relationship pattern is of a "leader" and a "follower."

What do these axioms mean in terms of family systems? Despite the different emphases of Jackson, Satir, and Haley, common core concepts, which embody these axioms, are evident in their work. These concepts may be summarized as follows:

1. The primary need of individuals within a relationship is to *form and maintain the relationship itself.*
2. There are two major tasks involved in this process: deciding *what* the *rules* of the relationship are, and negotiating *who* actually makes the decisions regarding the rules.
3. The tasks of *setting rules* and *negotiating who has control* over the rules are accomplished through the exchange of *messages.*
4. *Messages* form the substance of the communications between people in the relationship and, as such, are the *basic element* of the *interactional process.*
5. Messages have two major aspects: the *communicational,* dealing with the *content* of the message itself, and the *metacommunicational,* dealing with the *message about the message.* The latter seeks to impose behavior or to define the self and the nature of the relationship.

Thus, the core concept of the communication theorists is that relationships can be understood by analyzing the communicational and metacommunicational aspects of their interactions.

Family System Properties and Communication

Before we look further at rule setting and message units themselves and at the components of communication, let us look again at those *system properties* that characterize the communication system:

1. *System-subsystem relations.* The interactions between subsystems and between the system and any subsystem can alter the characteristics of the system.
2. *Wholeness.* A change in the communicative behavior of one part of the system will change the interactions of all parts of the system and of the larger system.
3. *Feedback.* The circular feedback can alter communicative behavior at any point. This feedback can be sequential or spontaneous. *Sequential* feedback occurs when messages are communicated through a clear chain. For example, Mother may tell daughter something that she knows daughter will pass along to older brother, who, in turn, will pass the message along to Father. Mother knows that this is the path to delivering a message to Father. *Spontaneous* feedback occurs when each member of a system has communicational access to all other members and messages are delivered via any combination of communicators, or even directly. Feedback can be negative or positive. *Negative* feedback is information about the system performance that serves to decrease the deviation from the set norm or bias of the system, to reduce change. *Positive* feedback is information about the system performance that serves to increase the deviation from the set norm or bias of the system, to increase change.
4. *Equifinality.* The final results of the interaction systems will depend upon the process of interaction, not on the number or characteristics of the individual members in the system.

Another property to consider is the *time variable.* Time can limit the number of possible communicative interactions and can alter the context in which communications occur.

The process of rule setting and change requires further elaboration of *homeostasis,* a major concept of systems theory.

Homeostasis.   The purpose of negative feedback is to maintain the homeostatic balance within a system. Homeostasis is the dynamic equilibrium that is established as the family evolves; it is continuously threatened by external stresses (for example, job loss, economic depression, war, geographical relocation, fire) and internal stresses (for example, birth of a new child, death or serious illness, developmental crisis of individual family member).

As an example of family homeostasis, let us look at a case in which a thirty-five-year-old woman, suffering from anxiety and depression, enters therapy at her husband's urging. Her depression and anxiety have kept her so immobilized that she has been unable to attend to child care and housework. After a couple of months of therapy, she begins to behave more assertively, demanding that her husband and children share more of the housework and taking time for her own interests and activities. At this time her husband begins to feel depressed and anxious, and chides her for "getting sicker rather than better" because of her therapy.

Thus, the behavioral change of one person in this family system has affected the equilibrium (homeostasis) of the system and caused an imbalance to occur. When such an imbalance occurs, there is an extremely strong impulse on the part of the system to *revert* to its former homeostatic state, that which is known and customary. Whether or not the former homeostatic state is comfortable or painful is immaterial. A system would rather retain its familiar pain than subject itself to the vulnerability of change, even when the outcome of that change is likely to alleviate the pain.

Change agents must consider the *homeostatis* of the system and the *strong resistance to change* that occurs when the homeostasis is disrupted. This principle cannot be overstressed. It is a cornerstone for the family systems theorist.

Messages

Remembering the axioms we have cited, let us now look more carefully at the nature of messages, which form the substance of communications. Any observable behavior may transmit a message. The more obvious message is that conveyed through spoken language. This may be termed *verbal, digital,* or *report*. However, the nonverbal message, which may be termed *metacommunication, analog, command* and which is conveyed through specific action, tone of voice, facial expression, gesture, and posture, is also an effective means of communication. People are often unable to resolve disagreements because they have not understood each other's messages. One person may insist on arguing about the content, whereas the other is reacting to the relational aspect of the message.

Any message, whether it is verbal or nonverbal, contains *both* the report (verbal, digital) aspect and the command (metacommunication, analog) aspect. The *report* aspect intends to *convey information*, whereas the *command* aspect intends to *impose behavior and to control the relationship*. For example, a friend approaches us with tears in his eyes, holding a handkerchief soaked from crying, and says, "I'm so lonely living alone and so desperate for conversation." The report aspect of the message is clear: the information being conveyed may be considered biographical data about our friend's present living conditions. The command aspect of the message, being sent through many channels, is less obvious. It defines the sender as unhappy and intends to impose a certain type of behavioral response on us—that we should offer help and be sympathetic.

The command aspect of messages defines relationships and establishes the rules governing which behaviors are to be included or excluded in a relationship. The interaction of the sender's message and the receiver's acquiescence in accepting it is a process involving *both* members. In the example above, we, as the receiver, have a choice: we may *not* respond with sympathy and help, and so, when we do, it is an interaction for which we, together with the sender, are responsible (Rappaport 1976).

Many people claim ignorance about the command aspects of their communications and about the rules of their relationships. For example, a husband comes home and tells his wife that he has purchased tickets so that they may spend their vacation in Florida. He has not checked with her in advance because he "knew" she would want to go. As it happens, his wife becomes furious because she was not consulted first. The husband cannot understand her anger because she in fact agrees with the plan. An understanding of content versus relational levels of communication shows that the real argument focuses not on whether they should go to Florida (that is, the level of content), but on the wife's wanting to be consulted first (that is, the level of relationship). As long as the husband continues to focus on the content, on which there is no disagreement, the argument will continue because it does not address the issue, which is relational in nature. The wife's concern is that her husband should not define their relationship as one in which he makes unilateral decisions about what should occur, even though the decisions might be ones she would make herself, given the opportunity. The point is that these aspects of communication do exist, whether or not one is aware of them. The communication theorists believe that changing communicational behavior can alter relationships within the system.

Communication Components

Watzlawick, Beavin, and Jackson (1967), in developing further concepts of family communications, broke communication down into three component parts: syntactics, semantics, and pragmatics.

Syntactics focuses on the problems of transmitting *information*. These problems are related to the system's capacity and noise and include problems of coding, channels, redundancy, an other statistical properties of language. In other words, syntactics focuses on the grammatical properties of language. The symbolic meaning of messages is irrelevant to the "information" theorist who is concerned with syntactics.

Semantics, however, focuses on the *meaning* of communication. It emphasizes that it is possible to have syntactical (grammatical) accuracy and yet have a meaningless message unless sender and receiver understand beforehand the significance of the words and gestures. In this sense, convention often determines the meaning, and it is easy to see how two communicators who do not share semantic convention can send messages that neither really comprehends.

Pragmatics focuses on the *behavioral* effects of the communication, what it actually causes one to do or not to do. Pragmatics includes the content and the context of the message; it considers all behavior to be communicative and all communication to be behavior.

These three component parts of a message unit are interdependent; each component must be understood in order to assess the nature of the communicational problem. In the example of the friend in tears who is holding a handkerchief and saying, "I'm so lonely living alone and so desperate for conversation," the syntactics of the message is clear. The man is lonely and wants someone to talk to him. The grammar is accurate. The semantics depends on each person's understanding that the tears and loneliness represent sadness and a demand for comfort. The pragmatics of the message is the command that the receiver of the message stop and take the time to talk.

Using the conceptual framework we have described, the communication theorists focus on improving the ways a family system communicates. They concentrate on how a family sends and receives messages. By studying a family's metacommunications, its "messages about the message," the communication theorists inform themselves of the nature of the family's relationships. We will now examine in more detail the work of Jackson, Satir, and Haley.

DON JACKSON

Don Jackson, as we noted in chapter 2, was the psychiatric member of the original Bateson research group during the early 1950s. Until his untimely death in 1968, Jackson published more material on family therapy than any other theorist and, as Foley (1974) points out, "constantly intertwined his clinical experience with theory to produce a rich but subtle conception of family process." A list of Jackson's principal writings can be found at the end of this chapter.

Major Concepts

Jackson's major theoretical contributions deal with the organization of human interaction. It was Jackson (1957) who introduced the concept of *family homeostasis* to the Bateson research project. Jackson observed that disturbed families were particularly resistant to change. When the patient improved, the stability or equilibrium of the family was disturbed; when the patient again lapsed into illness, the comfortable, status-quo balance, or equilibrium, returned. Jackson theorized that over a period of time, a family develops certain repetitive, enduring interactional techniques for maintaining its equilibrium when confronted with stress. These techniques are characteristic of a given family and are what we call *homeostatic mechanisms.* They are similar to an individual's defense mechanisms and determine how a particular family will deal with imbalance. Jackson wrote:

> It is significant in the development of family theory that it was the observation of homeostatic mechanisms in the families of psychiatric patients that led to the hypothesis of the family as a homeostatic, and eventually specifically as a rule-governed system. For . . . [rules] become quickly apparent if one can observe the reaction to their abrogation and infer therefrom the rule which was broken. Tiresome long-term observation of the beaten path, with careful noting of possible routes which were *not* taken, can eventually yield a fair guess about the rules of the game. But the observable counteraction of a single deviation is like a marker to our goal. [Jackson 1965b, pp. 13–14]

Jackson believed that the stability of the relationship is maintained by the *rule of the relationship* (1965a). As we have noted, the axioms of the communication theorists state that in every communication the communicators offer to each other definitions of their relationship. The rules of the relationship apply to all aspects of the relationship—equality (symmetry), differences (complementarity), a particular style of relating, such as persecuting, defending, and so forth. Families are rule-governed systems; thus whether the rules of the relationship are implicit and underlying, or explicit and apparent, they nonetheless operate in all family systems. The following exchange shows how a family rule defines one aspect of a marital relationship:

Henry: Mom, can I have the car Saturday night? John is on the phone and we want to get some action going then.
Mom: We don't have any plans that I know of, but I'll ask Dad when he gets home tonight.
Henry: Gosh, Mom, he won't be getting home until late, and John and I need to know so we can let the girls know.
Mom: I'll let you know as soon as I speak to your father.

In this situation, we can see what the rule about permission for use of the car in this family is, namely, getting Dad's permission. This brief dialogue also defines Mom and Dad's relationship in this instance as a complementary one, with Mom taking a request to Dad for his action. The issue is not whether this is right, wrong, good, or bad, but what the rules are and how they impact upon the behavioral interactions of the system.

When the rules are set in such a way that they can never be changed, the family system must be considered dysfunctional. For example, there are systems that have conflicting sets of rules in that two rules paradoxically negate each other. These rules may consist of (1) an operating rule and (2) a "rule about the rules" that denies the operating rule. Consider a family who has an operating rule dictating that "everyone is entitled to privacy," as well as a rule that "you cannot lock the bathroom door at any time because it is a health hazard." These two rules set up a situation in which one or the other of the rules will be broken every time anyone uses the bathroom. The double bind is that one loses by breaking one rule no matter what one chooses to do: by not locking the bathroom door, one is breaking the rule that everyone is entitled to privacy; but if one locks the bathroom door to ensure privacy, one is breaking the rule about locking the bathroom door. Jackson points out that people often invoke values of health or morality to avoid the operating rules.

Jackson's concept of rule holds that a system operates within certain limits. To describe his concept, Jackson added a fourth characteristic of the family system to those of wholeness, nonsummativity, and homeostasis, namely, *calibration*. The concept of calibration refers to the "setting" of the system, the defining of the rule. If we think back to the example in chapter 1 of the thermostat being set (calibrated) to regulate the temperature in the room, we remember that when the thermostat temperature is changed, there is a difference in the output of heat from the furnace. If the thermostat is raised, more heat is released from the furnace and the temperature in the room increases; if the thermostat is lowered, less heat is released from the furnace and the temperature in the room decreases. In family systems, calibration is the behavior that allows the system to operate and control its range or function. Thus, calibration of customary or acceptable behavior is the act of setting the family rules by which individuals or families most often operate. Any change or deviation from the accepted rules is counteracted by a homeostatic mechanism that either restores the homeostasis and the accepted rules or recalibrates the system by changing the setting. Such recalibration is referred to as a *step-function*.

It is Jackson's emphasis on the *process of articulating relationships* through specific interactions that characterizes him as a communication theorist. Jackson focused on the relationships between the sender and receiver (the process), not on the messages themselves (the content) nor on the subsystem in which they take place (the context). In other words, Jackson was primarily interested in the "how," not the "why" or the "where." More specifically, Jackson focused on (1) observing interactional patterns and (2) investigating the lines of communication by looking at how the "rules" of the system have been violated, who has the right to do what to whom and when, and who makes the family rules. Jackson, after observing the pattern, looked for ways to *punctuate* the sequence differently.

Jackson believed that punctuation organizes behavioral events and is therefore vital to interactional systems. Disagreement about how to punctuate the sequence of events is the cause of innumerable relationship struggles. For example, Mrs. Smith feels that she has to nag Mr. Smith continually because he is so passive and weak that he won't do what he is supposed to do if she doesn't keep after him by nagging. Mr. Smith sees himself as reacting to Mrs. Smith's nagging by withdrawing and appearing passive. Each sees the other as the provoker of their respective responses. Thus, the two different views of a common experience derive from this couple's inability to metacommunicate about their respective patterns of communication. This type of conflict ("Do it," "I won't") can go on ad infinitum until each person is thoroughly convinced that the other is bad or crazy.

For Jackson, therefore, we can say that (1) key issues are the relationship rules and homeostatic mechanisms that maintain the homeostasis of the system; (2) these rules are formed and maintained through communication; (3) the principle strategy is to alter the punctuation of communications, to change rules, and to calibrate the system. We will now see how Jackson did this.

Process of Therapy

Jackson was an active therapist who believed that the therapist's first task should be to intervene in the family's communication system. As an active participant, Jackson used the first session to set ground rules (for example, rules about tape recording, talking only in the present context, attending future meetings) and to engage all the family members in the therapeutic process (Jackson 1967). Jackson's style was *directive* and *cognitive;* maintaining the stance of the "expert," he focused on his and the family's thinking. By concentrating on the interactional system, Jackson was able to assess the shifting of meaning, intent, and focus within the communication system, which clued him about the nature of the family homeostasis. He made no attempt to interpret individual behavior or to provide insight to family members.

Goal of Therapy. Jackson aimed at *behavioral* change, rather than at change in attitude or feeling. This behavioral change could be seen when the homeostasis and rules of the system had changed. Influenced by behavioral learning theory, Jackson focused on the present rather than on exploring the past. He was interested in history only insofar as it shed light on the current interactional process.

As Jackson intervened in a system, he paid particular attention to the family structure and its component parts, namely the marital dyad, the parent-child relationships, and the sibling subsystems. However, he did this by checking out lines of communication to determine the rules of the system and the homeostatic mechanisms. Jackson's goals as a therapist were to help the family establish a *new homeostasis* and to clarify the *rules* that operate within the family.

To achieve these goals, it is necessary to upset the existing homeostasis of the family by disturbing the existing system. This calls for a directive, active type of therapy, where the paradoxical manipulation of power becomes a curative technique.

Techniques of Therapy. Jackson's two major therapeutic techniques were "relabeling" and "prescribing the symptom."

1. *Relabeling*: Relabeling is a way of reframing the problem for the family. The therapist emphasizes the positive and appealing aspect of the most disturbing communications. He or she lets the family seem to define the situation, but, in the end, manipulates the family into considering the therapist's viewpoint and eventually following it. For example, a couple comes for therapy complaining about the husband's

apparent inability to make love without being stoned. According to the wife, the problem is the husband's dependence on marijuana. According to the husband, the problem is the wife's lack of interest in sex. The therapist suggests that perhaps the husband wants so much to please his wife that he smokes in the hope that it will make him more relaxed and spontaneous and that he will therefore be a better, more caring lover. This gives the couple a new framework for looking at their problem. Relabeling is a means of taking the focus off the identified patient and helping family members look at the dynamics of the interactions in a different way.

2. *Prescribing the Symptom*: In this technique, the therapist instructs the family to continue and exaggerate what is already going on. This instruction is given seriously and the family is told that they must follow it. Since this behavior is already occurring, nothing worse can occur. There are two levels to this instruction: (1) on the one level, it appears to be something that is not too difficult to do, since the behavior is already occurring; and (2) on the interpersonal level, it shifts the meaning of the symptom and/or the balance of power within the system. Ferber, Mendelsohn, and Napier (1973) point out that there is a "meta" feature of this instruction: the instruction comes from a therapist who is not crazy (after all, how can a therapist be crazy?), so the behavior must be all right; otherwise the therapist would not prescribe it. The technique of prescribing the symptom is based on the belief in the therapeutic effect of *paradoxical communication*. Usually, the targeted behavior wilts under intention.

The following example shows how one can relabel the symptom, reframing the perceptual set of the couple, and then prescribe the symptom:

> A couple seeks help because they feel they are arguing too much. Rather than concentrating his attention on an analysis of their conflicts, the therapist redefines their quarrels by telling them they are really in love and the more they argue, the more they are in love because they care enough to be at each other and because fighting the way they fight presupposes a deep, emotional involvement. . . . No matter how ridiculous the couple may consider this interpretation—or precisely because it is so ridiculous to them—they will set about to prove to the therapist how wrong he is. This can best be done by stopping their arguing just to show that they are *not* in love. But the moment they stop arguing, they find that they are getting along much better. [Watzlawick, Beavin, and Jackson 1967, p. 251]

Role of the Therapist.   The major quality to remember about Jackson's therapeutic process is that he believed in *disturbing the family system,* a much more active stance than sitting back and pointing out and interpreting problems. When the family system is disturbed, the homeostatic balance is upset, and the family is then forced to establish a new equilibrium.

The therapist becomes a model and a teacher in helping the family learn how to achieve these changes. Because he wanted to be "up front" about his desire to influence people, Jackson acknowledged that he was manipulative (Jackson 1967). At the same time, as a participant in the family system, he felt perfectly comfortable expressing his own confusion or private opinions to his clients. He did not see this openness as a manipulative ploy, but rather as a way of actively intervening in the system.

While viewing films or reading transcripts of Jackson's work, one is struck by the air of competence and concern that he was able to exude to families. He was comfortable establishing limits and firmly, yet kindly, refusing to allow family members to hurt him, themselves, or each other. One notes the following strategies: (1) Jackson let many pathological statements go by in early sessions because he saw patterns that were redundant and that would be repeated; he was concerned that someone would be so humiliated that he or she would break up the group or that the person's humiliation would result in a coalition between sides that would be impossible to break down. (2) When Jackson perceived that the identified patient was about to negate himself or herself with a directly self-expressive comment, Jackson broke in to cut the person off after the positive part of the communication. (3) Jackson did not want to elicit too much information too quickly because it could interfere with the therapeutic process. (4) He attempted to engage all members of the family by having each make a contribution and by not following up on each one's contribution so that all would have the opportunity to participate. (5) Jackson tried to relabel negatives into positives, especially emotions. (6) He sometimes reduced to absurdity an interpretation of an interaction. (7) He emphasized the equality of all family members throughout the entire interview.

Overview of Jackson

Within the axioms of communication theory, Jackson's special emphasis was on *meaning*. Jackson saw the report aspect of the communication as dealing cognitively with the individual's thoughts about who he or she is and what the relationship means and the command aspect as intending to determine who the individual is, and so, to control what the relationship should mean. As a therapist dealing with a troublesome relationship between two people, Jackson's emphasis was on *relabeling* the implications of the behavior, rather than on clarifying the affect or power aspects of the relationship. His type of intervention reconceptualizes the meaning of the relationship for involved parties. Such a reconceptualization gives people the opportunity either to accept present behavior because they now understand it differently or to change it because they knowingly choose to do so.

For Jackson, then, the nature of the double bind is to effect one's identity and the meaning of one's behavior within a system. Communications in general have more to do with meaning and the determination of an individual's identity than with affect or issues of power and control.

VIRGINIA SATIR

Although Satir, a social worker, does not really add any new theoretical concepts to those developed by Jackson, Haley, and the other MRI researchers, she does provide a different focus, interpretation, and application of theory to practice. It is because of this different focus, which is influenced more by phenomenological theory than by behavioral theory, that we include her as a major communication theorist. Her basic text, *Conjoint Family Therapy* (1964), abounds in illustrations that translate her growth-oriented philosophy into clinical practice.

Major Concepts

Satir's growth-oriented philosophy stresses that individuals are innately good and that they have the capacity to develop their full potential. It is when this development of potential is blocked or hindered that pathology occurs. (We can see the influence of Rogers and Maslow on Satir's philosophical values.)

The concept of *maturation* is central to Satir's viewpoint: "The most important concept in therapy, because it is a touchstone for all the rest, is that of maturation" (1967, p. 91). Satir explains that mature people are those who are able to take full charge of themselves by assuming responsibility for their own choices and decisions. Choices and decisions that lead to growth are based on people's having accurate perceptions about themselves and others, and on their finding affirmation of their perceptions within their environments. To develop this maturity, it is important to be able to separate oneself from one's family, to become a *differentiated self*. The mature person would thus be characterized by (1) the ability to be in touch with his or her own feelings; (2) the ability to communicate clearly with others; (3) the ability to accept others as different from oneself; and (4) the willingness to see differentness and differentiation as a potential for growth and learning rather than as a threat.

Maturation is closely related to Satir's other core concept of *self-esteem*, in that one cannot be mature without having a feeling of self-worth. Communications within a family system reflect the self-esteem of the individuals within the family system. Whereas Jackson emphasized thinking, Satir believes that the *feeling*, or emotional, system of the family is expressed through communications. Thus, the essence of communications lies in the feeling dimension. It is this emphasis that places Satir in the communication theory framework.

Satir believes that dysfunction occurs when communication is incongruent. By *incongruent* Satir means that the communicational and metacommunicational aspects of the message do not agree. In *Peoplemaking* (1972), she describes four types of dysfunctional communication that occur when people fear rejection, judgment, or exposure of weaknesses, when people's self-esteem is shaky and vulnerable. These types of dysfunctional communication are:

1. *Blaming:* when one defines the problem as being in others, omitting what one feels about the other persons, but sending "I'm OK—you're *not* OK" messages.
2. *Placating:* when one is apologetic, agreeable, and often ingratiating, looking for approval from others; when one denies oneself by omitting what one feels about oneself, sending "I'm not OK—you're OK" messages.
3. *Reasonable analyzing:* when one maintains complete neutrality and denies one's own feelings about the subject matter, distancing oneself and others.
4. *Distracting:* when one chatters irrelevantly, leaving out everything and hoping to distract people from the issues and the process.

People who communicate in any of these styles are not only reflecting low self-esteem, but are also communicating nonacceptance of the other person or persons. The individual whose low self-esteem has prevented him or her from learning to communicate effectively is a candidate for pathological symptomatology. Low self-esteem hinders maturation by impeding the development of a self separate from the family mass.

Satir develops the viewpoint that the inability to separate oneself from the family and the inability to give or receive clear messages are intertwined. In this viewpoint, early formative relations with parents are critical to healthy development. If the parents are poor communications models, if they do not help to validate their child so that he or she can develop self-esteem, or if the communications of the marital system are troubled, the child's self-esteem will be low, which will result in impaired development. Parents have a critical role in helping children to develop positive self-esteem. This role involves helping children to achieve mastery of their environments and showing them how to maintain caring, lasting interpersonal relationships. "If parents consistently show they consider their child a masterful, sexual person, and if they also demonstrate a gratifying, functional male-female relationship, the child acquires self-esteem and becomes increasingly independent of his parents" (Satir 1967, p. 53).

Observing the communication system helps Satir to understand the tight, interlocking system of the family. Satir emphasizes the congruence or incongruence between the literal (report) and metacommunicative (command) levels of messages, between the apparent and underlying aspects of the communication. Congruence implies harmony, whereas incongruence implies conflict. Thus, congruence or incongruence is a valuable clue in assessing the climate of the family's emotional system.

Satir looks at all the pieces in the family system to see how they fit together. She pays particular attention to dyadic, or two-person, relationships. Thus, the marital relationship becomes pivotal. Satir believes that if the marital relationship is functioning well, a child then has permission to have different relationships with each parent, to develop high self-esteem, and to separate eventually from the family mass.

In studying the communicative relationships between dyads within the family system, Satir, like Jackson, focuses on the *rules* of the system: the "shoulds" that are sometimes clear and explicit, and sometimes vague and implicit. These rules reflect the family's value system. Problems are caused by "bad" rules, not by bad people. Bad rules cause people to interact dysfunctionally and result in system problems. Satir is a systems communication therapist in that she discovers the rules by observing communications. Satir does this by (1) assessing whether or not there is freedom in the family to express what one sees or hears; (2) identifying those family members to whom one can talk; (3) assessing the degree of freedom to disagree or disapprove; and (4) observing how one asks questions when one does not understand (Satir 1972).

Satir has added a developmental view to the framework of communication theory. Her concepts of self-esteem and maturation highlight the importance of parenting within the family system. However, Satir, like Jackson and Haley, bases her access and interventions into the family system on communicative interactions. Satir's conceptions are particularly valuable for the practitioner. From her writings, one can learn how to apply the concepts of communication theory to the practice of family therapy. In Satir's view, self-esteem and how it is acquired, acceptance and rejection are major issues in working with families.

Process of Therapy

For Satir, the emphasis of therapy is on improving methods of communication by correcting discrepancies between the literal (report) message and the metacommunicational (command) message, and by teaching members of the family to send clear, congruent "I" messages. Satir focuses on the *feeling*, or emotional, level of the interactions between family members. She engages the family by responding tenderly and empathetically to their pain, which she allows them to feel and to express.

Goal of Therapy. Basically, Satir's therapeutic goal of improving methods of communication involves three outcomes: (1) Each member should be able to report congruently, completely, and obviously on what he or she sees and hears, feels and thinks about himself or herself and others in the presence of others. (2) Each person should be related to in his or her uniqueness so that decisions are made in terms of exploration and negotiation, rather than in terms of power. (3) Differentness should be openly acknowledged and used for growth (Satir 1971, p. 130).

Satir believes that the therapist should help the family become aware of its operating rules. These rules refer to underlying rules, such as who is allowed to speak for whom, what feelings are allowed to be expressed by whom, what topics may or may not be mentioned. Once the family is aware of its rules, it is then able to decide which rules it wishes to modify, retain, or discard. The therapeutic process is both affective and rational in that the therapist uses affective awareness to encourage rational decision making.

Techniques of Therapy.   The major techniques of the therapist are observation and *empathic response* to the pain in the family system. By becoming a member of the family system, the therapist is able to observe the interaction that belies the family rules. The therapist can then help the family to become aware of its rules and to make the appropriate changes.

The therapist is an expert role model and teacher. He or she helps the family to clarify its values and to change its rules so that family members can learn to communicate openly and directly with each other and with the therapist. The therapist's task is to spell out clearly the family's rules of communication and to help the family perceive discrepancies between the meanings intended and the meanings received. The therapist functions as the "official observer" of the family rules; he or she does not engage in the power struggles or other conflicts within the family.

Satir pays particular attention to the techniques that each family member uses to handle the differentness of other family members. She focuses on the roles that people play and how these roles relate to one's position in the family, as well as their relation to the demands of the other family members. Satir also examines the congruency and incongruency between each family member's feelings, thoughts, and behaviors. She is thus able to zero in on the marital relationship and on the triangulation of a child into an unhealthy marital system, which may be the cause of some type of symptomatic behavior.

In *Conjoint Family Therapy* (1967), Satir recommends two helpful tools for therapists. One is a method for taking a family chronology, for which Satir provides an excellent chart. Satir sees this method as a multipurpose tool. In taking the chronology, the therapist establishes that he or she will be active and directive; takes the focus off the identified patient; reveals differences among family members; and emphasizes the marital unit. The other tool is a list of therapeutic roles and techniques; its items clearly express Satir's process of therapy:

1. The therapist creates a setting where people can risk looking clearly at themselves and their behaviors.
2. The therapist asks questions about all subjects and is not afraid of any subject area.

3. The therapist shows the patient how he or she looks to others.
4. When the therapist asks for and gives information, he or she does so in a nonjudgmental, straightforward manner.
5. The therapist builds self-esteem.
6. The therapist sets the interactional rules, thereby reducing threat.
7. The therapist structures interviews, specifying goals and boundaries.
8. The therapist creates an empathic climate to reduce defenses.
9. The therapist teaches patients how to be accountable and mature.
10. The therapist helps patients to understand the influence of past models on their behaviors and expectations.
11. The therapist delineates roles and functions.
12. The therapist completes gaps in communication and interprets messages.

Role of the Therapist. Thus, Satir sees the therapist as active and directive, a well-integrated resource person who enters the family system as a loving, tender, expert teacher and model. The therapist takes the responsibility for creating the empathic conditions that allow people to learn and grow. Focus is on the perceptions and communication of feelings. Communication of feelings is the key to developing the positive self-esteem of family members, which in turn improves the interactional patterns of the family system. Because the therapist uses himself or herself as a vehicle for therapeutic change, the therapist as a person is a critical variable in the treatment.

Watching Satir work or reading her transcripts, one is awed by her skill in attending tenderly to each member of the family. She uses physical touch and moves people around as she "sculpts" different patterns of actions. One notes the following strategies: (1) Satir rephrases family members' passive statements so that they denote an active decision by that family member. (2) She takes the label off the identified patient and redistributes it upon the entire family. (3) She exaggerates the dysfunctional rules or defenses to make subtleties apparent and to facilitate recognition. (4) She sees to it that every member confirms that he or she makes a contribution to the family, good or bad, so that they all become committed to therapy. (5) She understates (as opposed to exaggerates) so that people will open up in response. (6) She analyzes rules. (7) She takes a history to find out about past models and influences and to teach children about their parents' history. (8) She pays close attention to the family's use of pronouns, as she believes that in dysfunctional families, all things, all people, and all ideas are a comment on the "me"—for example, if the oranges are rotten, their rottenness means "I am unloved."

Overview of Satir

Within the axioms of communication theory, Satir's special emphasis is on *affect*. For Satir, the report aspect of the communication deals with affect, with how one feels in the relationship; the intent of the command aspect is to define one's qualities as a care giver and care receiver. As a therapist, Satir's emphasis is on clarifying the expression of feeling within the relationship. This type of intervention allows communicators to become aware of the real feelings underlying their communications. This awareness gives them the opportunity to accept present behavior because they recognize the true feelings underlying these behaviors or to change behaviors in accordance with their new awareness.

For Satir, then, the nature of the double bind is to effect one's value as a nurturer or recipient of nurturance and consequently to compromise one's expression of feeling with a relationship. Communications in general have more to do with how one feels and how one gives or receives care than with identity and meaning or issues of power and control.

JAY HALEY

Jay Haley has been heavily influenced by his research in communications with the Bateson group, by the family therapists with whom he has worked, and by Milton Erickson's application of the principles of hypnosis to therapy. He has written extensively on communication theory, on different therapy approaches from a dyadic point of view, and, more recently, on directive problem-solving therapy with units of three or more. An up-to-date list of Haley's major writings appears at the end of this chapter.

Major Concepts

While Haley believes that relationships are defined by communications and that communications possess different levels of meanings, also he strongly believes that any relationship is by definition a *power struggle* (a battle for control). People in the relationship are always attempting and struggling to define or redefine the relationship.

The levels of relationship that Haley refers to are the digital and the analogic. *Digital* connotes the content (report, literal) of the communication, and *analogic* connotes the metacommunication (the communication about the communication). The metacommunication may affirm or negate the communication. For example, if someone smiles and hugs you while saying, "I'm glad to see you," you would feel differently than if that person scowled and shrugged his or her shoulders. Haley has also attended to the *metaphorical,* nonliteral content of the analogical message. For example, the communication from a client who complains that his family situation may cause him to have a heart attack may be viewed in two ways: (1) digitally, in terms of the reality of the physical stresses his heart experiences within the family; and (2) analogically, in terms of what the metaphor of "losing heart" may mean to him and his family.

Haley states that "when one person communicates a message to the other, he is by that act making a maneuver to define the relationship" (Haley 1963 p. 8). This is the result of the dual nature—the "report" and "command" aspects—of messages and cannot be avoided. The power struggle that Haley postulates between any two people is *not* a matter of who controls whom, but rather a matter of who controls the defining of the relationship and by what maneuvers. If you, in a helpless tone of voice, ask your sister to bring you supper in bed, you are attempting to define the relationship by placing her in a "helper," "caretaker" role and yourself in the "helpee," "cared-for" role. If your sister agrees to this, she is allowing you to control the definition of the relationship, and you may not know if she is caring for you out of love or merely allowing you to control the relationship. However, your sister has other options, and she must take responsibility for whichever option she chooses. She could tell you she won't be home; she could say, "No, you can get your own supper"; she could arrange for someone else to bring you supper. Should she choose any of these options, she would then be engaging in a power struggle with you over who is going to define the relationship.

Relationships can be classified as *symmetrical,* where both communicators behave equally, or *complementary,* where communicators exchange different types of behaviors—for example, one gives and the other receives. Haley notes that symmetrical relationships tend to be competitive, as both people strive to maintain the symmetry. *Maneuvers* are the kinds of messages that attempt to change the relationship. For example, a patient may willingly engage in a complementary relationship with a physician, expecting the physician to make all the decisions about treatment. If, at some point, the patient asks some questions about side effects and other aspects of the treatment in a way that indicates the patient knows something about the treatment and its implications, it would be a "maneuver," an attempt to change the relationship from a complementary one to a more symmetrical one. It would then be up to the physician either to redefine the relationship and accept it as a symmetrical one, or to respond in a way that would retain the complementary relationship.

Haley describes a third type of relationship as the *paradoxical* relationship (Haley 1963, p. 18). A paradoxical relationship exists when one person in a relationship offers conflicting directives and the other person cannot define the relationship by either obeying the directives or by refusing to obey them, since he or she is being asked to do both simultaneously. For example, if Mrs. Johns, tired of always initiating and planning the activities of her family, were to communicate to her husband the message "I wish you'd be more spontaneous," there is no way Mr. Johns can be spontaneous and still follow his wife's directive. Thus, a conflictual relationship would be perpetuated, since Mrs. Johns's control would always require a particular response from Mr. Johns.

Every message has four elements: (1) a subject, which tells us *who* is doing something; (2) a predicate, which tells us what is being *done;* (3) an object, which tells us *to whom* the action is directed; and (4) a prepositional phrase, which tells us the *context* of the action. The following sentence illustrates *all* the elements of a complete communication: (1) I, (2) am talking; (3) to you; (4) about your daughter. Haley points out that the only way one can avoid defining a relationship is by denying one or more of the four elements of a message. Schizophrenic symptoms frequently are manifest in this type of denial. Schizophrenics typically avoid defining a relationship by denying that they are speaking, and/or by denying that anything is being said, and/or by denying that it is being said to the other person, and/or by denying that the interchange is occurring in this place at this time.

Contrary to the more traditional view that symptoms serve to maintain an intrapsychic balance, Haley believes that symptoms maintain the homeostasis of the family system. Obviously, this necessitates looking at the symptoms in terms of how they maintain or challenge the power struggles within the system. Haley has observed that a psychiatric symptom meets two conditions: (1) the patient's behavior must have an extreme influence on himself or herself and/or on someone else; and (2) the patient must be seen as not responsible for the behavior. In our culture, chronic alcoholism meets Haley's criteria of a symptom: the alcoholic's drinking problem has an extreme influence on himself or herself and/or on others in the environment; and the alcoholic is not held responsible for the alcoholic behavior ("he can't help it; he's an alcoholic"). Similarly, the anxiety of an "agoraphobic" prevents him and his wife from attending social gatherings as a couple, but he "can't help it; he's afraid." In both cases, intended or not, the symptom's consequences allow the individual to *control* the relationship. From this viewpoint, the family therapist must examine the effect of the symptom on the relationships within the system, as well as work with the symptom itself.

Thus, to understand families, one must examine the governing process of the family. Haley indicates that there is not just one "governor" for the family system. Each family member functions as a governor of the others in order to maintain the system. Family conflicts ensue when someone from within the family system attempts to bring about some kind of change. There are two levels of the governing process that must be considered: the *error-activated response* by a member if any one member exceeds a certain range of behavior; and the attempt by family members to be *metagovernors*, the ones who set the limits (Haley 1963). Not only do these two levels of governing process result in confusion about who is governing and who is being governed, but they also trigger off a wave of resistance to change, as all governed systems have investments in diminishing change.

For Haley, therefore, a family is a system that involves power relationships. The power struggle exists between subsystems within the family and between subsystems and the larger family system in that each family member attempts to be the "metagovernor" who determines the limits of the behavior of the other family members. Each subsystem attempts to govern the other subsystems and the total family system. They may seek this power through maneuvers—that is, through messages that attempt to redefine the power relationships. Developing symptoms to change the power relationships is another type of maneuver, in that one of the characteristics of a symptom is that one does not have to take responsibility for the symptom.

We can say then that for Haley the key is *control;* control is achieved through *communication;* communication tells us whether relationships are *symmetrical* or *complementary;* people attempt to control each other through *maneuvers* and *symptoms;* change occurs through *renegotiation* and *redefinition* of the *power relationships.*

Process of Therapy

While Haley, like Jackson, focuses on the communicative behavior within the family system, his concern is with the power struggle in the relationships of family members. When the family therapist actively and directively intervenes in the family system, he or she becomes part of the power struggle, and it thus is essential that the therapist immediately assume the role of a powerful, benevolent implementer of change.

Goal of Therapy.   For Haley, the goal of family therapy is behavioral change that will result in a new homeostatic setting for the family system. Haley has described his therapy as "problem solving therapy," defining problems as "a type of behavior that is part of a sequence of acts between several people" (Haley 1976). The focus of therapy is on the repeating sequence of problem behavior. To change this behavior, the therapist aims to become a "metagovernor of the system" (Haley 1963) and to resolve the problems of the power struggles that are inherent in any relationship.

Techniques of Therapy.   Haley (1963) lists three major tactics used by family therapists to change the system:
   1. *Paradoxical Messages*:   These are directives to the family phrased in such a way as to be irresistible because of the double bind in which they place recipients. For example, the therapist asks family members to show their real feelings about a situation. Even members who refuse to speak show their feelings because the act of refusing to cooperate is a statement in itself.
   2. *Relabeling/Reframing:* Using this technique, the therapist emphasizes the positive aspects of behavior, redefining negative behavior as positive. For example, if a complaint is the constant bickering between mother and daughter, the therapist might redefine this as an attempt of the mother and daughter to relate to each other, to become closer.
   3. *Prescribing the Symptom:* In prescribing the symptom, the therapist encourages usual behavior so that the client's resistance is manifested as change. For example, the therapist asks a mother and daughter to continue their physical fighting for the next week (between sessions). The therapist points out that since the mother and daughter have not killed each other or even warranted medical treatment in the past fifteen years, it is unlikely they will do each other in within the next week. The only way the mother and daughter can resist the governing control of the therapist is to change their behavior and cease or lessen physical fighting.
   Haley points out that because dysfunctional patterns of interaction may be functional for some family members, or because the "sick" member helps define and maintain the family status quo, the dysfunctional family usually resists change. The therapist, who takes direct

control, must not only recognize such resistance, but must also use the above techniques to deal effectively with it.

To use paradoxical interventions to create change, the therapist (1) sets up a benevolent framework that is defined as one in which change is to take place; (2) permits or encourages the patient to continue with unchanged behavior; and (3) provides an ordeal that will continue as long as the patient continues with unchanged behavior (Haley 1963).

To illustrate these conditions for paradoxical intervention, let us consider the case of a family who is concerned about a nine-year-old son who resists going to bed every night. His behavior causes all sorts of aggravation, and each night the parents and the son end up fighting and being upset. Fulfilling the first condition for paradoxical intervention, which is to set up a benevolent framework, involves establishing a supportive therapeutic relationship with the members of the family. The second condition is fulfilled by allowing the youngster to stay up all night, without any argument or harassment. The third condition is fulfilled by insisting that if he does not go to bed at whatever hour has been agreed upon, he must spend the night in the dining room (where there is no television or outside stimulation). According to this model, the boy will eventually decrease his disruptive bedtime behavior.

Note that the therapist's relationship with each member of the family system must be nonjudgmental, trusting, encouraging, accepting, positive, potent in terms of skills and expertise, and directive. Giving directives is Haley's major therapeutic technique.

By developing a powerful yet benevolent relationship, the therapist is able to give directives that teach people to behave differently, that involve the therapist in the family action, and that gather information about the family system. According to Haley, there are two ways to give these directives: (1) telling people what to do when the therapist wants them to do it, and (2) telling them what to do when the therapist does *not* want them to do it, because the therapist wants them to change by rebelling (Haley 1976). The tasks that these directives involve may be metaphoric, such as selecting an activity that resembles the target behavior but is easier for the family to achieve; or they may be paradoxical, involving two conflicting messages —for example, "change" and "don't change." In a paradoxical message, a therapist might direct an insomniac to stay up all night and wax floors.

Role of the Therapist. In *Problem Solving Therapy* (1976), Haley clearly places the responsibility for change in the family system on the therapist. He defines the task of the therapist as the definition of the

social unit that must be changed to solve the client's presenting
problem. Remember that Haley's goal in therapy is to change the
family interactions so that the presenting problems are solved, not to
create insight about causality or to teach family communications. The
therapist must become an active member of this social unit and must
possess the skills and expertise needed to give directives that will result in change.

Haley is quite clear and explicit about the tasks of the therapist and
the types of strategies that are effective. He advocates brief, intensive
intervention and rapid disengagement of the therapist, focusing on the
present situation and on organizing the family to change what is
happening. The therapist must use the presenting problem as leverage
to set goals and to design directives. The difference between Haley's
problem-solving therapy and more conventional behavioral therapies is
that Haley's therapy includes the therapist in the social unit and makes
the therapist a part of the behavior that needs changing.

Watching Haley work, one is struck by the warm, caring relationship that he is quickly able to establish with family members and
by his manner of issuing directives without insult, sarcasm, or pa-
tronization. He appears to be an earnest therapist who is genuinely
concerned with his own responsibility and accountability as a member
of a larger social system.

Perhaps the best way to understand Haley's conception of the role
of the therapist is to quote from his list of questions that a supervisor
might ask about a training therapist's management of an initial
interview:

1. Does the therapist frame the interview situation so the family knows
   who he is, what the situation is, and why different kinds of questions
   are being asked?
2. Has the therapist organized the family in the room well so that
   business can be conducted, for example, by dealing with obstreperous
   children or chaotic interchanges?
3. Is the therapist sufficiently nonmoralistic so that family members are
   encouraged to talk about their problems?
4. Has the therapist shown the flexibility to shift his approach when one
   way of gathering information is not working?
5. Does the therapist show a range of behavior from being reflecting to
   being confronting?
6. Has the therapist avoided pursuing a personal interest that is not
   relevant to the family problem?
7. Is the therapist able to assume the posture of an expert while also able
   to express ignorance when appropriate?

8. Does the therapist avoid offering solutions before the problem is clarified?
9. Does the therapist seem to know when to encourage dissent among family members and when to soothe them?
10. Does the therapist avoid siding with one family member against another or one faction against another?
11. Does the therapist avoid being too personally involved with the family?
12. Does the therapist avoid being too professional and detached from the family?
13. Is the therapist attempting to get all family members participating in the interview?
14. Has the therapist shown he can tolerate unpleasant material or strong feelings from the family members?
15. Is the therapist gathering information about significant other people not present in the interview?
16. Is the therapist learning whether other social agencies are involved with the family?
17. Is the therapist motivating the family members to change? Is he engendering hope and a willingness to make an effort?
18. Has the therapist been more positive in his approach than negative, in the sense of putting down the family?
19. Has the therapist shown the family that he or she has something to offer them and can bring about change?*

From this list, we see that Haley has been heavily influenced by behavioral theory. He believes that these conditions are critical to setting up a framework wherein directives to change or not to change behavior can result in a new homeostatic setting for a family system.

Overview of Haley

Within the axioms of communication theory, Haley's special emphasis is on *power*. For Haley, the report aspect of the communication deals with power, with how one controls the dynamics of the relationship; the intent of the command aspect is to define one's efficacy and one's prerogatives in entering into complementary or symmetrical relationships. As a therapist, Haley's emphasis is on clarifying the nature of the power relationship. This type of intervention teaches

---

*Reprinted with permission from Haley, Jay, *Problem Solving Therapy* (San Francisco: Jossey-Bass, 1976), pp. 46–47.

communicators awareness of their actual intentions in using underlying or implicit maneuvers to win or share power in a relationship. This new awareness gives them the opportunity to accept or change behaviors.

For Haley, then, the nature of the double bind is to effect one's efficacy resulting in experiencing of powerlessness. Communications in general have more to do with control and the determination of one's options for control within the relationship than with identity or affect.

Comparison of Critical Issues

It is clear that all three communication theorists whom we have presented perceive the family as an interactional system and that their principal therapeutic focus is on the communication process among family members. All are concerned with the rules governing communications and with the consequences of these rules. They share the same theoretical core, although their emphases differ according to their ideas about interactional processes. Jackson emphasizes cognition, Satir emphasizes emotion, and Haley emphasizes power. None of these therapists would consider studying or treating an "identified patient" without involving the family in the actual process of study or treatment. They all believe that the symptoms or problems, although perhaps housed in an individual, result from a faulty interactional process and thus involve or affect each and every member of the family system.

All three of these communication theorists believe that the goal of family therapy is behavioral change in family interactional patterns. Whereas Haley wants people to change how they fight over who is going to control the definition of relationships, Jackson and Satir want to teach family members to recognize the family's rules so that the rules and the interactional patterns may be changed. It goes without saying that each of these therapists bring his or her own unique self and style into the therapy process. In addition, their different backgrounds and training affect their different emphases. Despite their different approaches and methods, all these therapists achieve similar outcomes in terms of effecting positive change in family interactional processes.

Let us now compare these therapists' views of specific therapeutic issues—namely, history, diagnosis, and the therapeutic relationship.

1. *History*: Satir is the only one of the three who actually conducts a history, which she calls the "family life chronology." Satir (1967) ex-

plains that taking this history helps acquaint all members of the family with the background of the current dilemmas, points out the relationship of current issues to past happenings, and helps to control anxiety in the initial session, as well as to take attention off the identified patient. In contrast, Jackson is interested in historical data only if it sheds light on the current interactional process of the family, and Haley generally does not find historical data relevant or pertinent to current power struggles.

2. *Diagnosis*: Neither Haley nor Satir finds diagnosis helpful or useful. Labeling interactional problems does not help to change them; diagnosis thus has no practical value. Jackson is interested in diagnosis only in terms of assessing the homeostasis of the family system, not in terms of identifying pathology. Diagnosis is really considered to be the concept of a medical model and, as such, has no relevance to a communication model. Assessment of dysfunctional communications is not considered the same as diagnosis, which refers to illness and implies a specific treatment for a specific illness.

3. *Therapeutic Relationship*: All three therapists recognize the importance of establishing warm, trusting relationships with family members. However, they acknowledge that they cannot be effective teachers and models if they are not perceived as potent and credible in terms of their expertise. Jackson injected himself into the family system in order to disrupt the homeostasis and to force the family into creating a new dynamic equilibrium. He appeared somewhat detached and cool, at all times maintaining the posture of the professional doctor. Haley also thrusts himself into the family system and, by assuming control and power of the system, forces the family to redefine its power system. Haley deals with emotions in terms of power struggles, but he projects a calm, controlling manner. For both Jackson and Haley, the therapist's role is manipulative and controlling. Satir, on the other hand, utilizes empathy and affect to enter the system as a caring teacher and friend who teaches the family to revise its rules and to communicate more clearly and effectively. Thus Satir becomes more personally engaged with family members than do Jackson and Haley. She appears to use herself as a therapeutic vehicle, and her relationship with family members is less manipulative than Jackson's and Haley's. Satir deals more with the conscious awareness, her own and family members' values than do the other two therapists.

In looking at these three therapists, we might remember that they all began their family work with schizophrenic families. Since then, they have found that their approaches are equally effective with a broad variety of family populations, although most of their work has been with middle-class American families. They all advocate short-term, directive treatment and deplore the dependency that can be facilitated in other types of treatment modalities.

Summary

In this chapter, we examined the theoretical concepts of communication theorists Don Jackson, Virginia Satir and Jay Haley. Before discussing their individual theoretical contributions and therapeutic styles and approaches, we explored their common theoretical orientation. Their core axioms underscore the importance of studying the verbal and nonverbal levels of communication as a way of understanding family rules, power dynamics, and negotiation processes. Thus, the central concept of the communication theorists is that relationships can be understood by analyzing the communicational and metacommunicational aspects of interactions.

We elaborated upon the concept of homeostasis, the nature of messages, and the communication components, namely, syntactics, semantics, and pragmatics. The communication theorists share an emphasis on improving the ways a family system communicates, concentrating on how messages are sent and received. They learn about family relationships by concentrating on metacommunication, the communication about the communication.

In elaborating upon the theoretical concepts and process of therapy for Jackson, Satir, and Haley, we paid particular attention to their notions of change, their goals of treatment, their particular techniques, and, finally, their beliefs about therapeutic relationships and the role of the therapist.

We pointed out that Jackson emphasized cognition and the relationship rules and homeostatic mechanisms that maintain the homeostasis of the system. Satir highlights the concepts of self-esteem and maturation, positing that a mature individual has learned to communicate effectively and has achieved a differentiation of self from the family system. Haley focuses on the power struggle among family system members who vie to define the nature of the relationship.

Despite their different styles, these theorists share the belief that an individual's symptoms or problems reflect a faulty interactional process and therefore affect each member of the family system.

When we compared these theorists' notions and approaches, we found that they reached the same ends, albeit by different means. They all focus on the same elements of the communication process, the message units with literal and metacommunicative levels and the process of setting and maintaining rules. They all practice an active, directive form of therapy that deals in the here and now and that has as its goal behavioral change. They all utilize the communication process to change the interactional system of the family.

For exercises that will help you integrate the conceptual frameworks of Jackson, Satir, and Haley, we refer you to chapter 4 in the manual. These exercises will also help you to increase your awareness of your own communication styles.

We will now take a look at the structural theorists and see how they achieve the same behavioral outcomes as the communication theorists, although their emphases and interventions differ.

References

Ferber, A., M. Mendelsohn, and A. Napier. 1973. *The Book of Family Therapy.* Boston: Houghton Mifflin.

Foley, V. 1974. *An Introduction to Family Therapy.* New York: Grune & Stratton.

Haley, J. 1963. *Strategies of Psychotherapy.* New York: Grune & Stratton.

———. 1976. *Problem Solving Therapy.* San Francisco: Jossey-Bass.

Jackson, D. 1957. "The Question of Family Homeostasis." *Psychiatric Quarterly Supplement* 31 (1):19–90.

———. 1965a. "Family Rules: The Marital Quid pro Quo." *Archives of General Psychiatry* 12:592.

———. 1965b. "The Study of the Family." *Family Process* 4 (1):13–14.

———. 1967. "The Eternal Triangle." In J. Haley and L. Hoffman, eds., *Techniques of Family Therapy.* New York: Basic Books.

Rappaport, L. 1976. "Role and Context Interaction in Families of Alcoholics:" Ph.D. dissertation. Boston College.

Satir, V. 1964. *Conjoint Family Therapy.* Palo Alto, Calif.: Science & Behavior Books.

———. 1967. *Conjoint Family Therapy,* 2nd ed. Palo Alto, Calif.: Science & Behavior Books.

———. 1971. "The Family as a Treatment Unit." In J. Haley, ed., *Changing Families.* New York: Grune & Stratton.

―――. 1972. *Peoplemaking.* Palo Alto, Calif.: Science & Behavior Books.

Watzlawick, P., J. Beavin, and D. Jackson. 1967. *Pragmatics of Human Communication.* New York: Norton.

Suggested Readings

Bandler, R., and J. Grinder. *The Structure of Magic I: A Book about Language and Therapy.* Palo Alto, Calif.: Science & Behavior Books, 1975.

Bateson, G. "Minimal Requirements for a Theory of Schizophrenia." *Archives of General Psychiatry* 2 (1960):477–91.

―――. "The Cybernetics of Self: A Theory of Alcoholism." *Psychiatry* 34 (1971):1–8.

Bateson, G., et al. "Toward a Theory of Schizophrenia." *Behavioral Science* 1 (1956):251–64.

―――. "A Note on the Double Bind." In D. Jackson, ed., *Communication, Family and Marriage.* Palo Atlo, Calif.: Science & Behavior Books, 1968.

Haley, J. *Uncommon Therapy.* New York: Ballantine Books, 1973.

―――. "Why a Mental Health Clinic Should Avoid Family Therapy." *Journal of Marriage and Family Counseling* 1, no. 1 (1975):3–13.

―――. "Development of a Theory: The Rise and Demise of a Research Project." In C.E. Sluzki and D. Ransom, eds., *Double Bind: The Foundation of the Communicational Approach to the Family.* New York: Grune & Stratton, 1976.

―――, ed. *Changing Families.* New York: Grune & Stratton, 1971.

Haley, J., and L. Hoffman. *Techniques of Family Therapy.* New York: Basic Books, 1967.

―――. *The Power Tactics of Jesus Christ and Other Essays.* New York: Grossman, 1969.

Jackson, D. "The Question of Family Homeostasis." *Psychiatric Quarterly Supplement* 31 (1959):79–90.

―――. "Differences between 'Normal' and 'Abnormal' Families." In N. Ackerman, F. Beatman, and S. Sherman, eds., *Expanding Theory and Practice in Family Therapy.* New York: Family Association of America, 1967.

―――. *Therapy, Communication and Change.* Palo Alto, Calif.: Science & Behavior Books, 1968.

―――, ed. *The Etiology of Schizophrenia.* New York: Basic Books, 1960.

Jackson, D., and V. Satir. "A Review of Psychiatric Developments in Family Diagnosis and Family Therapy." In N. Ackerman, F. Beatman, and S. Sherman, eds., *Exploring the Base for Family Therapy.* New York: Family Association of America, 1961.

Jackson, D., and J. Weakland. "Schizophrenic Symptoms and Family Interaction." *Archives of General Psychiatry* 1 (1959):618–21.

————. "Conjoint Family Therapy: Some Considerations on Theory, Technique and Results." *Psychiatry* 24 (1961):30–45.

Jackson, D., and I. Yalom. "Family Interaction, Family Homeostasis and Some Implications for Conjoint Family Psychotherapy." In J. H. Masserman, ed., *Individual and Family Dynamics*. New York: Grune & Stratton, 1959.

Satir, V. "A Family of Angels." In Haley and Hoffman, eds., *Techniques of Family Therapy*.

————. "The Family as a Treatment Unit." In Haley, ed., *Changing Families*.

Watzlawick, P. "A Review of the Double Bind Theory—1962." In D. Jackson, ed., *Communication, Family and Marriage*. Palo Alto, Calif.: Science & Behavior Books, 1968.

Watzlawick, P., J. Weakland, and R. Fisch. *Change: Principles of Problem Formation and Problem Resolution*. New York: Norton, 1974.

Structural Theorists

In this chapter, we will discuss those family therapy theorists and practitioners who focus on the "where" of the family interactional process. These structural theorists tend to emphasize the dynamic orderings of the system itself, the actual structure within which elements of communication take place. It is this emphasis on the "context" of family interaction that distinguishes the structural theorists from the communication theorists who, as we have seen, emphasize the "how" of the family interaction, the "bits and pieces" of communication.

The three theorists whose concepts we will study in this chapter are Murray Bowen, David Kantor, and Salvador Minuchin. Bowen, as we pointed out in chapter 2, was one of the pioneers of the family therapy movement. Kantor has contributed some original theoretical formulations that reframe intrapsychic theory within the family structure, and Minuchin has demonstrated expertise and skill in applying his interpretation of structural theory to actual clinical practice. Unlike Jackson, Haley, and Satir, however, these structural theorists have never worked together.

The format of chapter 5 is somewhat different from that of chapter 4 in order to introduce you to the less familiar theoretical tenets of these therapists. Before examining the contributions of each of them, let us examine the structural concepts to which they all subscribe.

Conceptual Framework

Although Bowen, Kantor, and Minuchin have different points of emphasis within a theory of family systems, they do share a common "structural" framework. For each of them, diagnosis is directed toward and treatment is predicated upon a *system's organizational dynamics*. The system might be one as large as the entire family itself or as small as any dyad within the family, such as the husband-wife dyad.

In addition to stressing the primary relevance of the internal dynamics of the system, they also agree upon the critical importance of the *boundaries* that exist both within the family system and between the family system and its external environment. Let us take a closer look at this structural notion of boundaries. It appears, with a different emphasis, as a key concept in the work of all three theorists.

In chapter 1 we noted that systems theory sees a system as not only having internal characteristics, but also as having a relationship (an interaction) with the larger environment of which it is a part. This interaction is characterized by an "exchange" in which things move in and out of the system. A *boundary* is defined as the rules and regulations that separate the system from its environment. The characteristics of the boundary substantially determine how exchanges are carried out. Boundaries may be seen as the manifestation of the system's rules and regulations.

In a family of two parents and three children, for example, there is a boundary between the parent subsystem and the subsystem of the three children. This structure regulates the transaction of interactions between these two subsystems. Although no physical limits may be present, there still may exist a *feeling* of limitations between the subsystems. That feeling in itself, as it filters people's perceptions, is a boundary.

A boundary can be highly *permeable* so that thoughts and feelings are easily exchanged, or it can be fairly *impermeable,* so that thoughts and feelings are either not exchanged at all or are exchanged with much difficulty. Permeability or impermeability of a boundary is neither good nor bad in itself. Its value is derived from the actual circumstances.

Consider, for example, the relationship between an adult and a child in the family we have just described. A permeable boundary in their relationship is functional if the communication it allows is the father's appropriate parenting of his child as a son. On the other hand, a permeable boundary is dysfunctional if it allows, with equal facility, "interference" from the father as the child attempts to interact as a brother with his siblings. The quality of impermeability can also vary in the same situation—that is, impermeability is functional if it restricts or blocks interference, but it is dysfunctional if it restricts or blocks necessary parenting.

Thus, the system's structural dynamics, especially the creation, maintenance, and modification of boundaries, are a central focus in the works of Bowen, Kantor, and Minuchin.

Bowen's theory is squarely in the forefront of structural family therapy in its notion of *normal family development,* its hypothesis concerning the *etiology* of dysfunctional behavior, and its recommendations for *treatment* interventions.

To date, neither Kantor nor Minuchin has formulated a theory that balances etiology and treatment as equally as Bowen's theory. David Kantor's work places more emphasis on the structural development of a variety of family systems and individual goals, on family strategies that attempt to integrate the systems and goals, and on the etiology of dysfunction within them. For this reason, Kantor's theory must be considered one of *structural analysis.* While treatment may be implicit in his theory, Kantor has yet to state it formally.

Minuchin, on the other hand, although contributing to the theory of structural therapy, tends to emphasize slightly the family contexts in which problems are currently manifest and the particular styles of intervention appropriate to various forms of dysfunction. For this reason, Minuchin's theory must be considered one of *structural therapy.* Moreover, as Kantor's therapy may be implicit in his theory of family, Minuchin's theory of family is equally implicit in his treatment strategies. To label one a "structural analyst" and the other a "structural therapist" is not to ignore the totality of a theory that each is working toward, but to focus on where Kantor or Minuchin is placing emphasis at this time.

Let us see now how each of these theorists develops structural concepts within his theory.

MURRAY BOWEN

In chapter 2 we reviewed Bowen's early studies of families of schizophrenics. In the 1960s, Bowen, who is a psychiatrist, increasingly focused on the relationship between the father and mother and the implications of that relationship for the emotional well-being of a particular child. He developed the notion of *triangles,* along with several other concepts that emerged between 1957 and 1963 as the "interlocking" concepts of Bowen's theory. Since 1975, other concepts have been added and today they form the keystone of what is known as the "Bowen Theory" (Bowen 1978).

Major Concepts

Although the Bowen Theory is built around several interlocking concepts, it has as its foundation two fundamental variables: degree of anxiety and degree of integration and differentiation of self. We need to look at these two variables before proceeding to the concepts themselves.

1. *Degree of Anxiety:* Bowen uses the biological model of anxiety management. According to this model, all organisms can reasonably adapt to anxiety, even when the anxiety is acute for a period of time. However, when the anxiety becomes chronic, the mechanisms that normally deal with brief acute anxiety no longer seem sufficient. Tension builds in the system, which often results in symptom formation, dysfunction, or illness. How family systems handle the tension that is produced by chronic anxiety determines whether members of the family system remain free from symptoms, dysfunction, or illness.

2. *Degree of Integration and Differentiation of Self:* Bowen sees the family as an "emotional relationship system"—that is, people are emotionally intermeshed. For Bowen, this emotional process of relating is more significant than either verbal or nonverbal language. Bowen originally called the "emotional relationship system" the "undifferentiated family ego mass" because he saw it as a context in which

emotionality could flood the intellect, creating an emotional climate from which the less differentiated adult and the emotionally ruled child would have difficulty achieving independence. In other words, to avoid falling victim to the emotional force of the family system and to be able to separate oneself from the family system's emotionality, one would have to be able to differentiate between emotional and intellectual functioning. The person in whom intellect and emotion are fused is ruled by emotionality and is controlled by his own and/or the prevailing emotional climate of the family. The person in whom emotion and intellect are differentiated is better able to choose emotional and/or intellectual interaction, rather than be chosen by it. When intellect and emotions are fused, the individual reacts on a more primitive, instinctual level. When intellect and emotions are differentiated, the individual responds in a manner that is based more on choice.

Higher degrees of differentiation of self allow for better integration of the individual within the family emotional relationship system. Similarly, a more fluid integration of the individual within the family emotional relationship system makes possible a higher degree of differentiation of intellect and emotion within the individual. In other words, integration and differentiation of self determine each other.

Let us turn now to Bowen's interlocking concepts to see how the concepts of anxiety and integration and differentiation of self are developed into what he calls the "Bowen Theory."

Differentiation of Self.   Bowen sees individual and system maturity hinging on the degree of fusion or differentiation achieved between emotionality and the intellect. In other words, people with low levels of differentiation are unable to separate themselves from their families of origin, whereas people with higher levels of differentiation are able to function effectively, independent of their family of origin.

Looking at figure 5–1, we see that Bowen conceptualizes differentiation of self along a continuum. At the low level of differentiation, people who are characterized by "emotional and intellectual fusion" exhibit two characteristics: (1) they are intensely fused with the undifferentiated family ego mass in a way that leaves them constantly vulnerable to any family dilemma; and (2) the fusion between their intellects and emotions is so complete that many of them are also fused with the greater "undifferentiated ego mass of the culture or society as a whole" (Bowen 1976, p. 66). Thus, these people are totally relationship-oriented, devoting enormous amounts of energy to seeking love, approval, and validation. They are likely to lead lives that move from

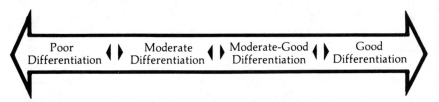

Low Level: Emotional and Intellectual Fusion   Toward High Level: Differentiation of Self

Figure 5–1   *Bowen's Continuum of Self-Differentiation*

one crisis to another, lives dominated by emotionality, in which they are unable to differentiate fact from feeling.

People at moderate levels of differentiation can begin to differentiate between intellect and emotions. Although still ruled by the emotional system, their lifestyles are more flexible. Relationships continue to be very important; many people at this level pursue a lifelong quest for the "ideal" relationship. Most are either frustrated in not finding this ideal relationship or, when real intimacy is possible, they are so threatened by fusion that they react with distance and alienation. Symptoms and problems occur when the relationship systems of these people are unbalanced. For example, between love affairs, a person with a moderate level of self differentiation may become ill or engage in impulsive or irresponsible behavior.

People who have moderate-to-good levels of differentiation are able to interact with others without being threatened by fusion—that is, by a loss of self in a relationship. At times, their intellects are truly capable of overruling their emotional systems, and they can thus make relevant and appropriate choices about their lives. They are able to live in the emotional world without having to fear that they will become victims of it.

Bowen chooses not to categorize those few individuals who have developed beyond "good differentiation." They are able to maintain various, flexible emotional relationships and at the same time maintain their own individuation.

It is important to note that any individual, at any place on this continuum, may revert to a lower position on the scale in time of crisis. The rapidity and ease with which an individual recovers his or her former lifestyle is an indication of the individual's level of self-differentiation. Highly differentiated individuals, for example, may slip into emotionality at the moment of crisis, but adjust rather quickly and come out of it as soon as the crisis has passed. Individuals whose differentiation is "moderate to good" may require some help in making such a recovery. On the other hand, crisis can plunge some moderately differentiated individuals, and certainly most poorly differentiated ones, into such a state of emotional fusion that they may need substantial help to recover, if they recover at all.

Bowen believes that an individual's place on this continuum is largely determined during childhood by a critical structural feature of family systems. This feature, triangles, is explicated in his next concept.

Triangles. An "automatic emotional response system" implies at least two people. When tension is low, most two-person systems operate fairly calmly and stably. However, when tension and anxiety increase beyond the level that the two-person system can manage, a third person is frequently "triangled in" to reduce the tension. The most vulnerable, least well differentiated person in the family is the person who is triangled into the two-person system in the attempt to diffuse the tension. Less well differentiated persons are more subject to the "emotionality" of the system, more likely to be seduced by the emotions of the highly tense two-person system, which accounts for their being the ones who are triangled in.

When tension in the triangle itself becomes too high, other people in the family system are triangled into a series of extending and interlocking triangles. Moreover, when all the available family members have been triangled in, the family may then reach outside of itself to the extended family, the neighborhood, and eventually to the police and other social agencies (Bowen 1976).

The fusion of a child with the emotional relationship system of a family triangle inhibits the child's normal process of differentiation of intellect and emotion. Growth that would enable the child to move out of the triangle would threaten the homeostasis of the system; and so differentiation of self is retarded and subordinated to the system's need to maintain its present level of functioning.

Triangulation, then, not only is made possible by poor differentiation of self and the vulnerability that poor differentiation implies, but also maintains poor differentiation and vulnerability during the time of triangulation. Triangulation frequently leaves the individual disabled long after the triangle has been broken. Let us now look at Bowen's concept of the type of family context that facilitates the formation of such triangles.

Nuclear Family Emotional System.   Bowen believes that the degree of self-differentiation determines marital choice. Individuals choose mates whose levels of differentiation resemble their own. Once the choices are made, once children are born and the family begins to evolve, it must manage the usual developmental tasks and crises that confront families.

Bowen identifies three major ways that families with lower levels of differentiation handle the anxiety in a two-person system that results from the intense fusion of the individual with the family emotional system: (1) marital conflict; (2) dysfunction in one spouse; and (3) impairment of one or more of the children.

Marital conflict is intense in a relationship in which neither spouse gives in to the other. Usually the undifferentiation is confined within the two-person marital power struggle, and the children are not involved in the battle. Tension is chronic, negative as well as positive feelings are high, and each spouse is primarily focused on the other.

Dysfunction in one spouse is an alternative to outright conflict. It begins with one spouse's adaptive posture absorbing most of the undifferentiation. The spouse who is adapting is unable to make decisions or take responsibility for self. Any substantial increase in stress and anxiety in the relationship can trigger some form of dysfunction on the part of the adapting member, such as physical, emotional, or social illness. Since many of the symptoms that occur in this type of relationship are socially sanctioned ("he can't help it, he has a drinking problem"), these relationships may endure for years or decades. The formation of such symptoms, for which no one can be blamed, absorbs most of the undifferentiation. (See chapter 4 for a description of Haley's concept of symptom formation.)

Impairment of one or more of the children may occur when the undifferentiation cannot be absorbed entirely by marital conflict or spouse dysfunction. The couple may then project the undifferentiation onto one or more of the children. Bowen sees the impairment that results as the consequence of the family projection process.

Family Projection Process.   Although the family projection process operates within the father-mother-child triangle, it begins with the mother-child relationship; the mother, Bowen argues, is the key figure in reproduction and in the early care of the child. For example, the undifferentiation that causes marital disharmony may in turn cause the mother to behave anxiously in the family system. The child, quite normally, may respond with anxiety to the mother's anxious behavior. The mother, sensing anxiety in the child, becomes more anxious. She misperceives a problem in the child and, responding with solicitous, "overnurturing" behavior, she establishes a pattern of "infantilizing" the child. Once begun, anxiety on the part of mother or child may trigger another cycle of overnurturance and overprotection, causing the child to become progressively impaired in terms of self-maintenance skills and emotional independence. The fusion between the mother and child can be intense for years.

It is important to note that this intense fusion may be experienced as positive and that the relationship between the mother and child may be problem-free for many years, perhaps even until the child enters adolescence. However, once the child, at whatever age, attempts to function on his or her own, the relationship can change to a negative one in which severe emotional or physical symptoms develop. This child lacks the degree of emotional differentiation required to become independent of the family system. As the child attempts to leave home and function independently, he or she may emerge as the identified patient in the family. In his clinical work, Bowen has coined the term *the triangled child* to identify that member of the family who has become ensnared in this family projection process. The Bowen Theory considers even schizophrenia to be the unfortunate consequence of several generations of this process, wherein children of succeeding generations become less and less differentiated, more and more intensely fused to the parent system, and eventually so severely impaired as to be dysfunctional.

The question arises as to what the alternative is to this process of fusion and impairment within the father-mother-child triangle. How does the healthy child emerge from the family's emotional system and pass into adulthood? Bowen addresses this issue in his concept of emotional cutoff.

Emotional Cutoff.   Bowen added the concept of emotional cutoff to his theory in 1975, after realizing that it had been implied, although never stated explicitly, in many of his other concepts.

In early life all people develop a certain degree of emotional connection to their parents and family of origin. As they grow up and leave their families, they must deal with the resolution of this emotional connection. The manner in which they resolve it or leave it unresolved determines what Bowen calls "emotional cutoff." How well people differentiate themselves from their original families, how much emotional attachment remains, is a critical determinant of how individuals handle all subsequent emotional relationships.

There are various gradations of emotional cutoff, just as there are various degrees of differentiation of self. Bowen would argue that these factors determine each other. We might point out that in terms of achieving appropriate emotional cutoff, running away from the family may be just as unsatisfactory as never leaving home. In either case, the emotional dependency may remain, for emotionality knows no boundaries of time and space.

Ideally, emotional cutoff is handled during late adolescence and early adulthood, when the individual is actually leaving the family system to go out into the world. If not negotiated successfully at that time, one may still return later to finish the job, perhaps during therapy. For Bowen, a goal of therapy is to "convert the cutoff with an orderly differentiation of a self from the extended family" (Bowen 1976, p. 84).

Sibling Position.   Bowen adapts Toman's work on sibling position to explicate the notions of differentiation and triangling. For example, in a normal sequential developmental hierarchy among five siblings, aged four, six, eight, ten, and twelve, one would expect to find the highest degree of differentiation of self in the oldest child and decreasing degrees of differentiation as one moves toward the youngest in the family. If the oldest child in this family turns out to be more like the four- or six-year-old in degree of differentiation of self, Bowen would interpret this as an indication that the twelve-year-old is a triangled child, one whose normal development of self has been retarded by the intensity of the father-mother-child triangle. However, emotional immaturity is not the only indication of low differentiation. If the oldest child were extremely autocratic in interpersonal relationships, Bowen would still see it as symptomatic of poor differentiation of self, an equally possible consequence of triangulation and emotional fusion with one or both parents.

Multigenerational Transmission Process.   The concept of a multigenerational transmission process is in many ways a synthesis of several concepts that precede it. Bowen sees the development of the dysfunctional individual as the consequence of several generations of poor-to-moderate differentiation, triangulation, family projection, and inadequate emotional cutoff.

Let us see how these processes all work together within a family to produce a dysfunctional individual. Imagine a family started in 1810 by

Mr. and Mrs. Bart. The Barts were both "moderately differentiated" and their relationship was thus anxious and tense. Because the mores of their time frowned upon outright fighting, the Barts were unable to engage in overt marital conflict as a way of handling their anxiety. Social factors also negated the possibility of their dealing with anxiety by the formation of dysfunctional symptoms in one spouse. Thus, when their first child was born, the Barts diffused their tension by triangling him into the emotionality of their relationship.

When Bart, Jr., emerged from that family, he was less well differentiated than his parents, the consequence of eighteen years of somewhat pleasant, but very restricting, emotional fusion.

In 1835 Bart, Jr., married a woman whose level of differentiation was similar to his own. They had three little Barts, two of whom were triangled into the parent subsystem, each in different ways. The oldest of the third generation of Barts was the least well differentiated of the three, but she never married or had children. The middle Bart, better differentiated than his older sister, but less well differentiated than his parents, and certainly much less well differentiated than his grandparents, went on to have a family.

Mr. Bart III married Mrs. Bart III in 1860. They had only one child, a very poorly differentiated daughter. At the age of sixteen, she had a son out of wedlock, who remained in the family and was raised as the "fifth-generation Bart."

In 1897, this Bart left the family, married someone whose level of differentiation was as poor as his own, and had several children. One of them, still living today, is known as "Grandpa Bart." As a young adult, Grandpa Bart was so poorly differentiated that he was capable of only marginal labor, lost jobs frequently, and developed a serious drinking problem. Ruled more by emotionality than reason, he managed to keep his family intact only by his autocratic style. He had eight children, several of whom emerged from the family system *better* differentiated than their father (Grandpa Bart) or mother, because they were seldom involved in the family emotional system. These children, having to rely early in life on their own resources, were allowed the autonomy to achieve levels of differentiation of self surpassed in this family only in the early nineteenth century. They went on to marry spouses as well differentiated as they, and to raise children who achieved even higher levels of differentiation.

However, the oldest son of one of Grandpa Bart's less well-differentiated children was involved for over twenty years as the triangled child in an intense relationship between his father and mother.

At the age of twenty-three, he represented the lowest level of differentiation of self achieved in eight generations of the Bart family. Sheltered all his life, emotionally fused with his mother, kept out of criminal action by his father, protected socially by his siblings, he was institutionalized and diagnosed as a "catatonic schizophrenic" when his parents died within one year of each other.

Although we have taken considerable liberty with Bowen's notion of the multigenerational transmission process, the spirit of it remains intact. The dysfunctional individuals who now populate many of our state and private institutions may be viewed as the end products of eight to ten generations of low degrees of differentiation. Thus, it is the multigenerational transmission process that produces "the level of impairment that goes with schizophrenia" (Bowen 1976, p. 86).

Changes in degrees of differentiation within families may occur rapidly or slowly from generation to generation. Even families with histories of poor differentiation may suddenly produce a generation of well-differentiated children. For example, several of Grandpa Bart's children emerged from the family with higher degrees of differentiation of self than their parents and went on to have children who achieved even higher levels of differentiation.

The process is quite flexible. A family with very high levels of differentiation of self can certainly, though perhaps imperceptibly, influence one of its children toward a lower differentiation of self. On the other hand, a family with very low levels of differentiation of self can influence one of its children toward a higher level of differentiation. Only the generations will experience the cumulative effects.

Societal Regression.   The concept of societal regression is included last not only because it is the one that Bowen added most recently, but also because it is the least well developed of his concepts.

Bowen contends that social factors—social groups, external crises, and chronic social anxiety—invoke automatic emotional responses in the same way that family members and families do, but on a larger scale. Thus, there is the potential for the logical extension of Bowen's theory of family to the larger emotional systems of society that contain the family itself. Societal dysfunction will result from societal crises, resulting in emotional band-aid types of legislation that can increase the problems, causing repeating cycles of social dysfunction.

Now that we have examined the fundamental concepts that Bowen has contributed to family systems theory, let us look at his contribution to family therapy practice.

Process of Therapy

Originally trained as a psychoanalyst, Bowen now considers himself a systems therapist. Since the triangle is such a key concept in the Bowen Theory, it is not surprising that Bowen postulates a therapy in which the triangle is the primary focus of intervention.

Goals of Therapy. For Bowen, the primary goal of therapy is to differentiate the self from the family ego mass. This differentiation is accomplished by helping people to detriangulate themselves out of the family system. Remember that the triangle is the manifestation of the lines of emotional fusion in a family system and that all triangles interact in some way. It stands to reason then that if one can modify the functioning of a single triangle within the emotional system of a family, one can effect change in the entire system.

Bowen postulates two ways to modify the triangle: (1) to place two people from a family emotional system in contact with a third person (the therapist perhaps) who is not vulnerable to their emotional maneuvers and who, by not changing, forces them to change; or (2) to change one member of a triangle (even through individual therapy), since that change, of necessity, will change the other relationships within the triangle.

The latter method, although superficially seeming to place Bowen in support of individual psychotherapy, in reality places him squarely among the structural family therapists, for, while his work may be with the individual, his goal is to modify the structure of the emotional system of the family through that individual change.

Techniques of Therapy and Role of the Therapist. Bowen believes that the therapist is a model and a teacher who has four main functions: defining and clarifying the relationship between the spouses; keeping self detriangled from the family emotional system; teaching the function of emotional systems; and actually demonstrating differentiation through his or her own behavior. Let us look at each of these functions a little more carefully to understand Bowen's view of the role of the therapist and the techniques of therapy.

1. *Defining and Clarifying the Relationship between Spouses*: As people develop longer and more intimate relationships with each other, they know more about what makes each other anxious, what is forbidden emotional turf. Very early in his own work, Bowen found that en-

couraging emotional disclosure often drove the spouses into deeper difficulty. He then began to discourage spouses from talking it out at home or even discussing issues with each other during the actual therapy session. Instead, he found it more helpful to have the spouses speak directly to the therapist. This technique resulted in the clarification and definition of the relationship. Thus, Bowen encourages people to talk about their feelings in calm, low-key ways. For example, if the wife, in speaking to the therapist, becomes enraged, the therapist asks the husband whether he noticed the anger, what his response is, and so forth. The therapist then asks the wife for her response to her husband's response. Bowen contends that in this intellectual, calm, conceptual approach with families, each spouse finally gets the opportunity to know the other in a way that their emotional system might not have allowed for decades.

2. *Keeping Self Detriangled from the Family Emotional System*: This technique rests upon the ability of the therapist to relate to each member of the couple without being too close or too distant, walking some line between emotional overinvolvement, on the one hand, too light a treatment of the couple's problems, on the other. Obviously, the therapist's own degree of differentiation of self is the critical factor in the ability to effect such a balance. If the therapist can achieve and maintain this detriangled state in the therapeutic relationship, the couple will find their emotional maneuvers futile, and it is they who will be forced to change. Bowen describes his therapeutic stance as follows: "The 'right' point for me is one between seriousness and humor, when I can make either a serious or a humorous response to facilitate the process in the family" (Bowen 1976).

3. *Teaching the Function of Emotional Systems*: Bowen believes that it is important for the therapist to teach the family members how to differentiate, how to clarify their values, and how to resolve family problems. Thus, intervening in an emotional triangle might involve some didactic instruction about individuation.

4. *Taking "I-Position" Stands*: The more the therapist models a high degree of differentiation of self by calmly stating his or her own convictions and beliefs, the greater the possibility that the spouses will understand their therapeutic goal. The effectiveness of the model will also encourage them to work toward that goal.

As we have already noted, the degree of differentiation of self that the therapist has obtained in his or her own life is the key to the effective implementation of Bowen's theory. To the extent that the therapist can respond, rather than react, to the emotionality of family members, the family members will themselves learn to respond in the same way, detriangulate themselves, and to lead more effective, self-differentiated lives.

Bowen cuts through the arbitrary dichotomy between the therapist's role and the therapist's personal life. Unless the therapist has undergone the process of effectively working on his or her own triangles in his or her own family system, he or she can only be too vulnerable, too easily triangulated into some other family's emotional system. Bowen's anonymous article (1972) on his work on his own family system remains one of the most awesome pieces of literature within the field.

In watching Bowen work, one notes that he takes a careful history in order to understand multigenerational transmissions. Because of his de-emphasis of affect and feeling, he appears to some to be disengaged and aloof, much like the authoritarian doctor. However, one observes his ability to create a calm, rational climate wherein family members can begin to respond to each other in a new and more effective way. He seems like a coach or director, teaching people how to hear and think about what they are experiencing.

Overview of Bowen

The two most basic concepts of Bowen's theory are triangles and differentiation of self. Bowen emphasizes the importance of the process of detriangulation both in the life of the family and in the work of the therapist. Within that process, the degree of differentiation of self is the critical factor, the determinant of an individual's vulnerability to attempts to fuse him or her into an intensely emotional relationship with other members of the system. Recalling our introduction to this chapter, we see that triangles are the *structures* in Bowen's conceptualization of family systems and that degree of differentiation of self determines the *permeability* or *impermeability* of an individual's *boundaries*.

DAVID KANTOR

David Kantor's formal graduate training is somewhat different from Bowen's and Minuchin's, both of whom are psychiatrists. Kantor's doctorate is in the area of social psychology. Nevertheless, his entry into family systems theory and therapy is similar to Bowen's and Minuchin's in that it began with research. Kantor's early studies focused on the effect of the structure of the psychiatric ward on patients, which logically led to his interest in patients' families. To conduct this type of research, Kantor, along with Fred Duhl, established the Boston Family Institute. More recently Kantor founded the Family Institute of Cambridge, which provides a setting for experimental and clinical research and the formal training of family therapists.

Although a relative newcomer to a field only two decades old, Kantor is included here as a major family structural theorist for two reasons: (1) He presents an original and comprehensive framework for the analysis of the structural development of a *variety* of family systems. (2) While being aware of the effects of the family system on an individual, he offers a theory that also recognizes the impact of the individual's intrapsychic needs and experiences on the system—that is, in Kantor's framework, some systems transform people, but there are also people (each of us has known some) who, by virtue of their own personal dynamics, transform systems.

Major Concepts

Like Bowen and Minuchin, Kantor focuses on the structures of family systems and management of the boundaries within them. Let us look first at Kantor's concepts of subsystems and family styles.

Subsystems.   Kantor begins with the levels of subsystems within the family system itself. He postulates three such levels: the family-unit subsystem, the interpersonal subsystem, and the personal subsystem. What separates these subsystems are boundaries. The point at which the boundaries of one person's subsystem meet the boundaries of another person's subsystem is called the *interface* of the boundaries.

When one subsystem interfaces with another subsystem, several things occur:

> Each system's traffic can be regulated in relation to the traffic of the other system, particularly as each system's members see what they might gain from members of another system or transmit to them. Meetings at the interface thus result in the shaping and reshaping of each unit's space, including the thickness of its boundary walls. Those inside each unit use their experiences in meeting members of another unit to define who and what they are as a unit among other units. [Kantor and Lehr 1975, p. 24]

Let us now look at the three subsystems with which an individual might interface.

1. *The Family-Unit Subsystem*: This subsystem is basically the "face" that the family unit presents to the outside world. The family-unit boundary is that place where an outsider initially interfaces with the family system. Figure 5–2a illustrates how an outsider can pass through the original exterior boundary to interact somewhere inside the family-unit space. Notice that now a new boundary exists for the outsider: the boundary of the interpersonal subsystem.

2. *The Interpersonal Subsystem*: The outsider in the family-unit space is now a member of the family, but at a superficial level. He or she is still a stranger to the interpersonal subsystem of the family. This interpersonal subsystem could be characterized as the "real life" of the family, its life as it carries out its daily transactions within the privacy and security of its own walls. This is the way a family really behaves at home, as opposed to the way it presents itself to an outsider. Entry into the interpersonal subsystem usually requires additional questions and decisions and depends on the outsider's ability to meet certain criteria. Figure 5–2b illustrates the outsider being let into some of the interactions of the interpersonal subsystem. Note that now another new boundary appears for the outsider: the boundary of the personal subsystem.

3. *The Personal Subsystem*: This subsystem represents how an individual would behave if he or she were not engaged in family interaction. Let us illustrate this with Mr. James. The family therapist might meet Mr. James in his family-unit subsystem posture. There, Mr. James might be friendly, considerate of all his children, a model father and husband. On the way home from the therapy session, however, Mr. James's son might meet Mr. James at his interpersonal subsystem space. There, Mr. James might be furious at his son for sharing so much at the session and embarassing the family in public. And beyond this, if we (or even Mr. James himself) knew him better, we might see that his chastising his son was part of the interpersonal role expected of him as the "father" within the family system. In fact, his *personal* subsystem position might really be one of personal anguish that his family needs therapy; he might actually be blaming himself, but not sharing it within the intimacy of his family. Clearly, to negotiate that final boundary, to know Mr. James on the "personal" level, might not only be a difficult task for the outsider, but an equally difficult task for Mr. James as well.

Here, then, is a man who has three postures as "father," all in reference to a particular situation. As a "family-unit-subsystem" father, he is open and understanding of public disclosure of family difficulties. As an "interpersonal-subsystem" father, he is critical of the son who initiated the disclosure. And as a "personal-subsystem" father, he is critical of himself. Figure 5–3 illustrates these three postures. Note that a different type of behavior occurs at each level—that is, within the

a. Family - Unit Space

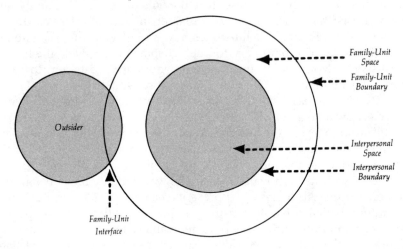

b. Interpersonal Space

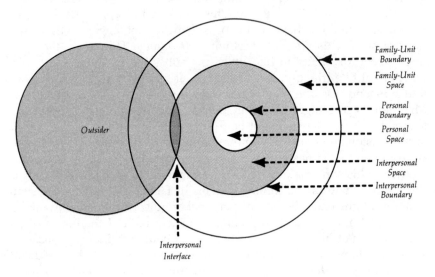

Figure 5–2   *Outsider's Interface with Family Subsystems*

family-unit space, the interpersonal space, and the personal space. Subsystems, therefore, consist of roles, acts, and levels.

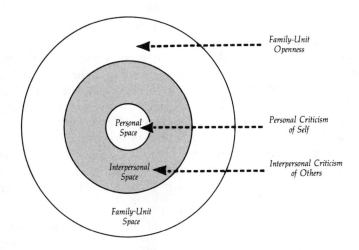

Figure 5–3 *Three Subsystem "Postures" of Father*

Family Styles. A family's particular *style* of structural arrangement, of structure and boundary management and negotiation, may differ substantially from that of other families. Kantor postulates three models of structural family arrangement: *closed, open,* and *random.*

While every family typically evolves a unique configuration of patterns, strategies, and rules, often blending characteristics of each pure style, most families tend toward one or another of the three styles. All three are "good" and "workable" models. Each has its own successful and unsuccessful variety.

The three models differ in several important ways. First, each model defines its *core purpose* differently. The closed style seeks *stability* and relies on the certainties of *tradition*; the open style espouses *adaptation*, which it arrives at through *dialectic* and *consensus*; and the random style prefers *exploration* with a reliance on *intuition*.

The second difference is that each model has a different *homeostatic ideal*. The system of the closed style relies on *negative feedback* or *constancy loops*; the system of the open style stresses a *balance between negative and positive feedback*; and the system of the random style relies on *positive feedback* or *variety loops*.

A third distinction is that each model defines the *targets* within the major dimensions of family life in different ways and seeks *access* to them differently as well. For Kantor, the three "target dimensions" are *affect, power,* and *meaning*. The "access dimensions" through which family members and families work to reach their targets are those of *space, time,* and *energy.*

Table 5–1 presents a matrix of how each of the access dimensions differs in each type of family model. Let us see how the characteristics of the access dimensions translate into the realities of a family's life. If you grew up in a family in which the predominant structural style was closed, you probably had a living room (space) that was off limits except when guests arrived. The living room's furniture might even have been covered "to protect it." Dinner (time) was at six o'clock, whether or not you were hungry ("because that's when we eat"). And chores (energy) around the house were completed on schedule and with diligence.

Table 5–1   *Characteristics of Space, Time, and Energy in the Three Family Models*

	Space	*Time*	*Energy*
Closed Model	Fixed	Regular	Steady
Open Model	Movable	Variable	Flexible
Random Model	Dispersed	Irregular	Fluctuating

If you grew up in a family whose style of structure was more open, your living room might have been used on occasion, and by mutual agreement, for you and your friends to present "the world's greatest puppet theatre." The dinner hour was at times modified for "special events." And on some weekends, it was all right to rake fewer leaves.

If you grew up in a "random" family, you might have come home after school to find your brother's friends building their project for the science fair on the living room floor, after having moved the television to the kitchen ("so we won't disturb your watching the news"). Dinner might not have been cooked at all, or it might be an hour late ("I got into reading this article and I couldn't stop"). And in November, the back screen door might still be in the bathroom ("because if I put it downstairs, I'll forget to fix it").

Kantor acknowledges that although his matrix of structural styles and access-dimension characteristics is a valid way of organizing the family system, it is rare that a family exclusively employs only one style. These structural styles are stereotypically different ways of system organization and in reality families usually combine them.

The family's target dimensions, affect, power, and meaning, are really the same for all three models of family structures. The goals of affect are nurturance and a sense of intimacy; of power, a sense of efficacy and competency; and of meaning, validation and a sense of belonging.

However, each model sees these target dimensions and governs activity within them in different ways. In the closed model, power is organized vertically; rules are clear and opposition is discouraged. Strong loyalty to the family is characteristic. Affect is characterized by earnest and sincere emotions and control of public demonstrations of emotion. And meaning is generated and perpetuated through reliance on rationality, tradition, and traditional symbols.

In the open model, power is lateral and universal participation is expected. Dissent may be voiced or even encouraged, but loyalty to both the family's individualistic and collective ideals is still expected. Affect is expressed openly and is shared, rather than withheld. Meaning emerges from consideration of different points of view and the process of dialectic argument. Uniquely personal values and meanings are expressed and authenticity is expected.

In the random model, power is determined more experimentally than in other models, and charisma and personal ability prevail. Affect tends to be passionate, rapt, and quick. Meaning and reason tend to be dominated by personal inspiration; paradox and ambiguity are preferred modes of expression. "The random style is extravagant at paying tribute to potentiality" (personal communication from Kantor).

Kantor's model of the family system uses these six dimensions (the access dimensions of space, time, and energy and the target dimensions of affect, power, and meaning) in the following way: "Through the transmission of matter and information via energy in space and time, family members regulate each other's access to the targets of affect, power and meaning" (Kantor and Lehr 1975, p. 39). Figure 5–4 illustrates this interaction. For Kantor, this is the "structure" of the system through which communications are manifested as individuals pursue the targets of their lives.

At this point, the following questions arise: Why pursue one target as opposed to another? What propels the individual to move through this system seeking anything at all? Kantor's answers lie in his notions of *critical identity images, psychopolitics,* and the *four-player system.* Let us examine each of these concepts separately.

Critical Identity Images.   Kantor postulates two basic goals for the individual as he or she interacts with the members of the family system, or, for that matter, interacts with any social system. The individual's basic goals are: (1) to actualize his or her preferred self, to actually "be" who he or she would like to be in relationship with somebody; and (2) to

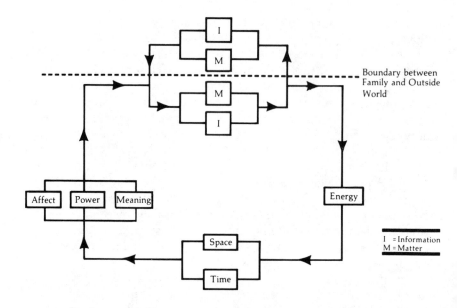

Figure 5–4   *The Interaction of Information and Matter with Access and Target Dimensions*

Source: Reprinted with permission from Kantor, David, and William Lehr, *Inside the Family* (San Francisco: Jossey-Bass, 1975), p. 39. Chart contributed by Larry Constantine.

actualize his or her preferred system, to actually live in his or her ideal social context. Kantor uses the term *operational identity* to refer to the actualization of preferred self and the term *collective identity* to refer to the actualization of the preferred system.

Kantor claims that the individual has internal imagery of his or her "operational" and "collective" identities. He defines the image as "an internalized memory picture" (personal communication from Kantor). It is an integration of sensory and cognitive experiences into pictorial thought. Some part of these images comes from experiences in families of origin, some from present family systems. At any one time, one has an image of one's operational identity and of one's collective identity. It is these images that propel people to move through the system as they seek to realize their ideal identities through interaction with the other members of the system.

Kantor contends that among these images there is a special subset of images, which he calls *critical identity images*. These are seen as providing the hidden energy that family members manifest as they attempt to conceive, nurture, and perfect a family that "works."

An individual's critical identity images are distinguished from the larger family of sensory images by eight features:

1. They are primarily visual and spatial.
2. While their derivations may be in past experience, they continue to influence present and future events to a significant degree and their formation does not stop in childhood or adolescence, but continues throughout life.
3. They are actional in nature, involving the self and at least one other significant person, who, together with the image-bearer compose a scenario of action that is either implicit or explicit.
4. The psychopolitics (the behavior of an individual in relation to others) embedded in the originating image action are as important in later identity struggles as the content of the image, sometimes more important.
5. Through their specific *contents* (for example, the *routine humiliation* of a child by a parent while another helplessly looks on) and through the *mood* climates associated with these contents (for example, *gloom*, or *heaviness*), critical identity images embody the thematic and qualitative character of the family system.
6. Within an individual's set of critical images, certain ones contain the instructions and formats for how the system's goals ought ideally to be defined (the model core purpose) and how the goals ought ideally to be realized (the homeostatic ideals). In other words, critical images contain the blueprints for model formation and thus they define the scope of the system's development.
7. Critical identity images tend to have unusual vividness and intensity, what Kantor calls their arousal value. What people store in memory experience, then, is not only the special memory content of the image and the psychopolitical configuration, but an energy component associated with the original experience, reinforced by new experiences along the way. And finally,
8. Any new context similar in structure to the original identity image can invoke an emotional response and a behavioral response similar to what was experienced earlier. (Therapists commonly try to neutralize the energies generated by these images and their collisions. Further, they even attempt to get rid of the images "Look at it from her point of view," etc.). Kantor believes that both are mistaken strategies. The model structure is derived from critical images.

Taken together, these special memory pictures constitute the individual's operational identity. Operational identity is that aspect of personal identity reserved for use in structuring our relationships with intimates.

Whereas individuals may acquire many images, they tend to have but a handful of critical identity images. Kantor argues that we acquire perhaps two or three key ones for each of the major dimensions of our lives—some for our affect relations, some for our power relations, and some for the spiritual-ideological relations through which we assert our meanings. Moreover, he believes that we are especially open to the formation of new critical identity images during the transition periods that mark development throughout the individual life cycle.

We can now supplement Kantor's description of the interactional structure of the system ("through the transmission of matter and information . . . members regulate each other's access to the targets of affect, power and meaning") by adding "in an attempt to actualize their critical images of their operational and collective identities."

Psychopolitics. In attempting to actualize their critical images, individuals must cope with two types of experience: *self-consciousness*, the experience of self in relation to others; and *system consciousness*, the experience of the relation of others to self. The style of coping with these experiences is what Kantor calls *psychopolitics* (Kantor and Lehr 1975). *Psycho* refers to the interior person, the individual's right to actualize himself. *Politics* refers to observable family interactions, the individual's style of coping with the institutional requirements of the family unit and interpersonal subsystems. Psychopolitics, then, consists of the *strategies* chosen in an attempt to satisfy the individual's and the family's needs simultaneously.

In the mid-1960s, Kantor, drawing upon his earlier experience with psychodrama, developed the therapeutic strategy of family sculpture (personal communication from Kantor). In family sculpture, a family member arranges the family, "sculpts them," in a way that reveals his or her perceptions of the psychopolitics of the family system. To do this, the family member, primarily without speaking, utilizes the physical space of the room and the physical gestures and movements of other family members. The carrying out of such a "sculpture" requires the participant to share his or her internal images and, by so doing, to clarify the relative degree of integration of his or her intrapsychic and interactional needs. Although Kantor originally developed sculpture as a diagnostic tool, other therapists have extended its use as a treatment tool within the context of several treatment modalities.

The Four-Player System. Kantor argues that in implementing one's critical images, one's psychopolitical choices are limited to four roles within the family interactional model: mover, follower, opposer, and bystander (Kantor and Lehr 1975). Kantor refers to this limitation of interactional roles as the *four-player system.*

A *mover* is someone who has initiated action within the system, who has started something going. Whether that something is positive or negative is irrelevant to the status of mover. Once someone has become a mover, only three roles remain for the other persons in the family system. One who supports the action of the mover is called a *follower*. One who takes action against the mover or follower is called an *opposer*. And one who neither supports nor opposes the movers, followers, and opposers is called a *bystander*. Being a bystander may involve no interaction whatsoever, or it may take the form of "process comments," which place the bystander in the position of not choosing sides (for example, "It seems as if you and Dad both wanted to relax this afternoon, but wound up having a fight about it.").

Kantor's notion of critical images is an attempt to answer the question of why one's psychopolitical choice of role might be to function as a mover, while another person might choose to function as an opposer. Each choice, each interaction, is an attempt to implement one's ideal system by resolving the competing needs of the individual and the needs of the family system.

We can now return to Kantor's early definition of the structure of the family system, which explained the operation of the six dimensions, and, by adding to it the concepts of critical identity images, psychopolitics, and the four-player system, present a more complete summary of his theory of family interaction:

> Through the transmission of matter and information via energy in space and time, family members regulate each other's access to the targets of affect, power, and meaning. They achieve this regulation through their psychopolitical choices of interactional roles (mover, follower, opposer, or bystander) and are motivated to do so by their need to implement, in actual relationships with others, the critical identity images they have of their ideal selves and their ideal social environments.

Strategies.   When the models of individual family members are in disagreement, when critical identity images are in competition, the family members' individual psychopolitical choices—that is, their actual interactions with each other—produce instability and possibly crisis.

Kantor integrates these concepts into daily family interactions, which he calls *strategies*. Strategies fall into categories that are determined by their function within the development of the family. There are strategies for *maintenance* of the family system (to keep it in equilibrium), strategies for times of *stress* (to encounter and begin to integrate structure transformations), and strategies for *repair* (to consolidate transformations and move on). Strategies that help an individual, a subsystem, or an entire family to actualize the target ideals are called *enabling strategies*. Strategies that are associated with the failure of an individual, a subsystem, or an entire family to achieve the target ideals are called *disabling strategies*.

Obviously, with several individuals all attempting to implement their own critical identity images within the context of a family's interactions, there are bound to be competing and conflicting strategies. These competing and conflicting strategies may very well have unforeseen and/or unintended results. When the unforeseen and unintended results have unfortunate consequences for family members, they are called *ironic displacements*. The notion is: "Isn't it ironic with three people basically caring as much about each other as these three people do, that something as unfortunate as this should have happened instead of what they actually wanted to have happen?"

Implications for Therapy

Let us attempt to see how Kantor's theoretical material applies to the actual practice of family therapy. Consider an example from a present generation of the Elliot family. This generation consists of a father, Mr. Elliot; a mother, Mrs. Elliot; and their six-year-old son, Elliot, Jr.

Recently, with much trepidation, Elliot, Jr. informed his elementary school counselor that over the past few months his mother has engaged in a type of sexual activity with him that one might describe as "incestuous." These advances took place on evenings when Mr. Elliot was not at home and was working extra time at his job.

Rather than simply assuming that "Oedipus has struck again," the counselor, working with other school personnel and outside agencies who knew the Elliots, pieced together the following case of *ironic displacement:*

The Elliots' family system conforms to the *closed* model, in which the members of the husband-wife *interpersonal subsystem* are fairly inflexible in *communicating* with each other. In an attempt to implement a *critical identity image* of his own efficacy (*power*), Mr. Elliot has been working late (*time*) at his office (*space*) and has had no inclination whatsoever toward sexuality (*energy*) with his wife. Mr. Elliot sees his wife's constant demands in the area of sexuality as a threat to his already depleted energy reserves at work, where he has been fairly ineffective (*power*). Mrs. Elliot, on the other hand, sees his ignoring her sexual advances as a rejection of her *critical identity image* of herself as a "lovable, caring person" (*affect*).

In her lonely moments on the evenings when her husband had not been home, Mrs. Elliot had begun crying in the presence of her son. He had responded with sympathy and love, bringing her tissues, rubbing her back, and telling her, "It's OK, Mom. I love you and I'll take care of you" (*affect*). Within a few months, their loving, caring relationship had blossomed into the incest described to the counselor. Table 5–2 outlines this strategy and its ironic displacement.

Although Kantor does not explicitly indicate the therapeutic implications of a family's interactional strategy, let us see what it offers. We can see that there are several "choice points," that is, several places at which the therapist might choose to intervene in the Elliot's family system.

To begin with, it is clear that the incest is symptomatic of some dysfunction in the husband-wife relationship. Thus, individual therapy with the son or the mother, or even therapy with both of them together, although potentially supportive, is not to the point. Where, then, does one intervene in the structure of this system? In this case, there are at least three possible points of intervention:

1. *Theme*: One possible point of intervention is in the theme, which in this family is sexuality—that is, sexuality is (by tradition, default, or whatever) the primary means for implementing nurturance in the husband-wife subsystem. Perhaps through therapeutic intervention at this point, the variety of themes for giving and receiving nurturance in this system could be expanded so that Mrs. Elliot could feel lovable and caring through behaviors other than sexuality (for example, getting a baby sitter so that she could share some evening work with her husband at his job).

2. *Blocking Mechanism*: Another possible point of intervention is in the blocking mechanism. As we see in table 5–2, the blocking mechanism in this family strategy is impotence. The therapist might recommend a physical examination to determine whether there are physiological bases for Mr. Elliot's impotence. The therapist might also recommend conjoint therapy with a time-limited behavioral contract to allow the Elliots to explore whether there is a relationship between sexual activity and job performance.

3. *Goal*: At least one more point of intervention remains. That is in the goal, which, in this case, is Mrs. Elliot's need to nurture and receive nurturance from her husband. Perhaps through individual or

138

Table 5-2 *The Elliot Family's Strategy and its Ironic Displacement*

System Type	Subsystem	Mrs. Elliot's Critical Identity Image	Target Dimension	Goal	Theme	Blocking Mechanism	Outcome
Closed	Inter-personal (husband-wife)	Herself as a "lovable, caring woman"	Affect	Nurtur-ance	Sexuality	Impotence of husband	Incest

conjoint therapy focusing on this point, Mrs. Elliot could determine whether as a person in her own right she needs to nurture and receive nurturance from her husband, or *any* man, or whether this is a sociocultural role out of which she may wish to move.

None of these points of intervention may be the most efficacious way to treat this family problem. Nevertheless, it is clear that Kantor's conceptual scheme of family interaction and structure facilitates *diagnosis* of family dysfunction. Although for purposes of illustration we have applied Kantor's model of analysis only to Mrs. Elliot's position in the family problem, his model could be equally as well applied to the positions of Mr. Elliot and Elliot, Jr.

Overview of Kantor

We have described Kantor's delineation of the complexities underlying the strategies that people choose in family interaction. In various types of systems and the subsystems within them, through the access dimensions of space, time, and energy, people move toward the targets of affect, power, and meaning. In this process, which involves psychopolitical choices of roles, they are motivated by the need to implement their critical identity images. Ironic displacements, which are symptomatic of family dysfunction, occur as unfortunate consequences of family members' attempts to implement these critical images.

Because dysfunction motivates system members to clarify their rules, to evolve more expedient strategies for reaching their developmental goals, and to perfect their model for living, the resolution of dysfunction can become the source of new system structures and can lead to an increase in structural complexity and efficiency. At the same time, private symbols, images, and themes of individual members may be complemented and creatively synthesized into a richer and more broadly sustaining collective identity. When dysfunction is not resolved, critical identity images are left unrealized, interactional structures rigidified, and family development thwarted.

Kantor's integration of these three critical areas—intrapsychic processes, systemic structural dynamics, and developmental challenges—is a major contribution to family systems theory.

Now that we have seen how Murray Bowen and David Kantor define and treat the structures and boundaries of family systems, let us turn to our third structural theorist, Salvador Minuchin, to see how he deals with these same concepts.

SALVADOR MINUCHIN

Minuchin was trained as a psychiatrist and early in his practice found it beneficial to include parents in the treatment of children. In his early work as a psychiatrist at the Wiltwick School for Boys, he began to recognize relationships between the boys' patterns of delinquency and the degrees of disorganization of the families from which they came. A grant from NIMH allowed Minuchin to study the structure and process of disorganized, socioeconomically disadvantaged families, each of whom had produced more than one delinquent.

Families of the Slums (Minuchin et al. 1967) is a superb pioneering work in the general field of family therapy, but especially in its specific treatment of the disorganized and disadvantaged family. The book summarizes the strategy of the Wiltwick project, the profiles of the families involved, and the specific implications for therapeutic intervention with families of this type. The concepts of this work have been incorporated into Minuchin's current approach to symptomatic dysfunction in individuals and families.

Major Concepts

A full understanding of Minuchin's approach requires an understanding of his model of family development, as well as his concepts of generic and idiosyncratic constraints, boundaries, and family adaptation to stress.

Family Development Model.   Minuchin sees the structure of the family as that of "an open sociocultural system in transformation" (Minuchin 1974, p. 14). The family structure is *sociocultural* in that it integrates the demands of society, as well as those of the internal family system, in shaping the individual. The process of birth, childhood, and adolescence, of leaving one's family of origin, coupling, and beginning the process all over again with a new generation of children, after which one moves on toward late adult life, decline, and death, is a circular, self-generating one. Minuchin postulates that the family *developmental* tasks in this process require the modification of the *structure* of the family. This structural modification is accomplished through *boundary negotiation and modification*. Minuchin's model of family development begins with the couple.

1. *The Couple*: In this primary stage of family development, the couple is engaged in a complex process of negotiation on three fronts: (1) Within the couple subsystem, the spouses must develop a series of mutually satisfying "patterned transactions"—for example, they must decide who will shop, how they will share a bathroom, closet, and so forth. (2) At the same time, the spouses must accomplish the task of separating from their families of origin and from other family systems. This task involves negotiating new boundaries (relationships) with parents, siblings, in-laws, divorced spouses, and so forth. (3) They must decide how they will reorganize and regulate the demands of the work world, as well as their previous leisure activities and commitments. The management of each of these three major tasks is difficult in and of itself. This stage of family development involves intense negotiation between the two members of the couple system.

2. *The Parents*: When the "coupling" tasks appear to have been successfully negotiated, the husband and wife may find that the two-person system they have effectively begun is about to become a three-person system. This calls for renewed and additional negotiations as they redefine their functions to meet the demands of the child or children. The couple must deal with the new subsystems that emerge in the process (mother-child dyad, for example), as well as with changes in their relationships to the outside world. One spouse may perhaps take an extra job to help out financially. The couple must also renegotiate their boundaries with their extended families, who are now grandparents, aunts, and uncles.

3. *The Siblings:* The sibling subsystem is described by Minuchin as the "first social laboratory in which children can experiment with peer relationships" (Minuchin 1974, p. 59). It is here that children begin to prepare themselves for the varieties of boundary negotiations that they will encounter for the rest of their lives. As the children grow into and through adolescence, the process of structural change and boundary negotiation continues. Minuchin's emphasis is always on "what happens" in this process, not on "why." He discusses what happens in terms of two major types of constraints on family development.

Generic and Idiosyncratic Constraints.   Within the changing structure of the family, Minuchin perceives that there are *generic* and *idiosyncratic constraints*. The generic constraints are so called because Minuchin feels that there are "universal rules governing family organization" (Minuchin 1974, p. 52). For example, in any family system with children, there must be a power hierarchy. *How* the levels of authority are eventually negotiated may differ among families, but this negotiation is a generic constraint in that *all* families with children must work it through (successfully or unsuccessfully).

The idiosyncratic constraints, on the other hand, are composed of the unique individual expectations and intentions of each family member. Through them, patterns are explicitly or implicitly formed, sometimes continuing for years after the reason for them is no longer present. For example, a hierarchy established between the members of the original couple, but based on their role as parents, may continue between them long after the children have grown and left home. Mother may continue to assume full responsibility for keeping the house and maintaining contact with the adult children, while Father continues to be the breadwinner and to play cards with the boys once a week, maintaining his authority and decision-making power with regard to family activities and functioning. The hierarchy in this case is idiosyncratic in that it is based on this particular family's matrix of values, expectations, and intentions.

The concept of boundaries is a key to understanding the nature of the particular developmental task of the family.

Boundaries.   For Minuchin, the boundaries of a subsystem are the "rules defining who participates and how." Moreover,

> the function of boundaries is to protect the differentiation of the system. Every family subsystem has specific functions and makes specific demands on its members; and the development of interpersonal skills achieved in these subsystems is predicated on the subsystem's freedom from interference from other subsystems. [Minuchin 1974, p. 53]

Who is a member of the subsystem—that is, its actual composition—is not nearly so important to the system's functioning as the *clarity of the boundaries* within the subsystem itself. A parenting subsystem consisting of a child, her mother, and her grandmother is no better or worse than a parenting subsystem consisting of a child and two parents. The critical issues in determining the clarity of the boundaries are how well the lines of responsibility have been thought out and how clearly the designation of authority has been defined.

Minuchin postulates three basic types of boundaries: (1) *enmeshed boundaries*, where relationships are diffuse and too close; (2) *disengaged boundaries*, where relationships are inappropriately rigid and too distant; and (3) *clear boundaries*, where relationships are within the "normal range." Minuchin conceptualizes these three types of boundaries as constituting a continuum, which is illustrated in figure 5–5.

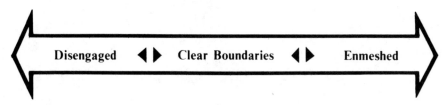

Figure 5–5 *Boundary Continuum*

It is important to understand that Minuchin's concepts of enmeshment and disengagement refer to a relationship style. They do not imply function or dysfunction in themselves. Indeed, most families have enmeshed and/or disengaged subsystems at one time or another. For example, in the early months following childbirth, it is not unusual for the mother-child subsystem to become slightly enmeshed while the wife-husband subsystem becomes slightly disengaged. Later, the wife-husband subsystem rearranges itself. Figure 5–6 illustrates this kind of normal developmental adjustment.

However, the extremes of disengagement or enmeshment indicate the potential for symptom formation. For example, if the family illustrated in figure 5–6 were to continue in a pattern of enmeshment of mother and child and disengagement of father, the child might be retarded in developing a sense of independence, with resulting complications.

Minuchin points out that the enmeshed family system generally "responds to any variation from the accustomed with excessive speed and intensity. The disengaged family tends not to respond when a response is necessary" (Minuchin 1974, p. 55).

The major subsystems in which boundary negotiation is a generic constraint are (1) the couple subsystem; (2) the parent subsystem; and (3) the sibling subsystem.

Family Adaptation to Stress. Within the whole cycle of family development, there are a variety of stresses impinging on the family. How well a family handles its stresses determines its healthful development. Minuchin sees four major types of stresses:

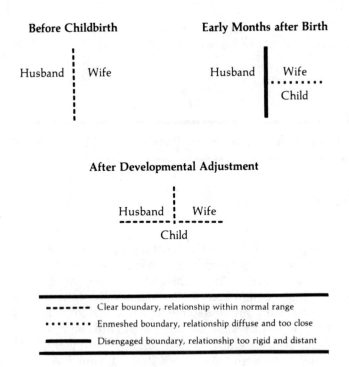

Figure 5–6 *Normal Developmental Adjustment*

1. *Stressful Contact of One Member with Extrafamilial Forces*: Extra-familial stress may impact on only one family member and may be contained there. On the other hand, this type of stress may affect other family members as well. For example, a spouse may bring the stress of a deteriorating job situation into the husband-wife relationship. This stress may perhaps even spill over into the father-mother-child subsystem and result in "triangling," to use Bowen's term.

In some cases, the entire family may be stressed by one member's extrafamilial difficulties. For example, one spouse's job loss may necessitate the other spouse's taking on a job, which in turn may cause stress in the parenting relationship (or even in the sibling relationship, if one of the older children has to take on a part-time job or assume some of the child-care responsibilities). The nature of the "executive subsystem" may change if an in-law moves into the home to help during the crisis.

2. *Stressful Contact of the Whole Family with Extrafamilial Forces*: In an example of this type of stress a poor family might come into contact with

so many different societal agencies (extrafamilial forces) that its coping mechanisms become overloaded. Minuchin also cites examples of "culture shock"—immigrant families who functioned quite well before coming to this country but who, faced with the stresses of an unfamiliar culture, needed to make a sudden adaptation.

   3. *Stress at Transition Points in a Family*: Examples of stressful transition points are the birth of the first child, the emergence of the oldest child into adolescence, and the oldest child's leaving home to go away to college. When the oldest child enters adolescence, the structural arrangement of mother and father in relation to children usually becomes mother and father in relation to adolescent child and children. Figure 5–7 illustrates this particular type of structural rearrangement. An inappropriate resolution to the stresses arising around the emergence of an adolescent in the family would be a father's refusal to recognize his son as an adolescent. The father's attacks on the boy might cause the mother to respond by engaging in a protective, enmeshed relationship with her son. A cross-generational conflict would then ensue and, if it persisted could precede some serious dysfunction in the adolescent .or in the family system as a whole.

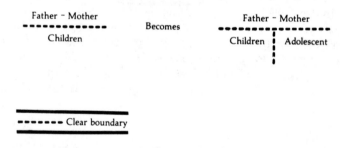

Figure 5–7   *Structural Rearrangement as Oldest Child Reaches Adolescence*

   Transitional stresses may also arise from decreased, as well as increased, family membership. Decreased membership may be the result of death, divorce, or imprisonment, while increased membership may result from an unexpected pregnancy or the addition of an in-law or elderly parent to the home.

   4. *Stress around Idiosyncratic Problems*: A family with a retarded child provides us with an example of stress arising from an idiosyncratic problem. The family may function quite well while the child is young,

but as the child emerges into adolescence, or even earlier when the disparity between the child and his or her peers becomes apparent, the stress involved may overload the system's capacity to respond, resulting in dysfunction.

In each of these four major types of stressful situations, Minuchin sees the *transformation of structure* through *boundary negotiation* as the key to successful adaptation.

In summary, then, Minuchin's theoretical concepts include the couple, parent, and sibling subsystems as part of an overall model of family development; the generic and idiosyncratic constraints that operate on the boundary negotiations within the structures of the family subsystems; and the impact of stress on the family from extra-familial forces, as well as from internal transitional and idiosyncratic problems. Minuchin would refer to a consideration of these concepts as "structural analysis."

Process of Therapy

Minuchin sees the family as a matrix of structures that respond to the external and internal demands made upon it. Dysfunction occurs when, in response to such demands, the family "stereotypes" its functions. In other words, regardless of whether family relationships are too enmeshed or too disengaged, if the family is unable to adapt to stress by renegotiating its boundaries and modifying its structure, the family becomes dysfunctional. It will remain so until alternative, effective means of boundary negotiation and structure modification are found.

Goals of Therapy and Role of the Therapist. Minuchin charges the therapist with three major tasks: to join the family as a leader; to unearth and evaluate the underlying family structure; and to create circumstances that will allow for the transformation of this structure. Thus, it is the therapist who is responsible for the healing and growth of the family members. Minuchin divides the therapist's task of facilitation into two major parts: forming the therapeutic system and restructuring the family.

1. *Forming the Therapeutic System*: The forming of the therapeutic system is characterized by moves that decrease the distance between the therapist and the family system. These moves are more often than not *accommodating* to the dysfunctional system "because a successful

restructuring often requires support of the structures that eventually must be changed" (Minuchin 1974).

Minuchin describes three styles of accommodating: (1) *maintenance,* in which the therapist supports the existing dysfunctional family structure; (2) *tracking,* in which the therapist merely attends to the family's communication and behavior patterns; and (3) *mimesis,* in which the therapist in a sense joins the family by adopting its pace of communication, by being jovial with a jovial family, and even by sharing something of his or her own life with them ("I have an uncle in Bayonne who's like that!").

This work is done without challenging the existing family structure so that the therapist can experience the current dynamics and thereby form a *diagnosis.* The actual diagnosis should consider six areas:

1. The family structure in terms of its major subsystems.
2. The system's flexibility and its capacity for elaboration and restructuring, as revealed by the reshuffling of the alliances, coalitions, and subsystems in response to changing circumstances.
3. The system's resonance, its sensitivity to individual member's actions.
4. The system's context, its life-support systems and the sources of stress in its extrafamilial environment.
5. The family's developmental stage and its performance of tasks appropriate to that stage.
6. The ways in which the identified patient's symptoms are used to maintain the current transactional patterns.

Once the diagnosis has been made, a *contract* must be established between the therapist and the family. That contract may initially be something like, "I will help you with Joe." Once the focus has shifted from the identified patient to the dysfunctional family structure, the contract may be: "We need to explore this area together."

2. *Restructuring the Family System*: In attempting to restructure the family system, the therapist begins to challenge the family's current transactional style. Thus, the distance that was decreased during the formation of the therapeutic alliance may be increased during the restructuring process. We will see how this restructuring can be accomplished as we look at Minuchin's techniques of therapy.

Techniques of Therapy.   Minuchin postulates at least seven therapeutic strategies for facilitating the restructuring of the family system: (1) actualizing transactional patterns; (2) marking boundaries; (3) escalating stress; (4) assigning tasks; (5) utilizing symptoms; (6) manipulating mood; and (7) providing support, education, and guidance.

The *actualizing of transactional patterns* may involve the therapist's encouraging family members to actually *do* the thing that they are describing to the therapist—for example, encouraging an adolescent to verbalize complaints to a parent, rather than to the therapist. The therapist can also actualize transactional patterns by refusing to respond even when directly addressed, which forces the family to show what they actually do when left to their own resources.

In *marking boundaries* the therapist might instruct the parents of an enmeshed parent-child family with an "open-door policy" to "evict the children from the bedroom for one hour each evening."

Escalating stress can be achieved by emphasizing differences ("it seems that you two disagree") or by joining one family member against another (to do this, the therapist must have an accurate sense of the other member's threshhold of endurance). The pitfalls of escalating stress may very well outweigh its potential gains. A family may be overstressed or conflict may be stimulated to such an extent that the family withdraws from therapy before restructuring can be achieved.

Task assignment may take the form of specific requests on the part of the therapist during the session—for example, "Sit next to your wife and take her hand when she's anxious." It may also take the form of homework: "Grandma, I'd like you to visit your son in Chicago for two weeks."

To *utilize the symptom*, the therapist may exaggerate it—for example, by telling a child who steals to "steal something from your own family this week." The symptom can also be utilized by de-emphasizing it—for example, "I can set up a behavior modification program to trick your daughter into coming to school, but that would not really help you folks regain respect for each other as parents." This strategy may eventually "relabel" the symptom so that the family can see it as an unsuccessful attempt on the part of one member to solve a larger family problem.

Manipulating mood may involve changing the mood within the family itself, escalating the intensity so that the problem is seen as more than just another "here-we-go-again" situation. The therapist may also change his or her own mood—for example, by becoming highly critical of a child in a disengaged father-son relationship in a move to engage the father on the son's behalf. The therapist may relabel the mood of a family member, as in calling a mother's overcontrolling stance "concern" for the child. Here, as in escalating stress, the pitfalls are obvious, and the beginning therapist must tread very carefully.

The therapist provides *support, education, and guidance,* as he or she joins and restructures the family system. The therapist is a teacher and a model who helps, shows, educates. A session may be devoted to helping a youngster learn the tricks of getting along at the lunch table in school, instructing a couple in parenting, or teaching a family how to "deal with the welfare people."

Overview of Minuchin

Minuchin, like the other two theorists presented in this chapter, clearly has a structural approach to family systems. His emphasis is on the context of the interaction, and his interventions are always designed to modify the structures and boundaries within those contexts.

We want to point out that Minuchin's contributions are more in the area of therapeutic intervention than in the area of theoretical formulation. Particularly noteworthy is Minuchin's success with hitherto "untreatable cases," such as those of children or adolescents plagued with anorexia nervosa or intractable asthma (Liebman, Minuchin, and Baker 1974; Minuchin et al. 1975; Minuchin, Baker, and Rosman 1978). Stanton and his research group (Stanton and Todd 1976; Stanton 1977) have also demonstrated success in applying Minuchin's structural family therapy model to their work with hard-core heroin addicts. (See chapter 9 for further discussion of Minuchin's and Stanton's work in these areas.)

Minuchin's structural treatment model outlines two major tasks for the therapist: (1) forming a therapeutic system—joining the family as leader, accommodating to the dysfunctional system, diagnosing, and eventually agreeing on a contract; and (2) restructuring the family system through various strategies. Through these two major tasks, the therapist helps the family to challenge its current perceptions of reality; to accept alternative possibilities; and after the family has tried alternative transactional patterns, to develop new relationships and structures that are self-reinforcing.

Comparison of Critical Issues

Let us now examine the work of Bowen, Kantor, and Minuchin in terms of three criteria: (1) Does each theorist have a hypothesis concerning the etiology of dysfunction within the family system? (2) Does each have a conceptual framework that utilizes a structural approach to dysfunction? (3) Does each have an emphasis unique enough within the structural framework to merit inclusion in this chapter? This review is intended only as a summary. The reader is referred to the suggested readings at the conclusion of this chapter for in-depth coverage of these theorists.

1. *Etiology of Dysfunction*: For Bowen, the roots of dysfunction lie in the concept of the undifferentiated ego mass and its impact on the vulnerable individual whose task it is to develop a differentiated self. For Kantor, dysfunction is manifested as ironic displacements, the unfortunate consequences of the particular strategies that individuals use as they attempt to implement their critical identity images. For Minuchin, dysfunction is the result of a family's inability to adapt to stress through renegotiation of its boundaries and modification of its structure.

2. *Conceptual Framework*: Bowen's emphasis on triangulation as it is related to a lack of differentiation of self defines him as a structural theorist, as does Kantor's emphasis on closed, open, and random models of family systems as they are related to ironic displacements. Similarly, Minuchin's emphasis on internal and extrafamilial stresses on couple, parent, and sibling subsystems places him within the framework of structural theory. All three of these theorists are primarily interested in the structure of the family system and the boundary negotiation that structural maintenance implies.

3. *Uniqueness of Emphasis*: All of these theorists believe that structure and boundary negotiation are ultimately more significant than the specifics of communication; yet each has his special contribution to make within the framework of structural family theory. Part of Bowen's special contribution is his emphasis on the multigenerational transmission process in the development of family dysfunction. Kantor has contributed his concept of the critical identity images of the individual, his belief that although people are transformed by the system, they at times transform the system itself according to their intrapsychic needs. Part of Minuchin's unique contribution is his emphasis on sociocultural stress that impacts on individuals and their families.

A composite of these theorists might view the family as a structure of systems and subsystems that is constantly negotiating boundaries and relationships. In this structure, the multigenerational family history, the individual's internal goals and aspirations, and the needs of the family, as well as the demands of the society and culture, would all be integrated in an attempt to maintain simultaneously the well-being of the entire system and the individuals within it.

Bowen, Kantor, and Minuchin are still actively writing and developing their theoretical viewpoints. We expect that the coming decade will be a period of substantial development in structural family therapy.

Summary

In this chapter, we presented the theoretical concepts of the major structural family theorists, namely, Bowen, Kantor, and Minuchin. We explained their theoretical concepts, emphasizing their common focus on systems and subsystems and boundaries, the context in which relationships and interactions occur. As opposed to the communication theorists, these theorists focus on the family system's structural dynamics, particularly the creation, maintenance, and modification of boundaries.

We outlined Murray Bowen's major interlocking concepts, which are based on the fundamental variables of degree of anxiety and degree of integration of self. We were then able to see how Bowen postulates a therapy in which the triangle is the primary point of intervention. For Bowen, the goal of therapy is to differentiate the self from the family ego mass. We showed how Bowen translates his theoretical concepts into the process of therapy.

We presented David Kantor as an innovative systems theorist whose work has major implications for the assessment of family systems. We delineated the types of subsystems and family styles that Kantor postulates and explained his notions of critical identity images, psychopolitics, and the four-player system. We described Kantor's delineation of the complexities underlying the strategies that people choose in family interaction. We determined that Kantor's conceptual scheme of family interaction and structure facilitates the diagnosis of family dysfunction.

In discussing Salvador Minuchin's major concepts, we reviewed his family development model and the tasks that accompany each stage of family development. We discussed disengaged, clear, and enmeshed boundaries and showed how these boundaries are affected by different types of stress. Minuchin's goals of therapy are achieved when the therapist is able to form the therapeutic system and restructure the family. We described Minuchin's techniques for achieving these goals.

The exercises in chapter 5 in the manual will provide you with an experiential way of integrating the major theoretical concepts of each of the theorists whom we have studied in this chapter.

Having explored in section II the communication and structural approaches to family therapy theory and practice, we are now ready to integrate them in section III in two ways: (1) by viewing their implications for assessment of and intervention in family developmental crises, especially those in which the locus of control is within the marital dyad; and (2) by viewing their implications for a number of family crises that are not part of normal family development.

References

Bowen, Murray. 1972. "Toward the Differentiation of a Self in One's Own Family." In J. Framo, ed., *Family Interaction: A Dialogue between Family Researchers and Family Therapists*. New York: Springer.

———. 1976. "Theory and Practice of Psychotherapy." In P.J. Guerin, ed., *Family Therapy*. New York: Gardner Press.

———. 1978. *Family Therapy and Clinical Practice: Collected Papers of Murray Bowen*. New York: Aronson.

Kantor, David, and William Lehr. 1975. *Inside the Family*. San Francisco: Jossey-Bass.

Liebman, R., S. Minuchin, and L. Baker. 1974. "An Integrated Treatment Program for Anorexia Nervosa." *American Journal of Psychiatry* 131.

Minuchin, S. 1974. *Families and Family Therapy*. Cambridge, Mass.: Harvard University Press.

Minuchin, S., et al. 1967. *Families of the Slums*. New York: Basic Books.

Minuchin, S., et al. 1975. "A Conceptual Model of Psychosomatic Illness in Children." *Archives of General Psychiatry* 32.

Minuchin, S., L. Baker, and B. Rosman. 1978. *Psychosomatic Families: Anorexia Nervosa in Context*. Cambridge, Mass.: Harvard University Press.

Stanton, M.D. 1977. "Some Outcome Results and Aspects of Structural Family Therapy with Drug Addicts." Paper read at the National Drug Abuse Conference, San Francisco (May 1977).

Stanton, M.D., and T.C. Todd. 1976. "Structural Family Therapy with Heroin Addicts: Some Outcome Data." Paper presented at the Society of Psychotherapy Research, San Diego (June 1976).

Suggested Readings

Bowen, Murray. "The Use of Family Theory in Clinical Practice." *Comprehensive Psychiatry* 7 (1966):345–74.

————. "Family Therapy and Family Group Therapy." In H.I. Kaplan and B.J. Sadock, eds., *Comparative Group Therapies*. Baltimore: Williams & Wilkins, 1971.

————. "Principles and Techniques of Multiple Family Therapy." In J.O. Bradt and C. Moynihan, eds., *Systems Therapy*. Washington, D.C.: Groome Child Guidance Center, 1971.

Camp, H. "Structural Family Therapy: An Outsider's Perspective." *Family Process* 12, no. 3 (1973).

Duhl, F., B. Duhl, and D. Kantor. "Learning Space and Action in Family Therapy: A Primer of Sculpture." In D. Bloch, ed., *Techniques of Family Therapy*. New York: Grune & Stratton, 1973.

Klugman, Jeffrey. "Enmeshment and Fusion." *Family Process*, January 1976: 321–23.

Minuchin, S. "Conflict Resolution Family Therapy." In J. Haley, ed., *Changing Families*. New York: Grune & Stratton, 1971.

Minuchin, S., et al. "Anorexia Nervosa: Successful Application of a Family Approach." *Pediatric Research* 7 (1973):294.

Minuchin, S., and P. Minuchin. "The Child in Context: A Systems Approach to Growth and Treatment." In N. Talbot, ed., *Raising Children in Modern America: Problems and Prospective Solutions*. Boston: Little, Brown, 1975.

III

Developmental
Theory and Practice

Erikson (1963) uses the term *crisis* "to connote not a threat of catastrophe but a turning point and a crucial period of increasing vulnerability and heightened potential." His model of the individual client struggling with the *critical* challenges of a *developmental* transition has been readily integrated into family systems theory and practice. However, in a family system, the client with the crisis is not necessarily the individual, but is more often the family system itself or an entire subsystem within it. Many communication and structural theorists and practitioners not only support the notion that family crisis is a time of danger and opportunity, but also even advocate *inducing* crisis within the family system to facilitate therapeutic outcomes (Haley 1973; Rabkin 1977).

Two types of family crises may be conceptualized. One type, which is the type more commonly associated with the term *crisis*, occurs as the immediate consequence of an accident or emergency. This type of *crisis* requires a rapid response, yet its resolution produces no changes within the family system's structures and communication styles. The other type is the *family growth crisis*, in which a challenge to the system's structures and communication styles generates stress. The resolution of the family growth crisis requires a transformation of those structures and styles, either through therapeutic intervention or through the family's own resources.

Although an accident or emergency within the family may be quite disruptive and may require immediate therapeutic intervention, such crises produce no transformations of the family system's communication styles or structures, and their resolution implies a return to the status quo. It is beyond the scope of this text to examine this type of crisis primarily because the origins and resolutions of these crises are idiosyncratic to each family's particular social context. They therefore evolve patterns based on variables too complex for analysis here, or they evolve no patterns whatsoever.

Family growth crises, on the other hand, do involve system transformations and, at the same time, present some patterns that can be categorized. Two types of family growth crises may be conceptualized: (1) crises of regular *development,* such as those examined in chapter 1; and (2) a variety of *nondevelopmental* crises, so called because they do not evolve out of a family's regular developmental challenges. These nondevelopmental crises nevertheless require system transformations and occur with enough regularity in our culture to allow categorization. Let us look at each of these types of crises.

1. *Developmental Crises:* The developmental stages in the family life cycle begin and end with just two people—the members of the marital dyad. Moreover, although the other stages of development involve other family members, in all stages of family development the locus of control seems to reside within the marital dyad (Rappaport 1976). In other words, whether as a relationship of husband and wife or as a relationship of father and mother, that subsystem holds and exercises substantial power. Certainly, individuals and other subsystems may challenge the authority of the marital dyad, sometimes successfully. Nevertheless, in each developmental stage, and consequently in each developmental crisis, considerable responsibility for crisis resolution rests

with these two people. For this reason, this section examines developmental crises within the family life cycle by focusing on the marital dyad. Chapter 6 explores one special feature of the marital dyad—the couple system; chapter 7 explores another special feature of that dyad—the parent system.

2. *Nondevelopmental Crises*: Although nondevelopmental crises do not evolve out of the regular developmental challenges of the family life cycle, family members nonetheless "develop" by resolving them. Indeed, the family member who successfully resolves a crisis precipitated by chronic abuse from a spouse, or by the birth of a mentally retarded child, may develop and mature into an individual who has a deeper capacity for sustaining and fulfilling relationships.

Nondevelopmental crises, like developmental crises, differ in degree, as well as in kind. They may be partially, moderately, or substantially disruptive and intense. They may be as different as the temporary layoff from a job and the permanent amputation of both legs. Furthermore, a variety of factors—for example, culture, education, financial resources, idiosyncratic family mythologies—affect the way in which different families subjectively view a particular event as changing or having the potential to change their present or future lives (Price-Bonham and Addison 1978).

Despite the variety of nondevelopmental crisis, family crisis classification is sufficiently developed to present some general criteria for sorting among the various disruptions to normal family development. For example, Adams (1975) uses the criteria of the permanent versus temporary nature of the crisis to make some very general but highly useful distinctions among family crises. More specific criteria help us to delineate further. Farber (1964) distinguishes between role organization crisis (such as might be precipitated by adolescent rebellion) and tragic crisis (for example, an uncontrollable event that prevents the fulfillment of the parent's hopes and aspirations for a child). Ganz and Gubrium (1972) distinguish between instrumental crisis (for example, the financing of the care of a mentally retarded offspring) and expressive crisis (the emotional strain of that caretaking).

For the purpose of this section, we will use a criterion that divides nondevelopmental crises into the categories of voluntary and involuntary. *Voluntary nondevelopmental crises* have their etiology, or at least their sustaining dynamics, within the family system. Wife abuse, child abuse, and other types of family violence are some of the more obvious types of voluntary crises. Chronic alcoholism, as we shall see later, once considered an involuntary illness, is now seen by many theorists and practitioners as a voluntary crisis, with its roots and symptoms being maintained within the dynamics of the family. *Involuntary nondevelopmental crises,* on the other hand, may impact on the family even more heavily than the voluntary type, but they are not events of choice in any sense of the word. Mental retardation, chronic illness, and death are obvious examples of involuntary crises thrust upon the family as it interfaces with the outside world. Chapter 8 is devoted to an exploration of the distinctions between voluntary and involuntary nondevelopmental crisis.

References

Adams, B. 1975. *The Family*. Chicago: Rand McNally.

Erikson, Erik H. 1963. *Childhood and Society*. New York: Norton.

Farber, B. 1964. *Family Organization and Interaction*. San Francisco: Chandler.

Ganz, E.J., and J.F. Gubrium. 1972. "Comparative Parental Perceptions of a Mentally Retarded Child." *American Journal of Mental Deficiency* 77.

Haley, J. 1973. *Uncommon Therapy*. New York: Ballantine Books.

Price-Bonham, Sharon, and Susan Addison. 1978. "Families and Mentally Retarded Children: Emphasis on the Father." *Family Coordinator* 27.

Rabkin, Richard. 1977. *Strategic Psychotherapy: Brief and Symptomatic Treatment*. New York: Basic Books.

Rappaport, Louis J. 1976. "Role and Context Interaction in Families of Alcoholics." Ph.D. dissertation. Boston College.

The Couple System

Chapter

6

In sections I and II we saw that many family theorists view the marital relationship as the cornerstone of the family system. Its importance was especially highlighted in chapter 1 in our discussion of the "beginning family" developmental stage. Foley has described Satir's view of its central role in the family system:

The key to success of the family system is the marital relationship. If this is working reasonably well, each can allow the other to have a relationship with the child. When the marital dyad is dysfunctional, when the parental coalition nonexistent, both mates look to the child to satisfy their unmet needs in the marital relationship. [Foley 1974, p. 97]

Most systems theorists agree that when the marital relationship is dysfunctional, the resulting stress in the family system is often expressed in the symptomatology of one member, usually a particularly vulnerable child. Family therapists do not examine the symptom in terms of the pathology of the individual who carries it, but instead attempt to identify the family subsystem from which the stress is emanating. When the stress is seen to emanate from the marital dyad, the focus of treatment may be on the couple system or on the parent system, depending on the nature of the problem. Another reason for paying particular attention to the marital dyad is that it is, as we have noted, the usual locus of control.

In this chapter we will focus on the nature of the couple relationship and on the process of working with couples. We will begin our study by exploring the nature of the marital relationship and various types of marriages. We will then look at the developmental life cycle of a marital relationship from a systems perspective. The bulk of this chapter will focus on the process and practice of treatment of couples. This treatment is known by several terms: marriage counseling or therapy, couples work, divorce counseling, sex counseling. We will use the term *couples work* to refer to any type of work with the couple system.

In addition to exploring the systems theory approach to couples work, we will consider more conventional psychotherapeutic approaches. One may use whatever strategies and techniques are appropriate and still maintain a systems perspective of the relationship. Because of their relevance to contemporary family work, we will also consider the specialized therapeutic areas of separation, divorce, and sex.

The Marital Relationship

The *institution* of marriage affects the couple system as much as does the relationship between the partners. Although we recognize that many couples today are not legally married, for the purpose of this book we are choosing to deal only with legally constituted families. Therefore, the couple relationship that we are about to explore will be a legitimate marital relationship.

The institution of marriage in our culture is continuously challenged by the media and various art forms. It is ridiculed, disparaged, exalted, and revered. The idea and reality of marriage seem to cause great anxiety among young people. This fear and yearning, operating simultaneously, cause the marital relationship to be the most vulnerable of all human relations. Yet, despite the overwhelming focus of attention on marriage and divorce and the dire predictions of the extinction of the marital relationship, marriage and remarriage rates continue to rise (Bane 1976). It is apparent that while mates may be discarded, there is a continual search for a satisfying marital relationship. This search does not just include looking for the "perfect mate," but also involves a continuous reassessment and redefinition of the institution of marriage and the nature of the marital relationship.

How can we describe this relationship? We know that it is a very unique, intense way of relating. Two separate individuals must learn to live with each other and relate to each other in a special and intimate way, involving close emotional interaction and a sexual relationship. The emotional and sexual dimensions of their relationship in turn affect their financial, political, religious, and domestic relationships.

The marital relationship proceeds from an intensive, romantic infatuation to an extensive, problem-solving relationship that is based on the needs and expectations of each partner. From a family systems viewpoint, we know that both individuals bring to this relationship themes and patterns from their own families of origin, as well as their own individual perceptions, feelings, needs, and expectations. Jackson and Lederer (1968) describe marriage as a complex unity made up of at least three different, but interdependent systems: the male system, the female system, and the marital system. Each system incorporates cultural expectations, individual expectations, and expectations stemming from the family of origin. In other words, each partner brings to the marriage a self-concept, a concept of the spouse, a concept of the spouse's concepts, and a concept of marriage. Therefore, there are at least eight concepts (all based on perceptions, feelings, needs, and expectations) that mesh into the marital relationship.

Reasons for Marrying

Why do people get married? We really do not have a sound theory of attraction and interaction to explain people's motivations for marrying. However, a review of the literature indicates that the following variables are certainly influential: (1) societal expectations; (2) loneliness; (3) parental pressures; (4) romantic literature, tradition, and social hysteria; (5) economic insecurity; (6) desire for upward mobility; (7) neurosis; and (8) escape from family of origin or current work or living systems. Whereas in past centuries, physical, religious, and economic factors provided the strongest motivations for marriage, today it appears that psychological and emotional factors outweigh all others.

Sager (1976) defines marriage as involving three motivational contracts, namely, the male's contract, the female's contract, and the interactional contract. These contracts incorporate underlying expectations of marriage, which reflect internal and external motivations for marrying. Each contract includes expectations of marriage, intrapsychic and biological needs, and external focuses. Intrapsychic and biological needs include cognitive style, independence-dependence needs, closeness-distance needs, use and/or abuse of power, fear of loneliness, need to possess and control, level of anxiety, defense mechanisms, gender identity, self-acceptance, and acceptance of others. External focuses include communication skills, lifestyles, families of origin, family myths, values, sex, roles, and interests.

Sager's contracts have three aspects: (1) one that is conscious and verbalized; (2) one that is conscious, but not verbalized (because of fear or shame); and (3) one that is beyond awareness, consisting of those desires and needs, often contradictory and unrealistic, of which the partner has no awareness. The interactional contract "provides the operational field in which each struggles with the other to achieve fulfillment of his own individual contract, including all the realistic, unrealistic and ambivalent clauses that it contains" (Sager 1976, p. 28).

The point is that each relationship has a contract, whether implicit or explicit. What is meant by the term *contract* is that each relationship has a set of rules, as postulated by the communication theorists. These rules are based on expectations and reflect motivations. The parties to these rules may or may not be aware of what these rules are, how they operate, and who sets them.

Love

The focus on psychological and emotional factors leads us to the concept of love and what part it does or does not play in marriage. Jackson and Lederer (1968) label as a myth the belief that love is a cornerstone of marriage. They believe that the four major elements necessary for a satisfactory marriage are (1) tolerance, (2) respect, (3) honesty, and (4) a desire to stay together for mutual advantage. When talking about "love," they use Harry Stack Sullivan's definition:

> When the satisfaction or security of another person becomes as significant to one as is one's own satisfaction or security, then a state of love exists. [Jackson and Lederer 1968]

This definition of love makes it an underlying ingredient to Jackson and Lederer's four major elements. It is not surprising that Jackson, a communication theorist, would posit four interactional elements as the cornerstone of a successful marriage.

Representing the psychoanalytic viewpoint, Fromm (1956) believes that "mature love" is a necessary ingredient for a satisfactory marriage. He defines this love as an active relationship in which two people become one, yet remain two. Fromm points out that mature love cannot develop if there is not a basis of "self-love." If one cannot love oneself, how can one love another, and, further, how can one expect someone else to love oneself if one cannot love oneself? This belief is similar to that of Carl Rogers (1972), in that Rogers agrees that a positive self-concept is necessary to be able to accept and care for another person.

Rogers believes that a good partnership requires that one discover oneself, accept oneself, drop masks, and experience values for oneself. If individuals can achieve this kind of autonomy, they are then able to give positive regard and acceptance to another person, to "love." According to Rogers, both mates must have the freedom to grow together, as well as individually, within a marital relationship. Interestingly, Rogers concerns himself more with the development of self-acceptance and self-love as a prerequisite for loving others, whereas Fromm focuses more on altruism, the giving of oneself to and for another.

The point is that "relationship love" is different from romantic and erotic love. The core ingredients of relationship love appear to be self-acceptance, equal caring about self and spouse, and commitment to the relationship. Relationship love focuses more on autonomy than on symbiosis, on being two separate individuals who share much of their lives, but who are not glued together or stuck together in such a way that they lose their individuality. This kind of love is a process and continues to develop, grow, and change as the relationship develops, grows, and changes. In Satir's, Jackson's, Haley's, Bowen's, Kantor's, and Minuchin's terms, it allows for differentiation of self and reciprocity, as opposed to fusion and enmeshment. It is dynamic and expansive, rather than static and restrictive. It includes romance, fun, and ritual and adds an exciting dimension to the marital relationship. Relationship love differs from father love, mother love, and sibling love because of its sexual nature, as well as because of its dimension of choice. (One cannot, after all, choose one's parents and siblings.)

Healthy Marriage

It is important to consider one's own values and attitudes about marital relationships before attempting to assess the strength or health of another's marital relationship. We sometimes tend to confuse "idealism" with "health." In other words, in looking at a marital relationship, we need to assess its strengths in terms of its functionalism, compatibility, and effectiveness for the total family system, rather than in terms of how much "love" appears to exist and whether or not it is the type of relationship we would choose for ourselves.

In recent articles, Mace (1976) and Ellis (1976) have questioned the attitude that a marriage is good only if it is conflict-free. Similarly Bach and Wyden (1969) argue that a healthy marriage involves love *and* hate, caring *and* conflict and that marital partners can learn to use and resolve conflicts creatively and constructively. It is the process of conflict resolution that tells us more about a marital relationship than the content or amount of conflict itself. Bach and Wyden's thinking obviously has much in common with that of the communication theorists.

Our point is that as therapists we must separate our ideal concepts of marriage from our functional concepts of marriage and learn that there are many different types of marital relationships that work, just as there are many different types of family systems that work. The criteria for a functional marriage that we can derive from the theorists whom we have studied in this book are: (1) flexibility of role performance; (2) clear communications; (3) sensitivity to each other's needs; (4) mutual respect for each other's individuation; (5) use of crisis as a means of growth; and (6) commitment to the couple relationship.

Types of Marriages

In the search for a satisfying marital relationship, people are actually looking at the qualitative characteristics of the type of relationship they desire. A review of the literature indicates that there are basically three major types of marriages:

1. *Traditional Marriage*: This type of marriage has a complementary power struggle, stereotyped gender roles, and conventional expectations and functions. For example, Mr. Jones is the wage earner and makes all the big decisions for the family, administers discipline to the children, and sees himself as the "stable provider." Mrs. Jones is responsible for the couple's social life, for all household chores, and for most of the child care. Similarly, the children are clear about their functions and boundaries. Johnny Jones is likely to be encouraged to excel in athletics, and Susie Jones is likely to take piano lessons and help

Mom around the house. This type of marriage usually exists in what Kantor describes as a "closed" family system.

2. *Shared-Role Marriage*: This type of marriage has a more symmetrical power structure and more egalitarian expectations and functions than the traditional marriage. Whether or not Mrs. Jones works, she and Mr. Jones share the economic and political power in the family, and their functions are by choice, rather than by sex-role stereotype. Mr. Jones participates in the household chores, and Mrs. Jones helps him with the garden and painting the house. Both feel equally responsible for child care. The children themselves are not bound by preconceived ideas about what is appropriate in terms of expectations and role functions. This type of marriage could exist in any of Kantor's models of family systems, but is most likely to be found in the open model.

3. *Intimate-Network Marriage*: The intimate network might involve group marriage or communal living situations. In this type of marriage, several adults live together and share the marital and parental responsibilities and role functions. Thus, Mrs. Jones may be responsible for cooking for everyone one week, for raking the garden the next week, for doing the laundry the third week. Mr. Jones's income may be divided equally among all members of the system. Johnny and Susie Jones may have several different adults to go to for mothering and fathering. Again, this type of marriage could exist in any of the three types of family systems that Kantor describes.

Although each of these three types of marriage involves different roles, all involve sexual, emotional, practical, and social needs. The power systems of each differ according to the needs, motivations, self-concepts, and ideologies of the marital relationship.

Clinical View of Marriage

Another way of looking at types of marriages is from a clinical point of view. Stahmann and Hiebert (1977a) cite seven patterns of couple interaction that they most frequently encounter in clinical practice: (1) half marriage, where both mates want to be taken care of, but simultaneously dislike their dependencies and continuously struggle with their investment in the relationship; (2) attaching-detaching marriage, where the more one mate pursues emotional closeness, the more the other mate withdraws, highlighting their struggle to meet dependency/intimacy needs; (3) sadomasochistic marriage, where the partners handle their insecurity and mutual dependency by one attacking and the other being helpless; (4) child marriage, where both mates are dependent, each looking to the other to be a good "parent" and fighting childishly throughout the struggle; (5) neurotic marriage, where one spouse is the caretaker and the other the patient; (6) therapeutic marriage, where both mates try to behave as if he or she were the doctor and the other the patient; and (7) pseudomarriage, where the relationship is void of intimacy and the marriage is either for convenience or for appearance.

Many of the marital struggles that we see today center around the attempts of one or both partners either to change their interactional pattern or to develop a traditional marital "contract" into a more symmetrical, shared-role type of relationship. These marital struggles seem to be a response to the rapid cultural and social changes of the past decade. While these changes have increased the options available to individuals, they have also increased the demands and stresses on the marital relationship.

It is not at all unusual today for a couple who has been married for several years with an implicit traditional contract to seek counseling when one person wants to change that contract. For example, Dr. and Mrs. Wood had been married for eight years and had one child, aged six. Mrs. Wood initiated the counseling, declaring that she was tired of being a physician's wife, that she had total child-care and household responsibilities, and that she wanted to return to school for a master's degree and begin to lead more of a life of her own. Dr. Wood appeared confused and puzzled. As far as he was concerned, everything was "just as it should be." He had established a professional base in the community and provided a lifestyle of luxury. He could not understand his wife's angry accusations. Had she not always shared his goals and values? It turned out that they had both accepted the same initial relationship contract. But she grew and changed in such a way that she unilaterally wanted to revise the contract. The counseling sessions helped them both to understand the nature of the changes that had occurred and to learn how to renegotiate their relationship contract.

Developmental View of Marriage

Haley (1973) delineates the transition points in a marital relationship, points at which crises are likely to be precipitated by the way in which personal relationships are handled. Although we presented Duvall's eight stages in chapter 1, let us see how closely Haley's eight stages resemble hers and how they focus more on the couple as a system. As we review the stages in a marriage, we will highlight the particular issues that accompany each stage.

1. *Voluntary relationship of courtship*: Usually a time of romantic attraction, when each partner is trying to test out own and other's apparent expectations for the relationship. Period characterized by high energy and motivation.

2. *Commitment of marriage*: Relationship becomes compulsory, rather than voluntary, the moment marriage occurs. Both partners must change and adapt. Merger of two individual systems requires high energy, compromise, and negotiation. Development of new rules for relationship interactions essential.

3. *First child born*: Marital relationship now characterized by even less reversible commitment. Development of new needs of family system members and parenting role behavior. If marital system has not had time to stabilize, anxieties and tensions may be deflected onto child. Less time and energy for marital relationship, requiring more concrete determination and mutual assignment of areas of competence and responsibility.

4. *Sharing of influence with other authorities when child enters school*: Marital and family systems now open to speculation and evaluation by outsiders. Values, attitudes, and ways of operating open to reassessment, defending, and/or growth and development. Power struggles can develop in parenting and/or marital systems. Energy for marital system tends to lessen as parenting system usurps more.

5. *Sharing authority with adolescents and their peers*: Period of upheaval in that parents undergo individual mid-life crises and turmoil at same time adolescents experience turmoil and identity crisis. Influence system changes from compliance (no longer workable) to identification and internalization. Struggles for power and control escalate. Marital system strained by internal and external stresses. Marital partners begin to reflect on their relationship and divert some energy from parent system back to marital system.

6. *Shift from child-oriented marital relationship to two-party system when children leave home*: Reassessment of marital commitment, goals, expectations, emerging needs, and desires. Reestablishment of marital contract, including future goals and directions. Unfinished business from earlier stages resurfaces and requires some type of resolution.

7. *Intensification of two-party system at retirement*: Shifts in roles, balance of power, goals, and expectations, accompanied by aging variables involving physical, psychological, and economic well-being. Renegotiation of roles, rules, relationships to extended family and community, use of time and energy.

8. *Return to single life at death of spouse*: Passage through mourning

involving working through unfinished business with partner, establishing new lifestyle and way of operating.

Although Haley's eight stages are essentially complete, you will
recall from chapter 5 that Minuchin more explicitly delineates some
developmental issues to be renegotiated during his primary stage of
family development, which corresponds to Haley's stages of voluntary
relationship of courtship and commitment of marriage. For Minuchin,
this stage calls for complex negotiations that need to be handled on three
fronts: (1) The spouses must develop boundary relationships that allow
satisfying patterns of transactions between themselves so that they can
adequately handle positions around such mundane issues as shopping,
who uses the bathroom at what time, what time the reading light gets
turned out, and so on. (2) They must decide how they will separate from
their families of origin and other previous family systems, how to
renegotiate boundaries with parents, siblings, and so forth. (3) They
must decide how the demands of the work world, as well as their
previous leisure activities and commitments, will be reorganized and
regulated. The management of each of these three major tasks is difficult
in and of itself and involves intense negotiation between the two
members of the couple system.

Haley's third stage, the birth of the first child, obviously requires
additional boundary negotiations. Here Bowen's concept of triangulation is again applicable. In all these stages, the way in which the couple
defines its relationship tasks and goals, resolves its conflicts, and nurtures its relationship will affect its transition to the next stage and its
functioning as a couple system throughout the life of the relationship.

Troll (1975) identifies three ways in which the family system
can react to the change that comes with normal development: (1) by
compensating for change in order to maintain the system's homeostasis;
(2) by incorporating changes to produce growth and development
within the system; or (3) by breaking up as a system. For example, when
children are born, the family may react by differentiating their roles,
with the husband becoming absorbed in his job and in providing for his
family financially and the wife becoming absorbed in child care and
housework. When the children leave home, the marriage may undergo
a great deal of stress and may not survive. The type of strategy the
family selects to deal with change will depend on the stages of
individual and family development. The developmental perspective
enables us to view both the internal and external variables operating
during any particular period of the relationship.

It is important to keep in mind that the individual development of one mate may or may not synchronize with the other mate's individual development, and that one or both may be out of sync with the development of the marital relationship. Understanding individual adult development is as important as understanding the developmental stages of the marital relationship.

The Couple as a System

It is clear that our earlier definition of a system as a set of mutually interacting elements, wherein a change in one element affects all elements in the system, applies to the couple. The couple also fits the system definition that the system is more than the sum of its parts, as the couple is more than the sum of the individual dynamics of its two partners. Each mate may act differently outside the couple relationship than within it.

The system's attributes of equifinality and homeostasis also apply to the couple. We know, for example, that information processing can be a major problem for couples and that no matter what the input of information to the system is, the outcome will be the same unless the customary processing rules of the system are altered. This is the concept of equifinality. As an example, let us suppose that Mr. Smith is told by his individual therapist that his wife's flirtatious behavior with other men is an attempt on her part to obtain more attention from her husband. Even though this may be an accurate interpretation, when Mr. Smith goes home and tells Mrs. Smith what his therapist said, she may become defensive, retorting, "That's ridiculous!" The processing rules have not been altered, and thus no change will occur.

Similarly, we know that if we see only one member of the couple system in counseling and changes occur in this one member, the effect on the couple system may be heightened stress. This stress will, in turn, trigger off homeostatic mechanisms to restore the original homeostasis. Premature termination of counseling or some other form of sabotage of treatment is likely to result. If Mrs. Glass is coached by her therapist to behave more assertively with her husband, and if Mr. Glass finds this threatening and disruptive to the marriage, he may acquiesce to some of her demands for attention just long enough to wean her away from therapy and then slowly let the old situation recur.

Thus, the couple system is seen as an *interactional system*, as a *rule-governed system*, and as a *conditioning system*. By "conditioning system," we mean that one person's behavior reinforces (and shapes) the other person's behavior, which results in the formation of a circular feedback system.

With this orientation, let us now consider how intervention in the couple's information-processing system or in the structure of the couple's relationship can lead to system change.

Working with Couples

Treatment of the couple relationship within family systems stems from two different, but related fields. Olson (1970) describes marital therapy and family therapy as young "fraternal twins" that have developed along parallel, but separate lines. His extensive review of these fields delimits their different literatures, sources of theory, clientele, and the professional affiliations of their respective practitioners. For example, marital therapy grew out of a social need for therapists to work with marital problems; marriage counselors and/or marital therapists have traditionally been social workers or pastoral counselors, utilizing the theoretical work of family sociology or clinical psychology. Family therapy, on the other hand, moved toward "systems work" when practitioners sought alternatives to the inadequacy of individual treatment techniques. The pioneers in family therapy, as we know, were psychiatrists who utilized their former psychodynamic training and integrated it with systems theory. From the development of marital therapy, however, came the emphasis on the marital relationship (without disregarding the value of individual psychology) and on the technique of conjoint marital therapy. Marital therapists began to use conjoint forms of therapy to treat the marital relationship, whereas family therapists began to see couples because of the inefficacy of individual therapy. Regardless of its origins, conjoint therapy is today an accepted and effective format for treating relationships.

Olson and Sprenkle (1976) have pointed out that a more synergistic relationship now exists between marital and family therapy. They depict a continuum of treatment, with the choice of treatment unit being more pragmatic than ideological. Today, people who consider themselves "marriage and family counselors or therapists" have access to similar training and theoretical and research sources. As it is impossible for anyone working with families to ignore the couple relationship (regardless of who is actually seen in treatment), the approaches and strategies of couples work are pertinent for all family workers.

Treatment Units in Couples Work

When the focus of treatment is on the couple relationship, we term that work *couples work*. The unit of treatment may or may not be the partners of the couple, depending upon the motivation and accessibility of each mate. A review of the literature indicates that four most frequent forms of couples work are:

1. *Concurrent marital therapy*, in which each spouse is seen individually by the same therapist. Occasionally there may be conjoint sessions. This type of therapy is indicated when there are other major issues to be worked through concurrently with the marital issues, when one partner is particularly immature or has a specific neurotic or psychotic symptom, or when the therapist is inexperienced and feels insecure working with a couple system conjointly.
2. *Individual therapy for each partner with separate therapists*, in which each spouse is seen individually by different therapists. Usually when this occurs, the focus on the couple relationship is not clarified at the onset of treatment. In other words, an individual initially seeks individual therapy, and the couple relationship only becomes an important focus as the therapy progresses. Another indication for this type of treatment may be that only one mate wants to work on the couple relationship, while the other prefers focusing on individual concerns. In addition, there are many therapists who do not choose to focus on relationships as their major therapeutic orientation.
3. *Conjoint marital therapy*, in which the couple is seen together by one or more therapists. This type of treatment is indicated when there are adequate communications between the mates and when their motivation is reasonably high. Conjoint marital therapy has the highest chance for success when both partners mutually recognize the need for treatment, rather than one coming to therapy in response to an ultimatum, looking for permission to exit or for an ally, or to avoid self-observation.
4. *Couples group therapy*, in which several couples are seen together by one or more therapists. This form of treatment is often indicated to defuse an intense emotional climate so that the mates can learn to hear each other (people tend to behave more rationally in groups than individually), when other forms of de-escalation are necessary, when role models are desirable, and when economics of treatment are a factor. The group setting can offer a social context in which trust can

develop and from which support can be drawn. The multiple models for relating and multiple sources of feedback can provide an important reference point for perspective on marital difficulties.

It is important to note that although many therapists prefer *conjoint* marital therapy when working with couples, other forms of treatment can be effective. An example of *concurrent* marital therapy might evolve in the following way: Debra Porter, aged fifteen, is referred for treatment because of anxious, depressed classroom behavior. The female therapist requests a family assessment meeting and determines that Debra is indeed the symptom carrier of a depressed family system. The family agrees to family therapy sessions. During the course of these sessions, it becomes apparent to the therapist that the marital relationship between Mr. and Mrs. Porter is conflicted. It also becomes apparent to the therapist that Debra becomes less anxious as her mother's attention turns toward Mr. Porter. However, Mr. Porter refuses to deal with any marital issues, whereas Mrs. Porter appears to be relieved when the therapist focuses on these issues. Mr. and Mrs. Porter refuse to see the therapist as a couple, but Mrs. Porter indicates that she would be grateful for some individual sessions focusing on her feelings and concerns about her marriage. Note that the focus on the identified patient, Debra, is diminished when the marital issues surface. Mr. Porter prefers to stop therapy unless the focus is completely on Debra. The therapist chooses to keep Mr. Porter engaged by holding occasional family sessions dealing with the issues of the entire family system, but also begins to see Mrs. Porter individually to give her the chance to deal with the marital issues as she sees them. As Mrs. Porter begins to concentrate more on her own issues as a woman and wife and less on her role as a mother, she alleviates much of the pressure and anxiety that she has been focusing on Debra. Consequently, Debra is freer to interact with her peers and to become involved in school activities.

Individual therapy for each partner might have evolved out of Debra's family situation had the Porter family initially been seen by a co-therapy team that included a male therapist. At that point, with Mrs. Porter continuing to prefer that therapy focus on her feelings and concerns about her marriage, the availability of a male therapist might have facilitated Mr. Porter's engagement in individual therapy.

We, the authors, have frequently begun to work initially with a family, moved to working with a couple, and when individual work has seemed warranted, divided the couple and each of us has seen them separately. Eventually, we have moved them back as a couple, and then into family sessions that conclude the treatment.

Couples group therapy for the Porters would allow them to work not only on their relationship as husband and wife, but also on their relationship as father and mother. This therapy would take place within a climate of other adults, which might help to defuse some of the intensity of their relationship. Being with other adults would also give them an opportunity to learn some interactional and communication skills. A strong plus of couples group work is precisely that it does help couples develop communication and interactional skills with peers, not just with each other and their children. Peer relationships as adults sustain adults and sometimes give them the kind of nourishment they need to bring energy into the family system, to relate to spouses and children effectively.

Note that in all these treatment cases, the focus on the identified patient, Debra, is diminished when the marital issues surface. Each of these interventions is an effective way of getting to the locus of the conflict, that is, the marital relationship itself.

It has generally been our experience that when one mate is seen individually and the focus of treatment is the couple relationship, the change in the mate being seen can affect the couple system in such a way that eventually the other mate comes in, if for no reason other than to see "what the hell is going on here!" Remember that a change in one element of the system affects the entire system. Of course, it is also possible that the excluded mate will temporarily acquiesce until the treatment is over. This may result in a new request for treatment or in the treated mate's demanding renegotiation of the marital contract.

Theoretical Approaches to Couples Work

Olson and Sprenkle (1976) suggest that currently there are three major theoretical approaches to working with couples: social learning theory, general systems theory, and client-centered approaches. Rather than just focusing on the general systems theory approach, we also want to review social learning and client-centered approaches as many of these strategies and approaches are useful within the systems theory framework. In actual practice, these three approaches are not clearly separate and discrete.

Social Learning Theory. This behavioral approach to working with couples has become increasingly widespread, perhaps because one can measure and observe whether the behavioral goals of treatment have in fact been realized. Based on operant conditioning principles, the social learning approach sees marital difficulties as the result of inadequate or poor mutual reinforcement. Perhaps there are too few reinforcers; or there may be an imbalance in that one party does most of the reinforcing and the other partner takes that for granted. Often reinforcers lose their value, especially as new needs and desires arise. And sometimes the outside sources of reinforcement change by becoming restricted or by being used too frequently.

The therapist working with a couple from a behavioral framework would first attempt to define the relationship issues behaviorally. What behaviors of yours and your mate need to be changed in order for this relationship to work out for you? In other words, what are the specific behaviors that drive you up a wall? The therapist must also find out what the reinforcement system is. What happens when he or she does that? What are the payoffs that maintain these behaviors? How frequently do these behaviors actually occur and what conditions precede them? What are the consequences?

When target behaviors are identified and agreed upon, various behavioral strategies can be applied to bring about change. Different types of *behavioral therapy strategies* include the token economy, behavioral contracting, and assertiveness training.

1. *Token Economy:* When there are several specific behaviors that are causing friction in the relationship, the couple may design a token economy to try to effect quick relief and change, as well as reciprocal interaction. A token economy is

> a behavioral reinforcement program whereby desired behaviors are rewarded with tokens having reinforcement value by association with a variety of backup rewards. The tokens can be awarded immediately after the behavior is emitted and the exchange can occur later. [Okun 1976, p. 218]

Let us consider a case in which the establishment of a token economy was an appropriate and effective therapeutic strategy. Mr. and Mrs. Strong had found that so many petty irritations were getting in the way of their relating that they were constantly bickering and arguing. Mrs. Strong listed her irritations for the therapist: Mr. Strong's leaving his dirty clothes on the floor; not phoning when he was going to be home late in the evening; leaving his breakfast dishes on the table; leaving the newspaper scattered all over the house; leaving toothpaste smeared over the bathroom sink. Mr. Strong claimed that Mrs. Strong emptied the ashtrays before he even finished his cigarette; rushed him through breakfast so she could clean the kitchen before she left for work; cleaned his bureau and desk even though he had specifically asked her to leave them alone (causing him to become disorganized and to misplace important valuables); met him at the door every evening with a list of complaints and accusations.

The therapist helped the Strongs design a program whereby each partner could collect points for performing certain desired behavioral tasks. "Negative" behaviors were to be ignored and not to be reinforced by the attention of arguing or scolding. The points collected for positive behavior could be converted to joint or individual activities over the weekend, depending upon the preference of the individual. Mr. Strong liked to have a couple of hours of "free time" every weekend without having his wife nagging him to perform certain chores or demanding that he do something with her. He could choose to collect enough points to earn this privilege, whereas Mrs. Strong could earn enough points to claim a couple of hours over the weekend for some joint, mutually agreed upon endeavor.

Thus, both Mr. and Mrs. Strong were able to get what they wanted and needed in a reasonable manner. At the end of a six-week period, the Strongs felt that their petty irritations had diminished to the point that they were able to provide more positive feedback and reinforcement to each other. With the petty irritations reduced, Mr. and Mrs. Strong were able to engage in activities that enhanced their appreciation and enjoyment of each other. Note the shift from concrete (material) to social reinforcement; the Strongs were learning to acknowledge appreciation that became, in itself, a vital form of reinforcement. Their behavioral changes led to increased satisfaction in their attitudes and feelings toward themselves and each other.

2. *Behavioral Contracting*: The process of negotiating role responsibilities and the terms of behavioral contracts help the couple to spell out their needs and expectations. A behavioral contract clearly explicates the desired target behavior, the conditions under which this behavior is to occur, and the consequential reinforcement. The contract is always open to reassessment and renegotiation. Once the targeted behavior has been achieved, new contracts for maintenance may be needed until the behavior becomes a natural part of one's repertoire. Very often, behavioral contracts deal with one target behavior at a time, whereas token economies cover a broad array of behaviors. To be effective, behavioral contracts must be agreeable to both partners, must contain reinforcement that is meaningful to the recipient and unavailable outside the terms of the contract, and must encourage "shaping" by rewarding successive approximations of the desired behavior. The value

of behavioral contracts for couples lies in the focus on positive interactional behaviors and reinforcements, rather than on less observable attitudes and feelings. Changes in behavior can lead to increased
desire and energy to work on significant dynamic issues. Behavioral
contracts teach people what *to do*, rather than what *not* to do.

Mr. and Mrs. Phillips, who argue constantly over being places on
time, provide us with an illustration of the efficacy of the behavioral
contract. Mr. Phillips begins to nag his wife thirty minutes before
departure time. As his nagging increases, Mrs. Phillips finds herself
feeling resentful and rebelliously slows down, often delaying them for
over an hour. They usually end up arriving late at their destination,
arguing and carrying around a great deal of resentment for the next
several days. Mr. and Mrs. Phillips contract that either at breakfast or
dinner they will decide upon a mutually acceptable departure time. If
they are to leave, say, at 7:30 PM, Mrs. Phillips will be ready between
7:15 and 7:45. Every time that she meets the terms of this contract,
she receives coffee and her newspaper in bed the following morning.
This contract allows the Phillips to decrease the irritating behavior
(her tardiness and his nagging) so that they can begin to look at some
of the other aspects of their relationship without constantly engaging
in a power struggle.

3. *Assertiveness Training*: Assertiveness training is an effective behavioral approach when existing communications are inadequate. Alberti and Emmons (1976) describe a step-by-step process that focuses on
eye contact, body posture, gestures, facial expression, timing, flu-
ency, and content of communications. They advocate the use of role
play, covert rehearsal, modeling, coaching, and feedback strategies.
Assertiveness training is

> a behavioral technique whereby the client gradually learns progressively
> more assertive behaviors (standing up for one's own rights without
> impinging on the rights of others) through such means as modeling or
> role playing instruction. Assertive behaviors include saying "no" without
> feeling guilty and learning to "ask directly for what you want." [Okun,
> 1976 p. 210]

These techniques have been effective in increasing individual self-
esteem and in recalibrating the power balance within the couple or
family system.

Assertiveness training with Mr. and Mrs. Phillips would involve
helping Mrs. Phillips learn how to make a clear "I"-statement to her
husband about their leaving. An assertive statement might be: "Dear,

I'm aware of your need to be on time. I'm also aware that when you remind me half an hour before we're ready to leave that it's time to go, I remember my dad who used to rush me a lot to get me ready for school and that this brings up some unfinished resistance I have with that relationship, and I let that get in the way of my getting ready on time." What is assertive about this statement is its clear admission of the problem, which circumvents the power struggle. What remains is for the Phillips to design alternative solutions that may help them resolve this issue.

Very often a member of the couple system (or the family system for that matter) needs to learn how to say "no" in an acceptable way, how to ask for what he or she wants, how to resist being drawn into game-playing behavior that ends up with all parties feeling uncomfortable. Along with the behavioral component of assertiveness training, one uses a cognitive-restructuring approach (Ellis and Harper 1961; Ellis 1962, 1973) to teach people to change their thoughts about which behaviors are permissible and which are not—for example, helping a client learn how to say "no" without feeling guilty.

Thus we see that behavioral couples work focuses on the presenting problem in behavioral terms. The couple is encouraged to ventilate about the presenting problem, to assess the frequency and antecedent and consequent conditions of the problem behavior, and to help the therapist determine intermediate and long-range goals. During this assessment and clarification stage of treatment, the therapist is usually helping the couple to focus on their communication skills, encouraging them to learn to discriminate and record positive events (and not to focus solely on negative events) and to incorporate positive social and recreational activities into their couple system, thus creating a wider variety of positive reinforcements. After the particular target behavior has been treated, the situation is reevaluated, and the focus of treatment may shift to another set of behaviors. Behavioral therapy is specific, concrete, and short-term.

Regardless of their theoretical orientation, most therapists today utilize behavioral approaches and strategies in dealing with the management and behavioral components of relationship difficulties. Later in this chapter we will see how behavioral theory underlies the current approaches to working with couples in the area of sexual dysfunctioning.

General Systems Theory. As Olson and Sprenkle (1976) point out, the relationship between systems theory and practice is not so clear-cut as the relationship between social learning theory and practice. Systems theory gives us a model for viewing human behavior and human relationships, but it really does not spell out particular treatment approaches. Many therapists who have been influenced by systems theory incorporate behavioral and client-centered approaches with the systems theory principles of circular feedback, homeostasis, interdependence, and equifinality.

Let us look at couples work from the communication and structural framework that we developed in section II.

Communication Approaches. Increasingly, treatment approaches are utilizing the communication principles derived from systems theory. As we noted in chapter 4, these principles were pioneered by Jackson, Haley, and Satir, each of whom developed strategies focusing on the interactional processes. More recently, other theorists have developed new therapeutic approaches based on communication theory. After discussing the approaches of Jackson, Satir, and Haley, we will discuss two of these more recently developed approaches, namely, brief therapy and the Minnesota Couples Communication Program.

1. *Jackson:* In *The Mirages of Marriage* (1968), Jackson and Lederer focus on communications (report and command aspects of messages), as well as on the contextual aspects (social setting) of the messages. They believe that a lack of clarity in communications between people is the major cause of interpersonal discord. In addition to teaching couples new styles and processes of verbal and nonverbal communications, they deal with what the mates think about the relationship and expose the myths and irrational thoughts that contribute to the interpersonal discord. They advocate open, clear feedback and a "quid-pro-quo" (something-for-something) process, a step-by-step process of bargaining that helps each partner to satisfy his or her unconscious need and expectation of being equal in the relationship.

2. *Satir:* Satir, as we know, believes that there is a positive relationship between marital adjustment and a couple's ability to communicate. Her work with couples focuses on the expression of affect, on helping partners learn how to send "I"-messages and to recognize and tolerate the differentness of the other. She deals with the "you," the "me," and the "us" of the couple relationship. She helps couples to recognize the communication styles that she elaborates upon in *Peoplemaking* (1972), namely, blaming, placating, leveling, and distracting. She believes that such recognition enables people to recognize their own and each other's pain. Satir sees herself as an observer in the therapy triangle, having the power to intervene

by mediation, alliance, and/or collusion. Her interventions result in improved communications, improved self-esteem, and smoother functioning of the "us" aspects of the relationship.

3. *Haley*: Of the three communication theorists studied in this book, Haley has written the most extensively on marital therapy. He focuses on the family rules: those that the family recognizes and describes to the therapist; those that they do not initially perceive but are willing to acknowledge when pointed out by the therapist; and those that the therapist can see but that the family refuses to recognize or acknowledge. Haley is concerned with the power struggle between the couple, and he teaches them ways of dealing openly with this conflict.

In an article entitled "Marriage Therapy" (1963a), Haley states that each situation that a newly married couple meets must be dealt with by establishing explicit or implicit rules. A couple cannot avoid establishing rules; with the completion of any transaction, a rule has been established. The couple must also reach agreement on which of them is to be the one to set the rules in each area of the marriage. The process of working out a particular rule always occurs within a context of resolving who is setting the rule (who is in control). Thus, marriage is a process of defining relationships.

The process of working out conflicts over rules involves the establishment of a set of *metarules*—that is, a set of rules for making rules. These conflicts over establishing rules are influenced by each partner's own experiences in his or her original family. The transition from one's previous family to the new one requires some compromise and some inevitable conflict.

Any established rule defines a certain type of relationship (either *complementary or symmetrical*). You will recall from chapter 4 that a symmetrical relationship is one in which people relate to each other as equals. A symmetrical relationship may be either positive or negative; the sole criterion of this type of relationship is equality in relating. Complementary relationships are ones in which there are a leader and a follower, one person up and the other down. Again, this type of relationship is not necessarily positive or negative. Complementary teacher-student relationships can produce growth, while complementary sadomasochistic relationships can be destructive for both individuals.

According to Haley (1963b), the difficulty in complementary-symmetrical relationships concerns the ability to distinguish beween the content of the message and the way in which it is communicated, especially if incongruence exists. For example, a husband says to his wife, "Dear, I'm tired of bossing and controlling things around here.

From now on, we'll sit down for fifteen minutes every morning to work out through consensus who is going to do what and come to some agreement about how to control our lives." The content of the message, of course, is that the relationship will be a symmetrical one with equality for the responsibility of the course of their relationship. The style in which the message has been communicated, however, is still one of complementarity. The husband, in asking for symmetry, has in fact implictly stated that *he* has decided that things will now be on a symmetrical basis. This may leave the wife still feeling controlled.

In a reasonably successful relationship, the couple is capable of establishing mutually satisfying symmetrical and complementary relations in various areas of their marriage. If a marital partner has had unfortunate experiences in certain types of relationships in the past, he or she may be unable to tolerate simultaneous symmetrical and complementary relations within the marital relationship.

Thus, for Haley, marital conflict centers on disagreements about who is to set the rules for living together, disagreements about the specific rules, and attempts to enforce rules that conflict with each other. Fighting is often the means of resolving rule conflicts and reaching compromise. If a couple is unable to fight, they withdraw from each other and avoid discussing certain areas of their relationship. One function of the therapist, then, is to induce fighting to open up hidden areas of conflict. When a therapist tries to bring about change in the relationship, he or she encounters two tactics that inhibit a shift: the couple's persistence in protecting each other; and the development of a symptom in one or both partners. The symptom is used to avoid dealing with the distress, and may also serve to keep the marriage itself intact.

The therapist tries to promote change in a variety of ways: (1) by encouraging the couple to resolve conflict through discussion and by discouraging withdrawal and silence; (2) by being a reasonably impartial observer and judge; (3) by encouraging the couple to examine motivations that they may have but are beyond their awareness; (4) by explicating the couple's maneuvers; (5) by dealing with sensitive topics; and (6) by using paradoxical communications. In using this last technique, the therapist instructs the couple to continue and even to exaggerate their distress, while communicating to them, at another level, that he or she, as the expert, is helping them over that distress. Jackson would call this technique "prescribing the symptom." Its intent is to motivate the couple to discontinue the distressing behavior in order to show the therapist how ridiculous the instruction is.

Haley's approach takes into consideration the great investment that couples have in maintaining their equilibrium (homeostasis) regardless of how maladaptive it may be. In a later work, *Problem Solving Therapy* (1976), Haley develops his approach to marital therapy more pragmatically by stating that the marital therapist should (1) avoid minimizing the problem; (2) avoid abstractions; (3) avoid being in constant coalition with one partner; (4) avoid debates of life; (5) avoid the past; (6) avoid thinking that problems are identical; (7) avoid unformulated goals; (8) avoid crystallizing power struggles; and (9) avoid forcing a couple to ask explicitly what they want from each other.

Haley's current approach to marital therapy is somewhat different from the one that he described in his *Strategies of Psychotherapy* (1963 b). Whereas he previously focused on the dyadic relationship of the couple, he now focuses on a triangle that includes the dysfunctional couple and a third element. This third element may be a child, parent, friend, or therapist. Haley's current approach leads more toward a structural than a communication approach to intervention. As we noted in chapter 3, this trend in Haley's work forms a bridge between communication and structural theory.

Haley believes that the initial approach to a marital problem should be determined by the couple's presenting problem, which might be the symptom of an individual, the behavioral problem of a child, or a straightforward presentation of the marital problem. Whatever the approach, Haley believes that the marital therapist should form deliberate coalitions to tip the balance of power and to increase the flexibility of the rules so that the couple system can increase its options.

Let us now look at some more recently developed approaches based on communication theory.

4. *Brief Therapy*: The brief therapy developed by Weakland et al. (1974) and Watzlawick, Weakland, and Fisch (1974) is based on the early work of the MRI group. The focus of brief therapy is on the observable interaction of the couple in the therapy situation. Observed behavior is structured and maintained primarily by current communicative interaction within the couple system. Thus, "problems" consist of persisting, undesired communicative interactions.

In brief therapy the therapist makes deliberate interventions to alter the dysfunctional ongoing system. This approach is based on a belief that minor changes in overt behavior or its verbal labeling are sufficient to initiate a progressive development of change. The therapist attempts to change the behavior that is producing the problem behavior—that is, to change the feedback circles that produce and maintain the problem behaviors.

This therapy is symptom-oriented and begins with a behavioral definition of the problem and an estimate of what behaviors are maintaining (reinforcing) the problem. The therapists who developed this approach (Weakland, Fisch, Watzlawick, and Bodin) believe that the problem lies more in what people do about the problem, how they "handle" it, than in the problem itself. Thus, the overemphasis or underemphasis of the problem may be a problem in and of itself. Problem resolution requires a new set of behaviors to substitute for the dysfunctional circular feedback system. Often, paradoxical techniques focusing on symptom reversal lead to more beneficial circular feedback systems.

By the second session, Weakland et al. have set goals for treatment. These treatment goals are determined by asking the clients to state their own minimal goal of treatment, to specify what behavioral changes they need to see in order to feel that the therapy has been successful. Obviously, this implies to the clients that the therapist believes that change is possible. It also reflects the cybernetic view of Weakland et al. that a small initial change can lead to progressively greater changes in the system. The therapist's major task is to get people to change the behavior that they cling to most strongly, to get them to see that their previous problem-solving tactics have not worked.

It is important for the therapist to be sure that the target of treatment is the person who most wants to see real change in the problem situation. This person is not necessarily the identified patient or the person who initiates treatment. The theoretical rationale for this specification is that an interactional intervention is most likely to be effective with the person concerned enough or hurting enough to do something differently.

The therapist is active and a deliberate change agent. Therapeutic techniques include paradoxical suggestions, homework, and utilization of interpersonal influence with the most susceptible person in the system. Weakland et al. find that this type of reframing allows interventions to be effective in a short period of time, usually ten sessions.

5. *Minnesota Couples Communication Program*: Another recent approach to a communication couples therapy based on systems theory was developed by Miller, Nunnally, and Wachman (1976) at the University of Minnesota. Known as the Minnesota Couples Communications Program (MCCP), this approach focuses attention on four major

styles of communication, as well as on the intentions and behavioral characteristics associated with each style. Spouses are taught to recognize their own and their partner's style and to practice other styles.

Briefly, these four styles of communication are: (1) cognitive emphasis with low disclosure, characterized by sociability, friendliness, conventionality, playful intent, chitchat, descriptiveness; (2) emphasis on feeling with low disclosure, characterized by tendencies to direct, persuade, blame, demand, defend, assume, compete, withhold, evaluate, advise, praise, speak for the others, with a focus on use of such words as "should," "ought," "always," "never"; (3) emphasis on thinking and high receptivity, characterized by tentativeness, elaboration, exploration, speculation, search, reflection, with a focus on the past or future, a search for causes, and use of such words as "probably," "maybe/perhaps," "could/might"; (4) emphasis on feeling and high disclosure and energy, characterized by active awareness, acceptance of responsibility, disclosure, understanding, caring, cooperation, use of self-disclosure, with a focus on self and the here and now.

This program teaches couples to speak for themselves, to document, to make appropriate statements of feeling and intention. The purpose of this program is to enhance communications. Its emphasis on systems concepts, on recalibrating the homeostasis and learning about metacommunication and feedback, leads to further relationship changes.

What differentiates all the communication approaches that we have described from the client-centered communication approaches is an underlying belief in the concepts of general systems theory. The intent is to clarify communications at the report and command levels so that the system can learn to sustain change and develop flexibility, to recalibrate its homeostasis.

Structural Approaches. Structural theorists, as we saw in chapter 5, place greater emphasis upon boundaries and systemic structures than upon communications and metacommunications. Here we will examine how each of the theorists whom we studied in chapter 5 approaches the treatment of the couple system.

1. *Bowen*: Because of his emphasis on differentiation of self, Bowen as a therapist relates to each spouse as an individual. When meeting with a couple, he talks with each spouse separately. The other spouse is present and is able to observe the interaction between Bowen and the spouse, but may not enter into the exchange. Thus, Bowen utilizes an individual therapeutic technique in his couples work. He is

interested in helping each spouse attain an "I-position," a satisfactory degree of individual differentiation.

Bowen postulates four main functions for the couples therapist: (1) defining and clarifying the relationship between the spouses by calmly and intellectually talking to each individual so that the spouse can listen without reacting emotionally; (2) keeping self detriangled from the family emotional system while actively relating to each mate, but in a more intellectual than emotionally reactive way; (3) teaching the functioning of emotional systems by keeping self detriangled and by maintaining emotional contact with both spouses without becoming emotionally overinvolved; and (4) taking "I-position" stands, stating own convictions and beliefs and acting on these without criticizing others' beliefs or becoming involved in emotional debate.

Bowen (1966) believes that the marriage duplicates essential characteristics of the former ego masses of each spouse. Each uses mechanisms that were used in his or her family of origin to deal with the other spouse. The most common mechanism is an emotional distancing that allows each individual to function with a reasonable level of "pseudoself."

Within the family ego mass, spouses use three major mechanisms to control the intensity of ego fusion: (1) marital conflict, where each spouse fights for an equal share of the common self and neither gives in; (2) dysfunctions in one spouse, where a spouse gives in to relieve the conflict, functions at a low level of differentiation, and develops a physical, emotional, or social illness; (3) transmission of the problem to one or more children, whereby the family projection process focuses on certain children, leaving others relatively uninvolved. In most families, the problem between spouses will spread to all three areas or various combinations of the three.

Bowen postulates the progression of therapy through several different phases. In an early phase the spouses learn to know each other better, to differentiate themselves, and to deal with the emotional reaction that their self-differentiation evokes in their mates. This learning to differentiate does not follow an orderly, regular pattern; for some it is quicker and more regular than for others. Couples work is completed when both parties have achieved a reasonable level of differentiation of self from each other and from their families of origin, when they are able to cope with crisis, and when they have some reasonable motivation to continue working on differentiation.

Like Haley, Bowen conceives of the marital therapist as the third element in the triangle. However, for Bowen the role of the marital therapist is to remain emotionally detached and to teach the other two elements in the triangle to develop higher levels of self-differentiation.

2. *Minuchin*: Minuchin joins the couple system and uses his presence to realign coalitions and to strengthen or weaken boundaries. His attention is focused on changing the functions of the system, on getting individuals to act differently. Minuchin is concerned with helping the spouse subsystem establish a boundary that protects it from the demands of other subsystems and systems. By joining the couple system, the therapist is able to restructure it through a variety of interventions—for example, directing people to talk to each other; assigning tasks in which the couple system boundaries are intact (such as instructing the couple to take a walk by themselves for thirty minutes every evening); emphasizing differences by soliciting opinions from both individuals; forming a coalition with one member (a shifting, nonbinding coalition). Whereas Bowen focuses on individual functioning, Minuchin focuses on the systemic functioning. Minuchin sees couples work as successful when the couple system is able to function without being enmeshed with other subsystems.

3. *Kantor*: Kantor's approach to couples work is threefold. It begins by assessing the property dynamics of the system's structure: its style (open, closed, or random); its availability of roles (mover, follower, opposer, bystander); its operating mechanism. The second focus is on the critical identity images of each spouse—that is, the images of "ideal self" and "ideal context" that each partner is trying to implement in this relationship. Kantor's third focus is on the functional or dysfunctional ways in which the spouses integrate their critical images within the system structure. Thus, the couple's psychopolitics are seen to be the key in helping them restructure or abandon their dysfunctional strategies.

4. *Other Structural Therapists*: Other family therapists, such as Guerin and Fogarty, focus on the concept of triangles. They conceptualize the marital emotional system in terms of its relationship to each individual's family of origin, to a child, to a job, or to some third function or person. Like many therapists who are currently pursuing multigenerational themes, they may include families of origin and in-law families in the therapy sessions to explore those relationships. Fogarty has developed the concept of pursuer-distancer to explain the regulating of distance in the marital emotional system. By changing the pattern of this dynamic (never pursue a distancer), the boundaries and structures of the system change.

Basically, the structural therapist enters into the couple system, helps the partners to sort out their rules and roles, and separates the couple system from other subsystems. This allows for and encourages individuation of each spouse and helps the couple system to restructure.

Client-centered Approaches.   Client-centered, or skills-oriented, approaches are based on the beliefs that disturbed marital relationships stem from faulty perceptions, that change cannot occur if one or both members perceive themselves or the other in a distorted, negative way, that all people have strong, innate self-correcting and self-actualizing tendencies. Persons who have positive self-concepts, can accept themselves and other people. These individuals are able to communicate genuineness, concreteness, unconditional positive regard, and empathy and can thus help their mates to heighten their self-esteem and to develop positive self-concepts.

To correct negative distortions and faulty perceptions, client-centered approaches focus on improving clients' communication skills. Toward that end, the work of Carkhuff, Rogers, and Ivey has been used with couples to enhance the ability to communicate. Couples are taught reflective listening so that they can directly express their own feelings and empathetically hear both the apparent and underlying feelings of their mates. In this type of approach, therapists often model appropriate responsive listening skills in sessions, assign exercises to be done at home or in the session, and teach people how to send "I-feel," as opposed to "you-feel," messages.

Transactional analysis provides another format for teaching communication skills to couples. When people learn how to recognize their own and others' ego-state messages, how to recognize different forms of transactions (parallel, crossed, ulterior messages), they can consciously choose to enhance their communications.

There are many laboratory approaches to teaching communication skills. These approaches show clients how to apply communication skills to negotiation, conflict resolution and problem solving. For example, the "fair-fight-for-change" communication technique developed by Bach (Bach and Wyden 1969) has the marriage counselor serve as a coach and referee as the couple learns to fight openly, clearly, and specifically. The anger-management training developed by Mace (1976) teaches the client to acknowledge anger by sending "I-feel" messages, to own the anger as inappropriate, and to ask the partner for help in coping with it. Ellis (1976) adds his rational-emotive training techniques to Mace's interventions so that couples can learn to understand that their anger is usually based on irrational beliefs.

Whereas Bach feels that fighting fair and venting anger is beneficial, Mace and Ellis feel that couples need to learn to cope with their own and each other's anger, rather than venting it in the marital relationship.

Thus, the skills-oriented, client-centered approaches grow out of the belief that didactic training and practice in improved communications will clarify and enhance the relationship so that stored up resentments will not erupt into irresolvable conflict.

Couple Counseling Outcomes

There really are no substantive data to show that any one theoretical approach to working with couples is better than any other. In fact, Gurman and Kniskern (1976), Beck (1976), and Olson and Sprenkle (1976) point out that there is no comprehensive theoretical foundation for marital therapy. Weaknesses in the design of follow-up studies add to the difficulty of evaluating theoretical approaches. However, Beck, as well as Gurman and Kniskern, found that 62 to 66 percent of clients engaged in couple counseling improved. Gurman and Kniskern estimated that improvement from spontaneous remission is about 17 percent.

Beck points to the methodological weaknesses in the study designs of counseling outcome research as a whole. Of interest, however, is her finding of a close correlation between research findings (such as they are) and descriptions by clinicians. She found that both clinicians and researchers defined a positive couple counseling outcome as characterized by improved attitudes of the spouses toward each other, change in the patterns of communications, reduced hostility and conflict, increase of positive statements to and about the mate, and decrease of symptoms (such as nervousness, defensiveness, depression, self-preoccupation) in each spouse. Clinicians also cited more responsiveness, openness, and readiness for self-exploration, as well as improved self-concepts. Neither clinicians nor researchers found much correlation between a positive outcome and change in such areas as patterns of dominance and control.

Current research is attempting to correct the methodological weaknesses of early research, as well as to integrate research, theory, and practice. We will discuss these efforts further in chapter 9.

Issues in Couples Work

Regardless of one's theoretical approach to working with couples, one must take into consideration the couple's developmental process, the individual developmental process of each partner, and the impact of the latter on the couple system. To gain a fuller understanding of the developmental process of the couple system, let us look at the types of issues that one encounters in couples work.

New Marriage.   When newlyweds come for help, the situation is very different from when a couple whose marriage is in its second or third decade comes for help. The therapist who favors "structural" interventions had better well realize that when working with a couple married twenty-three years, he or she is intervening perhaps only 50 minutes a week in a "structure" that has had over two decades (over 10,483,200 minutes) in which to establish and solidify itself!

Not only will the issues that newlyweds present differ from those of couples who have been married longer, but the strategies and techniques that the therapist uses in each situation must also necessarily differ according to the nature of the presenting problems. The tasks of the young couple focus on their struggle to adapt to a new family system and to redefine their relationships with their respective families of origin. These tasks involve negotiating rules and issues of power and dependency. The struggles and conflicts of this stage seem to center on: (1) relationships to extended families; (2) friendships—new couple friendships and earlier, individual friendships; (3) money management; (4) sex; (5) use of time (leisure, individual time, couple time); (6) handling of career(s). Other concerns may include housing, religion, and deciding whether or not to have children. Symptoms may be physical abuse, alcoholism, lack of communication, or unsatisfactory sex.

Children.   With the birth of the first child, a new subsystem (the parenting subsystem) enters the family system, and new issues emerge. Pressures and limitations on the system increase and often cause an increase in dissatisfactions. Inevitably there are new economic pressures. In addition, issues of who is responsible for child care arise, and limitations of time and support strain the couple system. During this stage, growth of the marital partners may be unequal, sex roles may become more rigidly stereotyped, and one spouse may have a feeling of greater sacrifice than the other spouse. Because the childbearing stage may last for many years, a pattern may emerge in which the child is triangulated into the couple system to avoid outright conflict. Couples may seek help at this time because of a child's symptom, because one of the mates develops a symptom, or because the marriage itself appears to be dead. The career development of both spouses may be an issue.

It is sometimes difficult for the therapist to differentiate between couple system issues and parent system issues. It is important that the therapist take the time to distinguish these issues clearly so that he or she can apply an appropriate intervention strategy.

Middle Age. When the children enter adolescence, the parents may be simultaneously experiencing their own mid-life transitions. This stage can thus create turmoil within the family system. The adolescent children are dealing with their own identity issues, the influences of their peer system, and the need to begin to separate themselves from the family system. Mother may be thinking about her career development, her use of time, and how she can deal with her emerging needs and desires. Father may be dealing with the realities of his occupational status and success, with disappointment in earlier expectations and painful compromises. At the same time, both parents may be experiencing confusing changes in their levels of energy and body appearances. All these anxieties may be deflected onto the family, with the parents venting their frustrations on their adolescent children. As the children become more independent, parenting burdens lighten, and the parents may find that they now have more time and engery. This, in turn, may add stress to the couple system, causing old issues of power, competition, and dependency to resurface.

When the children actually leave home, the couple often must decide how or whether they wish to continue their relationship. Being no longer able to maintain the view that they must stay together "for the sake of the children," they must look anew at their relationship to decide whether or not it is worth the investment of the rest of their lives. At this time, it is helpful for the couple to reassess their potentialities and liabilities, to examine the options open to them in terms of career, lifestyle, and relationship. Many middle-aged couples find that their commitment to marriage is heightened and that, with renewed vigor and attention, they can develop a most satisfying, fulfilling relationship. Time orientation is different for the couple now; they must learn to focus more on the here-and-now, rather than project the impact of their decisions and commitment to the future as they might have done when younger.

Troll (1971) found three themes that seem to dominate the interaction of middle-aged couples: decrease in passion; increase in conventionality; and concern with health. Kerckhoff (1976) points out that the middle-aged individual is "sandwiched between the demands of youth and the needs of the aged . . . the middle-aged person often reports feeling caught, pressed, squeezed." It appears that the triangle between marriage, job, and parenthood changes with middle age. Upward mobility in one's occupation decreases or ceases, financial gains lessen, children leave home, and friends and relatives who comprise the peer system begin to die. This results in a transitional crisis—which does not necessarily imply negative outcomes. This transitional crisis can also result in recognition of the value of the relationship, reassessment of life and marital goals, and a focus on actualizing one's wants, desires, and needs. Obviously the character of the marital relationship will continue to change as the pressures from other subsystems decrease.

At this stage in their relationship, the middle-aged couple may find themselves on the other side of the very same boundary that they negotiated years ago when they first became a couple. Their children are now negotiating the boundaries of their own couple systems and in doing so are moving the middle-aged couple out of the parenting relationship. Later, with the birth of grandchildren, the boundaries of the new family system may be altered to include the couple as grand-parents. But more importantly, the middle-aged couple must now attend to the boundaries of their own marital relationship, which may have been neglected for years. While in the process of raising children, the couple may have developed boundaries that were perfectly adequate for the parent subsystem, but may have ignored or neglected their relationship as husband and wife. Now, as the children leave and the parents are "bounded in" or "bounded out" of the new family systems, they return again to the boundary of their own couple system. As they reexamine their relationship, they are possibly twenty to thirty years older than when they formed the relationship and thus are likely to be two quite different people.

The couples worker needs to consider the interaction of physio-logical changes, differential rates of individual development, and the couple system's definition of societal change. The presenting issues of a middle-aged couple are likely to concern change in financial and occupational status, sexual changes (both physiological and societal), role reversals, death of close friends, adjustment to the loss of the parental role, redefinition of relationships with growing children and extended families, adaptation to different levels of energy, pre-retirement considerations, and accommodation of emerging needs and interests.

Older Age.   At later stages, illness, retirement, and stresses of extended family tend to dominate couple issues. Much of what happens in the couple system at this time depends upon individual development and the ways in which the boundaries of the couple system were negotiated at earlier stages. Issues that were not resolved in earlier stages are likely to resurface in these later stages. At this time, counseling may focus on enrichment of emotional, intellectual, and social functioning, on helping people to enhance their communication skills and to develop new interests and friendships. Retirement groups, grandparenting groups, marriage enrichment groups, and activities groups have all proven helpful in reducing anxiety, depression, and other psychological symptoms of the elderly.

Interface of Individual and Couple Developmental Issues.   It is actually impossible to separate individual development from marital development. The case of Mr. and Mrs. Ellis illustrates this critical point.

Mr. and Mrs. Ellis came to therapy because Mrs. Ellis, aged forty, wanted to terminate the marriage and was very upset at Mr. Ellis's refusal to move out of the house. Married twenty-two years, Mr. Ellis was a successful businessman and Mrs. Ellis (with her husband's backing) had just opened her own antique store. They had four children, ranging in age from fourteen to twenty years. Both spouses were very attractive and lived comfortably in a suburban community. When they married, they had an implicit traditional marital contract. Both came from closed-system types of families with rigid sex-role stereotyping.

Mrs. Ellis now felt that she was missing out on a new world opened up to her by the women's movement and that she wanted to have the opportunity to try living on her own, to act out all her fantasies, before it was too late. Mr. Ellis was stunned by all of this, felt that he had changed with the times as much as possible, that he was supporting his wife's business endeavor, was trying to participate more actively in child care and household tasks, and felt sad that no matter what he did, he was not able to satisfy her. The therapist gave Mrs. Ellis some behavioral homework assignments, such as figuring out the economic costs of separation and looking at apartments. The therapist also asked Mrs. Ellis to interview a dozen women who had been separated or divorced at her age to find out about life for single women. In addition, the couple was asked to list the positive aspects of their relationship and to deal with some of the interactional issues presented in the sessions.

It turned out that some of Mrs. Ellis's complaints were no longer really valid. Although in the past Mr. Ellis had invested much of his time and energy in his own career development, in the last two years he had decided that he had gone as far as he could go and thus had begun to expend more of his time and energy on his family. His priorities had changed with his individual development. Mrs. Ellis came to realize that she was experiencing some panic about approaching middle life, about having her children grow up and leave. In short, both members of this couple system had been so engrossed in their own individual developmental issues, that they had projected their anxieties and concerns onto the relationship. Mr. Ellis, in his developmental stage of mid-life reassessment, was in the process of investing more time and energy in his family and less in his business; thus, he was now more available for relating. Mrs. Ellis's approach to mid-life reassessment was manifested in her yearning to refocus her energy from family relationships to outside relationships and achievement as a businesswoman. In a few sessions, both spouses were able to gain a different perspective of their fears and decided to focus on enhancing, rather than dismantling, their relationship.

Thus we see that regardless of the developmental stage of the marriage, the relationship is the focus of treatment. While clients may view their spouse as the problem, part of the therapist's task is to reeducate them to viewing the relationship as the problem and to considering both individual and relationship developments.

Qualities of the Couples Worker

It is obviously very important for counselors working with couples to be in touch with their own values, feelings, and attitudes. The types of questions that couples workers need to ask themselves concern their own "shoulds" and "oughts": Does marriage have such a value in itself that it should be preserved? Do I consider the marriage vows to be fully sacred? Do I feel that sex is pleasurable and fun? Do I believe that in deadlocked situations, one or the other mate should give in? How do I feel about the handling of money, religion, and politics in a marriage? Do I feel that all married couples should have children? Do I feel that divorce really indicates failure and should be avoided at all costs? For example, a counselor who has recently experienced a painful divorce might treat a couple with marital difficulties quite differently from the way one who is experiencing a fulfilling marital relationship would. By openly acknowledging one's own values and attitudes to self and clients, a counselor can become aware of whether or not he or she is imposing personal values upon clients.

Basically, the couples worker needs the following competencies: (1) the ability to assess and distinguish marital relationship problems from either individual or other subsystem problems; (2) the ability to understand the dynamics of interactional patterns in order to develop a workable treatment plan; and (3) the ability to establish a therapeutic relationship with the couple system. Establishing a therapeutic relationship with a couple is often difficult, as it is not easy for a couples worker to avoid judging or taking sides. The couples worker, like the family therapist, needs to develop enough sensitivity to people's feelings to know how to wait for an appropriate timing of an intervention. It is as if the couples worker, in addition to serving as a catalyst, orchestrates the ups and downs, ins and outs of the relationship.

In addition, the couples worker needs the patience and stamina to stick with the couple, even when things appear to be at a standstill. The therapist's confidence in his or her therapeutic skills and ability to provide beneficial guidance, combined with the couple's commitment to work on their relationship and individual ego strengths, can lead to successful therapeutic outcomes.

Preventive Couples Work

In recent years, educators and counselors have become more aware of the need to provide sex education and marriage enrichment programs before a crisis brings a family into the counselor's office. Several church groups, as well as other community-based groups, have developed preventive programs that have become prevalent throughout the country. For example, the Unitarian Church has developed a sophisticated sexuality program that is attended by youngsters and their parents. Many schools and other community agencies are providing the same type of educational services.

The marriage encounter movement, begun by Father Calvo in 1958, has been steadily growing and progressing. Currently, there are over fourteen national organizations offering some type of marriage enrichment program. Basically, these programs are designed for groups of married couples who are interested in improving and enhancing their relationships, but who are not experiencing any dysfunction or crisis at the moment. The groups are led by trained married couples and provide an experiential learning experience designed to foster commitment to and growth of the marital relationship. Tasks include private couple dialoguing, couple group interaction, and, sometimes, structured communications laboratory exercises.

The major benefits that couples report in the few studies that have been done on the outcomes of marriage encounter and growth groups (Mace 1977) are clearer understanding of the relationship; some agreement on future goals; feelings of reassurance; and perspective, modeling influence, and support gained from the other couples in the group.

When working with family systems in which the parents do not want to focus on their marital relationship in therapy, we have found that recommending a marriage enrichment program as a normal, developmental experience (rather than as a prescription for a problem) has indeed resulted in improved awareness and commitment to the relationship. Therefore, we are suggesting that the family worker can utilize community-based preventive programs as an effective supplement to family systems work, particularly with resistant clients who are likely to see these programs as less threatening than therapy.

Areas of Specialization

Although there are many areas of specialization within marital therapy, we will focus on only three major areas: separation, divorce, and sex. It is important for couples workers to be comfortable with each of these specialized areas as one never knows if and when one of them will become paramount in couples work.

Separation

A marital conflict may be so intense that a couple seems stuck at an impasse. In such cases, a therapist may feel that a "sabbatical" is in order, a physical distancing of the couple so that they can gain the space and energy needed to work through the couple relationship. This type of separation may be called *structured separation* (Weiss 1975) or *transient structured distance* (Greene 1973).

One of the first obstacles to a structured separation is the customary belief that separation is the first step toward divorce. Weiss (1975) points out that separation, if structured properly, results in just as many renewed marriages as it does divorces. We have found that a structured separation is helpful in terms of giving clients an opportunity for reality testing and enabling them to gain the distance and objectivity needed to decide whether or not to resume their marital relationship.

In structured separations, the therapist establishes the rules. These rules include the length of time of the separation, whether or not the spouse acts as a boarder in his or her own home or lives in another residence, the kinds and numbers of therapy sessions to be held during this period, whether or not a legal separation or legal consultation is necessary, and the terms and conditions for the couple seeing each other. Some therapists stipulate that the couple can be together only if, when, and as long as both are comfortable, making it a matter of choice. Others assign particular "courting" or "relating" tasks to each spouse. Most therapists stipulate that neither party needs to account for his or her use of time or distance, although there may be built into this statement the rule that neither spouse has the right to break existing secular or sacred laws governing their marriage.

The actual separation counseling may be conjoint and/or individual. It focuses on each party's response to the separation in terms of feelings, activities, thoughts. There is a focus on individual development, on how one feels about one's own life and choice of lifestyles, career, reactions to freedom, value systems, dependency, conflicts, control needs, ways of coping with loss and change, risk taking, and role change. When it becomes appropriate, when the client has achieved sufficient distance, the couple relationship is concurrently explored from this individual vantage point. At the end of the prescribed time for a separation, the couple (individually and as a couple) are asked to decide what they want to do.

Needless to say, there is a risk in this type of strategy. There are two parties who must contribute to the outcome, which can never be guaranteed. An example of the risk involved occurred in the case of Mr. and Mrs. Sapir: Mrs. Sapir had initiated the couples counseling, telling the therapist over the telephone that her marriage was a "disaster" and that there "was nothing right about it." During their first session, the couple sat at opposite sides of the room, glared at each other hostilely, and indicated no positive rapport whatsoever. They had been married nine years. Both agreed they had been miserable for at least eight of these nine years. They had had a child three years after they were married to see if that would help the marriage. Now, Mrs. Sapir was constantly angry and bitter, accusing Mr. Sapir of not listening and of deliberately sabotaging her every interest, need, and activity. As Mrs. Sapir ranted on, Mr. Sapir increasingly withdrew, and the passive-aggressive dynamic between them became more and more obvious. Mr. Sapir's replies to Mrs. Sapir's charges were that he had "given up years ago," that he refused to hear her harassments, and that he would never accede to her demands to earn more money to live up to the Joneses. When the therapist asked each party what would need to change in order for the marriage to work, the reply was a firm "Impossible! As far as each was concerned, nothing could possibly make their marriage work except for the spouse to become a different person."

After several assessment sessions, the therapist suggested a structured trial separation. Mrs. Sapir was very interested in this suggestion and readily agreed to several homework tasks, such as looking for employment and arranging for child care so that she could work. Mr. Sapir was also interested, but took several months to plan his departure from the household. Eventually, the couple agreed to separate for a period of six months. During this period, the therapist saw them individually, as the recriminations and hostilities were too fierce to permit conjoint sessions. During the six-month period, Mrs. Sapir discovered that it was difficult to meet eligible men, that full-time responsibility for child care was rather overwhelming, and that the economic realities of maintaining two households were distressing. Mr. Sapir, on the other hand, slowly began to find a new, exciting lifestyle for himself. He changed his style of dress, began to socialize and date, and developed a much more positive self-concept. After about four months of separation, he became involved in a relationship with another woman. Meanwhile, as he began to assert himself more openly and to do eagerly all the things that his wife had for years nagged him to do, Mrs. Sapir began to find him attractive and desirable and launched a concerted effort to woo him back. He refused and the separation ended in divorce with Mrs. Sapir angry and bitter, feeling that she had ruined her life, and with Mr. Sapir feeling that the separation was the best thing that could have happened to him and that his new relationship (and eventual remarriage) was more satisfying and fulfilling than he could ever have imagined.

It is important that therapists who suggest structured separations point out the risks involved in this strategy.

Divorce

Divorce therapy is quickly emerging as a specialty in its own right. It is the authors' belief that a couple needs to work through the process of terminating the marital relationship just as diligently as they need to work on developing the relationship. With the rising divorce rate, divorce counseling has become a more frequent component of couples work. Here we will discuss divorce counseling only as it applies to the couple system; the impact of divorce on the entire family system will be dealt with in a later chapter.

Although some couples have already decided to divorce before entering therapy, most couples do not enter therapy with that intent. Therefore, the predivorce decision period is an important phase of couples work. This period begins when one person begins to toy with the idea of separating. It may be a while before this idea is expressed and before the couple begins to ponder or consider divorce as a feasible alternative resolution of their relationship problems. In some instances, one mate makes a final decision before the other mate is even aware of a problem. This usually leads to some desperate strategies on the part of the reluctant mate and most frequently ends in a difficult divorce. In other instances, the verbalization of divorce as a possibility has been the cause of such anxiety in both partners that they have rushed into therapy for help and are highly motivated to put their marriage back on the tracks. The point is that individuals have different motivations for entering couples therapy, and the outcome of the therapy is somewhat dependent on this motivation. In some locations, lawyers and judges automatically recommend counseling for couples who are seeking a divorce. Whether or not the counseling is voluntary will certainly affect its outcomes.

Kressel and Deutsch (1977) point out that only recently have clinical accounts of divorce therapy appeared. There really is no research on the role of the psychotherapist or counselor in divorce. However, we do know from Krantzler (1973), Bohannon (1970), and Cline and Westman (1971) that divorce implies loss, the death of a relationship, and that the process of mourning and letting go is similar to that involved in loss by death. This process of mourning is a prerequisite to healthy reequilibration, to freeing oneself to build a new life. Many divorce therapists believe that the stages of mourning are similar to the stages elucidated by Kubler-Ross (1969) for the terminally ill: shock and denial, anger, bargaining, depression, and acceptance. We will examine the predivorce period, the mourning phase, and the phase of recalibration.

1. *Predivorce Period*: The predivorce decision period is most often characterized by ambivalence and shifting moods of guilt, anger, sadness, depression, and fear. Individuals in this phase are exploring their sense of identity, wondering who they will be if they are not married, fantasizing about what it might be like to be divorced. Usually

their focus is on all the negatives that have built up in the relationship, and there is a lot of blaming and exchange of recriminations. Another major characteristic of this period is the obsessive review of the relationship—what happened in the past, what could have been done by whom to make things better, who did what, who is to blame, what good times there once were. This review of the past often leads to strong resistance to the loss of attachment. There is much strong feeling about holding on to the image of the family, which is often more likely to be resistance to accepting the loss of attachment than to accepting the loss of a particular spouse.

The therapist usually attempts reconciliation, utilizing reflection and behavioral techniques. Most therapists believe that a relationship is not truly "dead" until it has been carefully tried and processed. He or she helps in the decision-making process, pointing out all the options open to the mates, weighing the negatives of the relationship against the strengths, exploring the possibilities of change within the relationship. In other words, the therapist helps the couple to focus on reality issues, on feelings and activities, and on examining their ambivalences in terms of losses and gains. The goal of therapy, whether it is divorce or reconciliation, is to be defined by the couple, not the therapist. When it is defined, the therapist may, or may not, agree to help the couple to move toward the accomplishment of that goal.

During the predivorce period most therapists try to clarify the sources of marital dysfunction and to promote understanding of current patterns of interaction. Depending upon orientation, the therapist may explicate the historical roots of the problems from a family-of-origin perspective, utilizing multigenerational themes and patterns. In most cases, the therapist helps to clarify the real sources of anger and helps the couple to shift the focus from the spouse to the self, by relabeling accusations (reframing the issues), encouraging positive interaction, and keeping the focus on substantive issues. Simultaneously, the therapist is also an information giver, suggesting resources where people can obtain help with the legal process and with financial and community affairs.

2. *Mourning Phase*: Once the decision to divorce is made, the objective of the therapist is to help the couple negotiate emotional and physical separations that will establish a favorable climate for legal and other types of negotiation. While being supportive, the therapist must also help the couple focus on loss and acceptance of change. It is not just the marital relationship that is lost, but often lifestyle and significant relationships with extended family and friends as well.

The therapist helps the couple to establish norms of equity, cooperation, and reasonableness in order to promote a satisfactory negotiation of the divorce. He or she actively discourages vengeance and revenge-seeking behaviors. Once lawyers enter the picture, the emotional climate can become very charged, and the therapist often finds himself or herself in the role of impartial stabilizer. The real task during this period is "letting go," working through the mourning process.

Much of this work can be done on an individual or group basis. Whichever modality is used, the person must work through the anger and begin to experience and mourn the loss of attachment. Increasingly, therapists are finding divorce adjustment groups helpful in that they provide clients with a way of draining off their intense emotions without overusing friends or family. These groups also help people to develop a sense of belonging and identity during this critical transition period and give them a context in which to share and contrast their past marital experiences and their current experiences of mourning.

Concrete planning may be difficult at this time because of confusion and the focus of whatever emotional energy there is on the self. Thus, the therapist's task during this phase is to help the individual focus on daily responsibilities and day-to-day living problems, while allowing ventilation of anger, depression, and sadness. The presence of children in the system, who will necessitate some type of couple relationship regardless of the marital status, will naturally affect the type of postmarital relationship that is established. It can be helpful to have occasional conjoint sessions, wherein the therapist maintains impartiality, already having established a trusting, confidential relationship with each partner.

Counseling during the mourning phase is usually a discouraging and depressing process, although there is a wide range of responses to separation and divorce, including relief and excitement about new opportunities and possibilities, as well as ambivalence and pain. This mourning phase can last from several months to several years, and counselors often feel useless and stuck. It has been our experience that very often the counselor serves an invaluable function just by being available for regular ventilation and support.

3. *Recalibration Phase*: When the mourning phase has been worked through, a recalibration stage, which involves the building and stabilizing of a new life, begins. The therapist encourages the client to establish new support groups, to develop individual social skills. In general, the therapist supports new behaviors of reaching out, supports change, and helps individuals to identify and examine alternative options. One way that the therapist knows that this stage has been reached is when clients are able to talk in terms of living for themselves,

rather than seeking replacement mates. At this point, they have accepted the deaths of their marriages, have achieved some insight and understanding of their marital conflicts and difficulties, and are now able to risk becoming emotionally involved and committed to new relationships and new lifestyles. These new relationships do not necessarily have to be heterosexual, potential marital relationships, but can be any friendships that provide emotional support and meet the needs for intimacy and caring that we all possess. In any case, the client is now involved in self-growth, and there is less focus on what happened in the former couple system.

Constructive Divorce.   Obviously, the major goal of working with a dissolving couple system is to help its members achieve a constructive divorce, where they can both feel OK about themselves and each other and about the dissolution of the couple system. Framo (1978, p. 76) says that the goal is to "disengage from the marriage with a minimum of destructiveness to selves and children and with the personal freedom to form new relationships." Needless to say, this is more likely to be the case if there is mutual acceptance of the need to divorce, if there is accompanying individual growth, and if there is minimal psychic injury to the children. The most frequent impediment to a so-called constructive divorce exists when one spouse wants to end the marriage and the other spouse is reluctant to do so. Divorce also often involves immediate family, extended families, and the rest of the couple's social network, who may be disapproving and censorious. Thus, the therapist may be called upon to help renegotiate these boundaries by dealing with the clients' underlying fears about loss and by disputing their negative self-assertions. In addition to helping clients face reality, the divorce therapist protects the welfare of the children and suggests workable compromises.

There are some therapists who continue to see both mates (individually and conjointly with or without the children) after the divorce. Some retain the custodial parent and children as primary clients and refer the noncustodial parent elsewhere for individual or group therapy. Obviously, many variables enter into this decision. Framo (1978) believes that seeing both spouses in individual sessions after the decision to divorce is made gives rise to suspicions and secrets, as well as to conflict of loyalties for the therapist. Stahmann and Hiebert (1977 b) recommend the use of consultants and co-therapists in conjoint and multigenerational sessions.

In situations where the tension is high, where the children are involved in the parents' power struggles, and where one or more of the children are exhibiting symptoms, it is helpful for the therapist to be present when the children are told of the impending separation. The purpose of such a family session is to facilitate an open, impartial discussion of issues and feelings without blame or vengeance and to prevent the children from being maneuvered into blaming and taking sides. The children, however, are likely to take a hostile view of the therapist as the agent of divorce. A family meeting with the therapist does not seem to be necessary when the couple is able to share with each other their concerns and desires for the children and when the parent system is not negatively affected by the tension in the couple system.

Lawyers and Divorce Therapists. Increasingly, divorce therapists are finding themselves in conflict with divorce lawyers. Surveying twenty-one highly experienced divorce therapists, Kressel and Deutsch (1977) found most of them critical of lawyers for the following reasons: (1) an adversary process hinders a constructive divorce; (2) lawyers become unwitting pawns in the escalation of marital conflict; (3) a lawyer's objectivity may be compromised by financial considerations, especially if the lawyer is operating on a contingency fee basis. In some cases, we have found it helpful to recommend that the couple first see another counselor for six sessions, where they can settle some of the property, custody, and financial issues, and then present their settlement to their respective attorneys. The rationale for referring the couple to another counselor is that the new counselor will not have been at all involved in the decision-making process that resulted in the divorce.

The divorce therapist should be familiar with community resources for specialized legal help with divorce. He or she should also recommend to clients that they use an experienced specialist as an attorney rather than a neighbor or friend who is not really experienced in divorce and custody cases. Some counselors prefer to delay the entry of lawyers into a case. Others, however, report that a preliminary legal consultation during the predivorce period is helpful in acquainting mates with the realities of divorce settlements and procedures.

Divorce Education. Divorce counseling may be emotionally draining and demoralizing for the therapist, who must have the stamina to absorb emotional assault and ventilation and to mediate in highly charged situations. For the client, divorce is a "psychological ampu-tation" (Stahmann and Hiebert 1977b) that impacts on all family relationships. A painless divorce is impossible, just as painless major surgery without side effects or aftereffects is impossible. Education about the process, its implications and ramifications, is surprisingly lacking in our culture. Many people have no idea of what they are getting into when they make this momentous decison. Although cultural acceptance of divorce has alleviated the stress that used to result from social ostracization, new types of stress appear to fill the void. One task of the divorce therapist is to educate the family about all the impending ramifications of the divorce process.

Sex Therapy

Sex therapy today is a short-term, behaviorally based psychother-apy that focuses on treating and curing specific sexual dysfunctions. It may be used exclusively to treat a psychosomatic or organically caused dysfunction or, as an adjunct to another type of therapy, it may be used to treat destructive interactional relationships and such sexual variations as fetishism, homosexuality, or unusual sexual object choices or practices (Birk 1978). Within the context of sex therapy with couples, therapists may find themselves treating boredom, diminished interest, and general, rather than specific, dissatisfaction.

Kinsey, Wolpe, Ellis, and Masters and Johnson have contributed significantly to the development of sex therapy as it is practiced today. Kinsey is noted for his sociological report on female and male sex-uality. Wolpe, perceiving that human sexual responses, like the sex-ual responses of other animals, are susceptible to conditioning, used reciprocal inhibition and other behavioral methodology in the effective treatment of sexual dysfunctions. Ellis began in the 1950s to examine reasons for male impotency and discovered that much sexual dysfunc-tion was related to misinformation, irrational ideas and beliefs, and, in general, poor sex education. Using rational-emotive therapy techniques, he developed strategies of cognitive restructuring to attack the irrational belief system and employed imagery and assertiveness techniques to teach people to feel more comfortable with their own sexuality.

Masters and Johnson. In the 1960s, Masters and Johnson gave a scientific explanation of the physiological components of sexual func-tioning that is the most significant to date. They were able to diagram the sex cycle to show the following phases:

1. *Excitement*: an arousal state of erotic feelings causing genital vaso-congestion and attainment of erection in men and vaginal lubrication in women.
2. *Plateau*: a more advanced stage of arousal, which occurs before orgasm and which is a state of intense sexual tension, with peak vasocongestion in both males and females.
3. *Orgasm*: consisting of involuntary, regular, climactic spasms of the bulbar muscles in the male and circumvaginal muscles in the female, resulting from sexual tensions.
4. *Resolution*: a gradual lessening of sexual tensions with a gradual return to the body's unaroused state.

Masters and Johnson (1970) discovered that a sexual response has two phases. In the first phase, genital vasocongestive reactions produce penile erection in the male and vaginal lubrication and swelling in the female. The second phase involves the reflex clonic muscular contractions that constitute orgasm.

Masters and Johnson emphasized that pleasure is the basic motivation of sex. They also determined that women have as strong a sex drive as men and that there is no difference between vaginal and clitoral orgasms in women. These findings were originally quite controversial in that they disagreed so sharply with previous conceptions.

After much research, Masters and Johnson identified four major sexual dysfunctions, which have either organic or psychosocial causes:

1. *Male impotence*, in which the male at one time may have experienced ejaculation (*secondary* impotence) or may never have experienced ejaculation (*primary* impotence).
2. *Premature ejaculation*, in which the male ejaculates before the female has time to become aroused.
3. *Nonorgasmic female response*, in which there is no response whatsoever to sexual stimuli or in which the female is aroused and lubricated but has difficulty reaching orgasm.
4. *Vaginismus*, in which a spasm of vaginal muscles prevents penetration.

Masters and Johnson found that the causes for these sexual dysfunctions were psychological in just about 90 percent of the cases and that sexual dysfunction reflects a relationship problem rather than individual pathology. Reasons for sexual dysfunction seem to include stresses on the family system when children reach adolescence, mid-life crisis of either mate, emotional immaturity, influence from repressive family of origin, misinformation, performance expectations, and lack of knowledge about body and sexual functioning. In examining the causes of sexual dysfunction, one must also consider congenital and medical factors; certain diseases and types of medication can affect both sex drive and sex functioning. Individual differences in sex drive are another consideration.

Masters and Johnson have had an important influence on the practice of sex therapy today. Their short-term directive counseling is aimed at symptom removal, as opposed to the conventional psychodynamic goal of insight and resolution of unconscious conflict. Major aspects of their contributions are: (1) the use of co-therapy teams of male and female therapists to work with both partners; (2) the view of sexual dysfunction as symptomatic of relationship difficulty, which therefore involves mutual responsibility; (3) the use of techniques stressing open communication, pleasure, information, and education; and (4) the taking of complete medical and sex histories. Their treatment is based upon behavioral theory, and their focus includes all aspects of sexual senses—olfactory, visual, auditory, tactile, and spatial.

The primary goal of Masters and Johnson's sex therapy is to teach the couple to relax and attend to giving and receiving erotic stimuli. Couples are assigned a gradual series of sexual tasks, requiring cooperation and mutual sharing. Most sex therapists do not feel that sex therapy can be effective if a high level of hostility exists between the partners. Therapists who have been influenced by Masters and Johnson usually assess the relationship before agreeing to sex therapy. Although it is possible to treat sex dysfunction without treating the relationship, many sex therapists want to be sure that the relationship is being treated concurrently.

Masters and Johnson have developed individualized techniques and exercises for specific dysfunctions. There is, however, one technique they recommend for all situations—that of sensate focus, or pleasuring. This technique is a process through which a couple learns to give and receive pleasure by touching and caressing each other's body. Intercourse is forbidden at the outset, and pressure to perform intercourse is thus removed from the situation. The couple is instructed to pick a time and place where they can relax freely and not be distracted or interrupted and where they can learn the pleasure of communicating both verbally and nonverbally about their likes and dislikes. The first few exercises forbid genital touching; gradually, genital areas are included and intercourse is allowed. An interesting aspect of this technique is that it teaches each partner to assume responsibility for his or her own sexuality. We have found this technique useful in treating boredom and dissatisfaction in that it tends to revitalize sensitivity and pleasure in giving and receiving.

Current Sex Therapy. Although Masters and Johnson have actually trained only a few sets of therapists, their techniques have been adopted as the basis of many current forms of sex therapy. Helen Singer Kaplan (1974) has developed a type of sex therapy that uses both psychodynamic and behavioral techniques to relieve the patient's sexual symptoms. Kaplan has applied this modification of the Masters and Johnson techniques to groups without the use of a co-therapist. Kaplan points out that (1) sex therapy benefits are usually limited to the patient's sexual functioning and that sex therapy will not necessarily cure a neurosis or a marriage that has failed for nonsexual reasons; (2) sexual dysfunctions can be cured even when neurotic personalities are involved, as basic defense mechanisms do not have to be altered in order for sexual dysfunctions to be alleviated; (3) sexual dysfunction is not necessarily symptomatic of either severe psychopathology in individuals or severe distress in the marital system; and (4) sex therapy involves both insight and behavioral changes.

Another team of prominent sex therapists are Hartman and Fithian (1972), who deviate from the Masters and Johnson format by using surrogate partners, by observing partially dressed couples caressing in order to provide accurate, on-the-spot instructions and evaluations, and by conducting conjoint sexological examinations for educational purposes. They also use videotape to provide immediate feedback on sexual performance.

Research studies and the experiences of sex therapy practitioners have shown us that sexual dysfunction can be treated quickly and economically. Although the sexual dysfunctioning is usually a part of the marital functioning, it is not necessary to treat the two together. However, as Sager (1974) points out, if sex is used as a weapon in a power struggle between mates, sex therapy can be counterproductive. Thus, many professional specialists in sex therapy prefer to have the couples whom they accept for treatment concurrently engaged in marital therapy.

One of us, with a co-therapist, once accepted a couple for treatment with a six-week contract for sex therapy. The presenting symptom was that in six years of marriage, the woman had never achieved an orgasm. During the six weeks of treatment, which was based on the Masters and Johnson model, the wife experienced her first orgasm. At the same time, both mates were learning a lot of accurate sex information that challenged many of their preconceived ideas. Relationship issues surfaced, and at the beginning of the sixth session, we attempted to deal with those issues. The couple became quite angry, as their contract was for sex therapy, not for marital therapy. We realized that as therapists we had erroneously crossed some forbidden boundaries. Although this couple did return for marital therapy two years later, it was important for us to learn that therapists must adhere to the original contract. In this case, the sexual dysfunction was cured, but the couple needed time to learn that the curing of a sexual dysfunction was not going to cure an ailing marriage.

What does this mean for couples workers and family therapists? We know that the work of Masters and Johnson and Kaplan has led to a new approach to sexual relations. Sexual problems are not necessarily deeply imbedded psychological problems, but are often a response to specific, current environmental factors. Counselors must realize that there is a vast range of expressions of normal sexual behavior and that treatment of the behavioral component of sexual dysfunction stresses the pleasurable aspects of these expressions. Counselors also need to comprehend the repercussions of the earlier repressive, moralistic views of sex so that they can devise educational techniques for teaching couples about current sexual knowledge and practice—for example, that there are other ways besides genital contact to obtain fulfillment, such as oral and manual manipulation. Counselors can help couples learn new coital positions that may be more effective in prolonging or stimulating erection and ejaculation. Counselors can help family members to realize that masturbation and fantasy are normal sexual practices, to feel more comfortable with themselves as sexual beings, and to give themselves permission to explore and get to know and like their own bodies.

In short, counselors should be aware of the following basic principles of direct treatment of sexual dysfunction as outlined by LoPiccolo and LoPiccolo (1978):

1. *Mutual responsibility*: Counselors should help clients to see that all sexual dysfunctions are shared disorders.
2. *Information and education*: Counselors should help clients overcome ignorance of their anatomies, their mate's anatomies, the biology of sex, and effective sexual techniques.
3. *Attitudes*: Counselors should help clients change negative attitudes toward sex, which may have been parentally or societally derived.
4. *Performance anxiety*: Counselors should help clients eliminate anxiety or pressure about their sexual performances.
5. *Communications and sexual technique*: Counselors should help clients increase their verbal and nonverbal effectiveness both in communications and sexual technique.
6. *Lifestyles and sex roles*: Counselors should help clients change patterns that are destructive to their sexual relationships.
7. *Behavioral change*: Counselors should offer clients appropriate pre-

scriptions for modifying behaviors that are destructive to their sexual relationships.

The area of sex counseling is certainly a specialty in its own right. Aware of the above principles, couples workers and family therapists will need to know which of these principles they can implement themselves, and when and to whom they should refer cases. The therapist will also obviously need to feel comfortable in talking and teaching about sex.

Summary

In this chapter, we focused on the couple system. In working with familes, we feel it is necessary to consider the nature of the marital relationship and to understand different types and patterns of marriages, as well as the reasons people marry. We also feel that family therapists and couples workers should understand the concepts of love and a healthy marriage. Each of these factors influences the values, attitudes, and beliefs of the individual members of the couple system and effects their motivations and expectations for couples work. In addition to looking at the impact of the institution of marriage and families of origin on the current couple system, we considered the impact of cultural changes and concepts of individual adult development.

With this background, we were able to outline the developmental stages of a marital relationship, along with concomitant issues and tasks. We described how the process of therapy must take into consideration not only the developmental stage of the marital relationship, but also the stage of individual development and the influence of cultural factors. It is our strong belief that the process of therapy must consider all these factors in order to understand how a couple system functions.

Reviewing the background of couples treatment as a development parallel to that of family therapy, we considered three major theoretical approaches to couples work: (1) social learning theory, (2) general systems theory, and (3) client-centered (skills-oriented) approaches. We believe that it is possible to incorporate the strategies of all these theoretical schools and yet maintain a systems perspective of the couple system. In our discussion of general systems theory, we elaborated upon how Jackson, Satir, Haley, Bowen, Kantor, and Minuchin view couples work. The other techniques and strategies that we included in our discussion of general systems theory illustrate how therapists can integrate eclectic approaches with the systems perspective.

Although the specialized areas of separation, divorce, and sex counseling are not usually covered within the field of family systems therapy, we strongly believe that current practices and issues within these areas are essential components of the family worker's knowledge. We would hope that family workers would have some basic skill in working within these specialized areas. While we recognize that further specialization would require further training and supervision, we are suggesting that family workers should be able to deal with presenting issues in these areas and then be prepared to refer clients for specialized help if necessary. It seems to us that separation, divorce, and sex are common areas of concerns among many couples who present themselves for couples work.

Our major focus in this chapter has been on the interfacing of individual and couple system development. Our emphasis has been more on the focus of treatment than on the unit of treatment, which is consistent with our integration of systems and developmental theory.

To increase your awareness of marriage and the marital issues that we have covered in this chapter, and to help you define and develop your personal and professional feelings and thoughts about these matters, we refer you to the exercises in chapter 6 in the manual. There you will also find lists of suggested readings in the areas of marriage and couples work, separation and divorce, and sex therapy.

References

Alberti, R., and M. Emmons. 1976. "Assertion Training in Marital Counseling." *Journal of Marriage and Family Counseling* 2 (1): 49–55.

Bach, G., and P. Wyden. 1969. *The Intimate Enemy.* New York: Morrow.

Bane, M.J. 1976. *Here to Stay.* New York: Basic Books.

Beck, D. F. 1976. "Research Findings on the Outcomes of Marital Counseling." In D. Olson, ed., *Treating Relationships.* Lake Mills, Iowa: Graphic.

Birk, A. 1978. "Sex Therapy." In A.M. Nicholi, Jr., ed., *The Harvard Guide to Modern Psychiatry.* Cambridge, Mass.: Harvard University Press.

Bohannon, P., ed. 1970. *Divorce and After.* New York: Doubleday.

Bowen, M. 1966. "The Use of Family Theory in Clinical Practice." *Comprehensive Psychiatry* 7:345–74.

Cline, D. W., and J. P. Westman. 1971. "The Impact of Divorce on the Family." *Child Psychiatry and Human Development* 2:78–83.

Ellis, A. 1962. *Reason and Emotion in Psychotherapy.* New York: Stuart.

———. 1973. "The No Cop-Out Therapy." *Psychology Today* 7:56–62.

———. 1976. "Techniques of Handling Anger in Marriage." *Journal of Marriage and Family Counseling* 2 (4):305–16.

Ellis, A., and R. Harper. 1961. *A Guide to Rational Living.* Englewood Cliffs, N.J.: Prentice-Hall.

Foley, V. 1974. *An Introduction to Family Therapy.* New York: Grune & Stratton.

Framo, J. 1978. "The Friendly Divorce." *Psychology Today* 11 (9):76ff.

Fromm, E. 1956. *The Art of Loving.* New York: Bantam Books.

Greene, B. 1973. "Transient Structured Distance." *The Family Coordinator* 22 (1).

Gurman, A. S., and D. P. Kniskern. 1976. "Research in Marital and Family Therapy." In S.L. Garfield and A.E. Bergin, eds., *Handbook of Psychotherapy and Behavior Change,* 2nd ed. New York: Wiley.

Haley, J. 1963a. "Marriage Therapy." *Archives of General Psychiatry* 8:213–34.

———. 1963b. *Strategies of Psychotherapy.* New York: Grune & Stratton.

———. 1973. *Uncommon Therapy.* New York: Norton.

———. 1976. *Problem Solving Therapy.* San Francisco: Jossey-Bass.

Hartman, W., and M. Fithian. 1972. *Treatment of Sexual Dysfunction.* Long Beach, California: Center for Marital and Sexual Studies.

Jackson, D., and W. Lederer. 1968. *The Mirages of Marriage.* New York: Norton.

Kaplan, H.S. 1974. *The New Sex Therapy.* New York: Brunner/Mazel.

Kerckhoff, R.K. 1976. "Marriage and Middle Age." *Family Coordinator* 25 (1):5–11.

Krantzler, M. 1973. *Creative Divorce.* New York: Evans.

Kressel, K., and M. Deutsch. 1977. "Divorce Therapy: An In-Depth Survey of Therapists' Views." *Family Process* 16 (4):413–45.

Kubler-Ross, E. 1969. *On Death and Dying.* New York: Macmillan.

LoPiccolo, J., and L. LoPiccolo. 1978. *Handbook of Sex Therapy.* New York: Plenum Press.

Mace, D. 1976. "Marital Intimacy and the Deadly Love-Anger Cycle." *Journal of Marriage and Family Counseling* 2 (2):131–37.

———. 1977. "Resources for Couple Growth and Enrichment." In Stahmann and Hiebert, eds., *Counseling in Marital and Sexual Problems.*

Masters, W., and V. Johnson. 1970. *Human Sexual Inadequacy.* Boston: Little, Brown.

Miller, S., E.W. Nunnally, and D. Wachman. 1976. "Minnesota Couples

Communication Program (MCCP): Premarital and Marital Groups." In D. Olson, ed., *Treating Relationships*. Lake Mills, Iowa: Graphic.

Okun, B. 1976. *Effective Helping*. North Scituate, Mass.: Duxbury Press.

Olson, D. 1970. "Marital and Family Therapy: Integrative Review and Critique." *Journal of Marriage and the Family* 32 (4):501–37.

Olson, D., and D. Sprenkle. 1976. "Emerging Trends in Treating Relationships." *Journal of Marriage and Family Counseling* 2 (4):317–29.

Rogers, C. 1972. *Becoming Partners*. New York: Delta.

Sager, C. J. 1974. "Sexual Dysfunctions and Marital Discord." In H. S. Kaplan, ed., *The New Sex Therapy*. New York: Brunner/Mazel.

––––––. 1976. *Marriage Contracts and Couples Therapy*. New York: Brunner/Mazel.

Satir, V. 1972. *Peoplemaking*. Palo Alto, Calif.: Science & Behavior Books.

Stahmann, R. F., and W. J. Hiebert, eds. 1977a. "Commonly Recurring Couple Interaction Patterns." In Stahmann and Hiebert, eds., *Klemer's Counseling in Marital and Sexual Problems: A Clinical Handbook*, 2nd ed. Baltimore: Williams & Wilkins.

––––––, eds. 1977b. *Klemer's Counseling in Marital and Sexual Problems: A Clinical Handbook*, 2nd ed. Baltimore: Williams & Wilkins.

Troll, L.E. 1971. "The Family of Later Life: A Decade Review." *Journal of Marriage and the Family* 33 (2):263–90.

––––––. 1975. *Early and Middle Adulthood*. Monterey, Calif.: Brooks/Cole.

Watzlawick, P., J. Weakland, and R. Fisch. 1974. *Change*. New York: Norton.

Weakland, J. et al. 1974. "Brief Therapy: Focused Problem Resolution." *Family Process* 13 (2):141–67.

Weiss, R.S. 1975. *Marital Separation*. New York: Basic Books.

The Parent System

Chapter 7

In this chapter, we will consider the parent system as the focus of treatment in certain developmental family crises. The unit of treatment may be one parent, both parents, parents together with one or more of the children, or any combination thereof. The major goals of treatment in working with the parent system are to improve the relationships between parents and children and to teach parents effective management so that the family system can function without continuous disruption.

Many families come to the attention of family workers via a child with a problem. When a child is referred for treatment, a therapist with a family systems orientation will view all of the members of the family as somehow, someway participating in whatever the problem of the referred child is. In other words, the child's problem is somehow meeting some need of the family system.

If you recall our discussion of homeostasis in chapter 1, you will remember that the family, like any other system, attempts to maintain a certain level of tension within the system—that is, a homeostatic balance. A child's problem, as difficult as it may be for that child, may also be a way of diffusing tension in the entire family and thus of "saving" the family at the expense of the child. In some instances, when the therapist determines that the child is acting out the tension in the marital relationship, the therapist will focus on the couple system. However, in some cases, the troubled relationships will clearly involve the parents and the children, and, therefore, primary focus will be on parent-child relationships.

Consider the following examples:

In desperation, Mrs. Hays requested help for her seventeen-year-old son, Guy, who had dropped out of school and whom she suspected was stealing money from her purse to purchase marijuana. She described a couple of years of increasing concern and stated that she "was at the end of her rope." At the initial assessment session, Mr. and Mrs. Hays and Guy were accompanied by Guy's two sisters, aged twenty-five and thirty-five, no longer living at home, but very concerned about the distress in the family system. During the session, which the therapist structured in a way that took the focus off Guy's delinquencies, it became clear that Mother did most of the talking and controlling; that Guy, while expressing confusion and unhappiness, had a protective mechanism that allowed him to go only so far in his acting out; and that there was genuine bonding and caring within the family system. At one point, when a sister was able to connect the onset of Guy's difficulties with the suicide of a beloved, father-figure family pastor, Guy began to sob. The therapist, observing that Mr. Hays had been agreeable, but detached, throughout the session, asked him to sit next to Guy and tell him how he felt about seeing his son cry and grieve. With this intervention, Mr. Hays was able to tell his family for the first time about the drowning of his father, which occurred during Mr. Hays's infancy (the family had always wondered what happened to Dad's father, but had assumed he had abandoned his wife). It quickly became apparent that Mr. Hays had had difficulty in his own fathering role and that a negative power struggle had been his and Guy's only way of communicating. Thus, the father-son relationship became the focus of subsequent sessions and, without any specific reference to drugs, stealing, or school dropout being made in the therapy sessions, dramatic changes in Guy's behavior occurred within a few weeks. A large part of the therapy focused on teaching Mr. Hays how to be a father and on helping father and son learn to communicate clearly and express positive caring, as opposed to their previous negative means of communication.

In our second example, Mrs. Rice requested help for her thirteen-year-old daughter, Penny, whom she felt was unhappy and always angry and rebellious. Penny, the oldest child of young parents, clearly verbalized her fear about feeling angry and her inability to control her anger. Mrs. Rice, who said that her own biggest contribution to the family was "doing for and helping everyone," realized that she was inconsistent in discipline and fearful of Penny's anger. Both parents recognized that whenever Penny had a tantrum, they changed whatever their position was and "gave in." Although Penny was frightened of her power, she continued to use it and became increasingly angry at her parents' inability to set limits on her. One of her specific complaints was that her parents treated her like a baby and did not seem to understand that she was growing up. During the first session, the therapist was able to determine that the parents in fact did not understand the difference between a thirteen-year old and a nine-year old. The therapist also realized that although the locus of the problem really was in Mrs. Rice's needing to be needed and fused with her daughter, access into this family system was best achieved by teaching effective parenting and helping the parents to change some of the rules—specifically, to change the rule that it is not OK to be angry, but to find ways that it is OK to be angry.

These two examples illustrate that in working with the parent system, there are usually two major focuses to consider simultaneously: (1) the child's functioning in the family system, the roles he or she plays, the needs he or she fulfills and generates, and the payoffs he or she receives from and provides to the system; and (2) the teaching of effective parent management techniques that provide children with the limits and security they need and that help them to develop self-esteem. Therefore, we are dealing with systems change, as well as with specific management techniques.

In this chapter, we will begin our study by exploring the nature of parent relationships and recent models of parenting, as well as the impact of current cultural changes on attitudes toward parenting and motivations for parenthood. We will then look at the stages of parenthood and their concomitant needs and tasks. The bulk of this chapter will focus on the process and practice of treatment of couples with regard to their parenting.

In addition to exploring the systems theory approach to working with parents, we will consider the social learning and client-centered approaches. We will conclude our discussion by focusing on the role and the requisite qualities of the therapist who deals with parenting issues.

Parent Relationships

Like marriage, parenthood is a highly charged state that is extremely vulnerable to cultural and societal pressures and changes. One cannot separate the needs of parents from the needs of children or from the responsibilities of marriage. One must also recognize that the needs of parents change as they pass through their adult developmental stages, just as the needs of children change as they develop through adolescence and into adulthood. In fact, children influence the psychological development of their parents, just as parents influence the psychological development of their children. Let us look at the state of parenthood, the myths and changing attitudes, before we elaborate upon work with the parent system.

Recent Models of Parenting

It has only been in the last two hundred years that the emotional climate of the family has become important, that the socialization and education of the child have become family functions. Before that, the church, the community, and the guild were the chief providers of childhood education and socialization. Change first occurred in the upper and middle classes and then spread to the working classes. Two models of parenting have been prevalent in the past century, the traditional-restrictive model and the rational-permissive model.

1. *Traditional-Restrictive Model*: This model held that children were empty slates on which parents could imprint their expectations and that children must be strictly trained for "unquestioning obedience and respect for authority" (Group for the Advancement of Psychiatry 1973). Thus, children were subject to the rule and authority of their parents, corporal punishment and chastisement were considered parental obligations, and it was the parent's duty to mold the child, by whatever means worked, to "achieve self-control, to acquire knowledge and to become a useful member of society" (Group for the Advancement of Psychiatry 1973).

2. *Rational-Permissive Model*: During the 1940s, a more rational-permissive model of parenting developed. The development of this model coincided with a surge of interest in child development. This model placed the child's interests first in parent-child relationships. Children began to be considered special, in their own separate category with their own psychology. Although dependency was discouraged, it was felt that using the right scientific approach to parenting would insure that children achieve their fullest individual innate potential. Few limits were set and few expectations imposed. This would result in the child's developing a healthy personality and a feeling of security (Gesell and Ilg 1943; Spock 1963).

Current Attitudes toward Parenting

There have been innumerable changes in parental attitudes in this century. From 1900 to 1910, the development of character and physical health were considered primary. Moral traits—such as courtesy, honesty, industriousness, orderliness, obedience, and cleanliness—were emphasized, and discipline was dispensed through love, religion, and imitation. From 1910 to 1930, "mother" became the primary parental force. Whereas around 1910 physical punishment and rigid schedules were customary, in the 1920s proper conditioning (for the sake of conditioning results) was emphasized and mother was told that strict control was in order. It was not until the 1930s that the influence of Freud and G. Stanley Hall resulted in an emphasis on personality development, rather than on character and moral development. The 1930s also saw an emphasis on proper nutrition, which resulted in mothers' evaluating their parenting by the way and amount their children ate.

Today, emotional climate and atmosphere are considered important ingredients of child development. There is a tendency to find a middle ground somewhere between strict discipline and permissiveness. The child is considered a full-fledged member of a family and an independent person with rights and responsibilities. Parenting is seen as more of an exemplary process than one based on authority or scientific principles. Limits are more often negotiated than imposed. The goal seems to be freedom with responsibility rather than license.

While children have become the focus of the family unit, other parental pressures, burdens, and responsibilities have increased. As society has increased its technology and complexity, expectations of parents' functioning have become more demanding. Psychologists have let parents know that their own words and actions and what they are themselves can and does affect their children and the way their children act. Parents are inundated with material about how children grow and develop, how to raise children, and how not to raise them. The key words that appear over and over are *flexibility, respect, love, patience, consistency, tolerance,* and *fairness.* The popularization of psychology has caused parents to feel overwhelmed with responsibility for the well-being of their offspring. In short, there is great pressure for parents to raise "model" children.

Two themes that seem to dominate current attitudes toward parenting are choice of whether or not to have a child—and, if so, when—and the perennial issue of discipline.

1. *Choice*: Until very recently, the decision of whether or not to have a child was not really possible. People got married to have children. In fact, until the middle of this century, the only legitimate aim of sex was procreation. In addition, there was an economic necessity for children. Thus, a marriage was not really a marriage unless children were born.

Only since the development of satisfactory methods of birth control has it been possible to choose whether to have a child, much less when to have a child or how many to have. Along with this dimension of choice, however, has come the dimension of responsibility. If one can choose whether or not to have children, then one must willingly accept the responsibilities and consequences of whatever choice one makes. In contrast, when one had children willy-nilly, one could more easily rationalize and avoid that responsibility. The fear of making a decision that will knowingly result in heavy responsibilities immobilizes many young couples who are unsure of their readiness to undertake those burdens.

2. *Discipline*: Discipline continues to cause confusion. Consider a recent newspaper column that reported on the development of "Advice to Parents" in this country: In 1910, the slogan was "spank them"; in 1920, it was "deprive them"; in 1930, it was "ignore them"; in 1940, it was "reason with them"; in 1950, it was "love them"; in 1960, it was "spank them lovingly"; and in 1970, it was "TO HELL WITH THEM!"

We see the trend from toughness to permissiveness resulting in angry frustration. And for each of these recommendations, there were well-known experts who exhorted parents to follow certain rules or guidelines to produce the perfect child. It is easy to see why so many parents today are confused, unsure, lacking in confidence. It is understandable why "parents' lib" groups and associations to promote childlessness have sprung up. Those who do choose parenthood seek answers about how to be the "perfect parent"; and if their children do not turn out to be "perfect children," the parents feel guilty, as if some lack in their parenting is responsible for this "imperfection." As parents strive more and more to do "the right thing," their expectations of their children become more intense, and much anxiety, guilt, and conflict result. Consequently, many young people today have negative attitudes toward parenthood and perceive it in frightening, negative terms. Obviously, young people's attitudes toward parenting are influenced by their parents' attitudes and by the type of parenting they themselves have received.

Impact of Cultural Changes

When we consider the numerous books and articles on the subject of parenting, we can easily understand why the prevailing feeling among parents is one of defensiveness. Wherever one goes, one fears a finger pointing and saying, "You are a bad parent. It is your fault that your child is. . . ." Many parents seem to carry around in their heads a little demon who is constantly reminding them of their weaknesses and faults. There is much fear, anxiety, and tremendous concern underlying this defensiveness.

Ackerman, in explaining the increased incidence of disturbed adolescent behavior, has described the manifestations of parental defensiveness:

> Parents seem to be afraid to love their children. It is as if loving is losing something they need for themselves. They function with an image of profit and loss in family relations. They fear to sacrifice that which they may need to spend on themselves. They feel that the demands of their children are exorbitant; they project to their children their fears and hates and unwanted qualities of their inner selves; they intimidate and scapegoat their children, and in turn are scapegoated by them. They do not give their children an appropriate sense of responsibility; often they are overprotective. They become self-conscious, stilted professional parents. They compete with their own children and sometimes try to play the role of big brothers and sisters rather than parents. Out of a sense of weakness and guilt they take recourse to manipulation and coercion. Their efforts to discipline the children are feeble and ineffective and they resort weakly and artificially to devices of deprivation, or so-called reasoning with the child but have no confidence that the discipline will work. [Ackerman 1962, p. 213]

Whereas parents are afraid of their children, children are often angry at them for not being effective parents. In the spring of 1978, one young man actually filed suit for several hundred thousand dollars of damages against his parents for poor parenting.

It is important to remember that most parents do care for their children, that they have good intentions and want to do the best job of parenting they can. Several factors interfere: (1) they do not know how to parent because they have never been taught; (2) they have unresolved conflicts with their own parents stemming from their upbringings, and these interfere with their own parenting abilities; and (3) they have difficulty separating their own needs and expectations from those of their children, in differentiating their own egos and ego ideals from those of their offspring.

In our culture, care of the young is valued above the needs of adults. As a result, parents often deny and ignore their own personal needs, especially those that conflict with their needs to be parents. This cultural value often results in two opposing attitudes: (1) the parent who feels total responsibility for the child's development; and (2) the parent who feels that social forces are the strong determinants of the child's personality and that he or she, as a parent, is absolved of all responsibility. Both attitudes cause guilt and anxiety and both ignore the developmental perspective of children, adolescents, and adults, which postulates that growth and change continue throughout life and that needs and expectations change as one goes through different develop- mental life stages.

There are certain specific cultural changes that have affected parental attitudes today. Two important cultural changes are a merging of sex roles and a greater perception of change as opportunity, rather than as threat. As a result of these cultural changes, fathers are becoming more and more involved in child rearing. This may be partially due to the decline in the involvement of grandparents, but it is also due to liberation from traditional sex-role stereotyping and the growing belief that fathers can be as nurturant as mothers.

LeMasters (1970) has summarized the conditions of cultural change that have made the parenting role so vulnerable today:

1. Higher standards for parents: societal expectations and pressures that cause parents to feel more and more inadequate and to judge them- selves very harshly.
2. Concept of progress: the belief that parents must rear children who will surpass their own social, educational, and economic achievements.
3. Cult of the child: the belief that children are more important than any other age group and the consequent emergence of a youth subculture with social, political, and economic power.

4. Emergence of professionals and experts on childhood: parental confusion over conflicting views among professional and experts.
5. Marital instability: increase in rate of divorce and one-parent families.
6. New roles for women: the feeling among women that they must assume responsibility for child rearing and occupation.
7. Increasing urbanization: greater interdependence of family with institutions of society.
8. Rise of mass media: power struggle between parents and television.
9. Limited preparation for parenting: lack of opportunity to learn about child rearing before children arrive because of fewer models from close extended families and neighborhoods.

As we mentioned earlier, the prevailing attitude toward parenting today appears to be fairly negative. Many young people feel children interfere too much with adult life, are too much of an economic and energetic burden, and that it would be impossible to experience any joy or pleasure in parenting. Economic stress, interference in marital interaction, restrictions on time and energy are all prices and sacrifices that many young adults are choosing not to incur.

On the other hand, many parents do experience their parenthood with a minimum of guilt, anxiety, and depression and find joy and stimulation in the challenges of parenting. For these parents, the stage of parenthood is an important part of their adult life, one in which interaction with children leads to mutual learning and growth.

It is impossible to know at this time which of these groups—the proparenting or antiparenting—is larger or whether there are patterns and themes in family backgrounds that predispose people toward one attitude or another.

Myths of Parenthood.   Our society has promulgated many myths of parenthood, similar to the myths of marriage. These myths are largely based on parents' needs and expectations. They have traditionally been reinforced by folklore, and more recently by the media. Some of these myths are:

1. The child is a possesssion and extension of the parent and will feel, think, and behave as the parent did as a child.
2. The child will hold a weak marriage together.
3. Having a child means that there will always be someone to love the parent.
4. Having a child means that when the parents are old, the child will take care of them.
5. The child owes love, respect, and total obedience to the parents. (The

child must meet the parents' expectations and needs at all times.)

6. The child is the parents' second chance to become and achieve what they feel they should have achieved.
7. The child should be the parent's best friend and vice versa.
8. Parents always know what is best for their child.
9. Parents can mold their children to be just what they want their children to be if they learn the right conditioning techniques.
10. Parents instinctively know how to parent.
11. If a child is not good, it is the parents' fault.
12. Mothers are by nature better parents than fathers.
13. There is one right way to raise children.
14. There can be no real substitute for a child's real parents.
15. A good child never argues with parents.

These myths can result in confusion and family dysfunction. The major theme underlying them is fusion—the child is not seen as an individual separate from the parent. And, as we know, the issue of separation, the differentiation of parent and child, is a very common and major therapeutic issue in both individual and family therapy.

Reasons for Having Children.   Many couples have children because of societal and cultural pressures; they cannot think of their marriage as complete without offspring. Until recently, most couples did not decide whether to have a child, but when to have a child. The current responsibility of deciding to become or not to become a parent has resulted in confusion, heightened guilt, and anxiety. It is a true dilemma in that the decision to have a child is irreversible once the child is born and that the decision not to have a child becomes biologically irreversible with time. Many couples in their thirties, feeling the press of biological time, reactively decide to have a child because they cannot decide not to have one. Because the couple is not really sure that they want a child or that the decision is the best one for them, such a decision can cause guilt and anxiety and can set up some obstacles to satisfying parenthood at the outset.

There has been little research on the motivation for parenthood. However, Moriarity (1970) identifies four major types of motivation:

1. Altruistic or unselfish motivation (where the couple feels nurturant, affectionate, and concerned).
2. Fatalistic motivation (where the couple has an obligation to procreate).
3. Narcissistic motivation (where one or both parents feel that the child will reflect glory on them).

4. Instrumental motivation (where the child may be able to serve some purpose, such as keeping the marriage intact or providing immortality by carrying on the family name, business, or tradition).

Pohlman (1969) adds conformity to pressures imposed by society as a fifth motive. This motivation may be reactive or proactive in that social pressures may motivate one to decide to have a child by refusing to decide not to have a child. The ambivalence that may accompany these various types of motivation for parenthood is easily recognized.

We also need to consider the motivation of the couple system. For example, one spouse may very much want children while the other may not. How the couple negotiates these differences and what the final decision is may set the tone for the experience of parenthood, if that is the course decided upon. Today, more and more couples are seeking professional help at this decision point because they do realize the enormous implications of the decision and its impact on the marital system. They need to decide who will be responsible for what, to anticipate the social, economic, psychological, and physical stresses, and to determine how they will deal with their changing roles. They also need to consider what changes parenthood will cause in the interaction between them as marital partners.

We have counseled many couples about these issues and have found that where the differences are irreconcilable, divorce is a possible alternative. On the other hand, counseling can help the couple to resolve their differences. Consider the following examples:

Mr. and Mrs. Poole came for counseling because they were in a deadlock concerning the issue of having children. Both were university faculty members, had married while in college, and had never discussed the possibility of having children. Now approaching the age of thirty, they had been married ten years and were well established in their respective careers and in their lifestyle. Mrs. Poole was thinking earnestly about having a child and taking a leave of absence for a year or two to do so. Mr. Poole, as he began to consider the idea, discovered that he was adamantly opposed to it, that he did not want to have his lifestyle or marriage disrupted in that way. In a reasonable manner, they tried to explore alternative possibilities. Until this conflict, they felt they had had a reasonably satisfactory marriage and they expressed great caring and concern for each other. By the time they came for counseling, they had been discussing and debating this issue for over a year, and each was becoming more resolute.

After six sessions of exploring their attitudes and the underlying reasons for their attitudes, the couple began to feel that the conflict had inflicted irreparable damage on their marriage. They decided to separate. Mrs. Poole initiated the separation, because she decided that she could not forego the experience or possible satisfaction of becoming a parent and wanted to have the opportunity to see if she could make another life for herself "while she was still young enough." Mr. Poole appeared to be simultaneously relieved and sad. While still proclaiming to care for each other, they did separate. Two years later, Mrs. Poole had remarried and was eagerly awaiting the birth of her first child. At the time of the follow-up, Mr. Poole was still experiencing feelings of loss and depression, but felt that he had made the right decision and that he was reasonably satisfied with his single lifestyle.

Our second example concerns Mr. and Mrs. Roth who came for counseling when they were in their early thirties, after having been married seven years. Mr. Roth had become established as a certified public accountant, and Mrs. Roth was a social worker. Mr. Roth wanted to have children, while Mrs. Roth was adamantly opposed to the idea. She did not want to stop work and be "saddled with the full responsibility of child care." In addition, she was concerned about preserving the status quo of the marital relationship. Again, it turned out that neither had discussed their feelings about children when they met and married, both believing that they had plenty of time to decide. Now they were finding that they had to decide within a time limit and that they each had some rather strong feelings about the issue.

In counseling, Mr. and Mrs. Roth learned to understand each other's fears and expectations. They were able to work out their difficulties conjointly and to decide that they would have a child. Mrs. Roth had strong fears about pregnancy and delivery, as well as much unfinished business with her own parents and upbringing. She had no desire to be put in a position in which she might have to relive her childhood. As she began to understand these fears, she began to see that she could choose a different style of parenting and that her husband could willingly and eagerly share much of the parenting responsibilities. Three years later, Mrs. Roth called to report that she was awaiting the birth of their second child and that her original fears and expectations had been unfounded.

Cases such as these two are quite typical today. It is helpful for a couple to take time and energy to explore their perceptions, needs, and expectations about children so that they can arrive at their decision together and can conjointly accept and deal with the consequences of their decision. In other words, the outcome of the decision is not so important as the process of making the decision and taking the responsibility for the decision and its consequences.

Now that we have explored the impact of cultural attitudes and changes on parenthood, let us look at the developmental stages of parenthood and their concomitant tasks and issues.

Stages of Parenthood

Although once begun the psychological state of parenthood never ceases, there are certainly differences in the needs and tasks of parents and children as they pass through different stages. It is important to remember that the stages of parenthood impact upon the individual developmental stages of the parents and the child, as well as on the developmental stage of the couple system.

The Group for the Advancement of Psychiatry (GAP 1973) divides parenthood into four developmental stages. We will look at these stages from a systems perspective, highlighting some of the issues that pertain to each stage and adding some substages. The four stages are: anticipatory, honeymoon, plateau, and disengagement.

1. *Anticipatory Stage*: This stage starts with the decision-making process, which may have begun early in the childhood of the parents when they fantasized about someday becoming parents. When decisions are completed and conception is attempted, another phase of this stage has been reached. This phase may be brief or lengthy. Sometimes conception occurs easily; sometimes it takes several months or years. How easily conception occurs can affect the level of anxiety associated with conception and pregnancy. For example, if conception is difficult, sex can become such an anxiety-arousing act that sexual satisfaction becomes secondary to conception, and the ensuing stresses on the couple system can lead to couple system dysfunction.

Once pregnancy occurs, the marital system has been affected. The attitudes and feelings of both parents are important. There is often a preoccupation with the woman's body changes and mood swings and with planning for the baby. How involved both partners are with the preparation for birth seems to influence the impact of the pregnancy on the couple system. Fein (1976) suggests that the father's preparation for parenting and his involvement in the birth process correlate positively with his adjustment to postpartum family life. During this period, the couple usually devotes a great deal of time to talking about how they will rear their child, what parenthood will mean to them and how it will affect their marriage. Needless to say, how the woman feels physically and whether or not she experiences pregnancy complications will have an impact on the couple system.

2. *Honeymoon Stage*: The parents' experience with the actual birth creates the immediate climate for the introduction of a third member into the couple system. From the moment of birth, the mother-child-father relationships involve much interpersonal adjustment and learning. The problems involved in this renegotiation are usually masked by the excitement and exhilaration surrounding the event and the congratulations heaped upon the couple by family and friends.

When the family returns home from the hospital, marital stress may develop around or be exaggerated by the presence of the baby. Often, the precipitating issue is the husband's jealousy and resentment at having been displaced from the central position in his wife's life. His feelings may be affected by the nature of his involvement in the anticipatory stage. The father may resent the physical bonding and involvement between the mother and child, especially if she is nursing the baby. As we noted in chapter 5, Minuchin postulates that a temporary enmeshment occurs between mother and child in the early months after birth. How the father handles this temporary distancing may depend upon his motivation for parenthood, as well as his preparation for it, and upon how fully developed the couple system was before the onset of parenthood.

3. *Plateau Stage*: This stage covers the period from infancy through adolescence and can occupy fifteen to thirty years of a marital life cycle.

The infancy stage requires a great deal of physical and emotional energy. The couple system revolves around the needs of the infant, who is completely dependent upon the parents for physical and emotional nurturance. The parents' level of confidence in their ability to understand the infant's needs and to respond to those needs with ease and affection will affect their experience as parents. This is a period of constant renegotiation during which both parents must redefine their expectations and responsibilities. Boundaries with each other, with families of origin, with the world of work and community of friends need to be renegotiated. Again, how the couple system responds to these demands for renegotiation and to the physical and emotional burdens of this stage is influenced by their motivation for parenthood.

The toddler stage increases both the physical exertions and the gratifications of the parents. Parents must be constantly on the alert, protecting and supervising their toddler as he or she begins to explore and wander out of the narrow confines of infancy. Parents must begin to let go of some of their control as the toddler learns to say "no" and embarks upon the quest for his or her own autonomy. Thus, the first power struggles between parent and child emerge during this stage.

In the preschool stage, the child's verbal ability increases; thus parents can supervise and protect on a more verbal level. This is a time when the youngster's demands and high levels of physical energy result in high levels of family activity. It is a time when parents and children begin to separate and deal with the anxiety that they all feel about separation. At the same time that they begin to let go, the parents must continue to set and enforce limits.

When the children enter school, the parents have the relief of having them in school for several hours during the day, but they are also faced with the power of outside influences. Teachers become significant role models, the child's achievements and productivity are now compared to those of their peers, and the parents become vulnerable to increasing anxiety about their parenting ability. They no longer maintain complete control over their children, and their philosophy and values are subject to scrutiny by outsiders. Thus, they need to "accept rejection without deserting" (GAP 1973). If the mother has been devoting full time to the care of the child, the child's entry into school means that she must now renegotiate her use of time.

During preadolescence, the balance of power begins to shift as children begin to argue and question their parents' pronouncements and authority. Triangulations begin to be accentuated, and unresolved fears about sexuality and control begin to resurface. The child's bonding with peer groups becomes stronger, and the couple system often finds itself separated by turmoil and arguments as the child and peer group pull one parent against the other.

Stress on the couple system can become more acute during adolescence when the issues of power and control become most overt. Masters and Johnson (1970) point out that it is during this stage that sexual dysfunction between the couple often coincides with the triangulation of an adolescent and the emergence of unresolved conflicts. In struggling to achieve separation from the parents the adolescent assigns greater importance to peer relationships than to parents. Parents often find it difficult to give support and help without intruding on adolescent growth. Another issue, of course, is the parent's ability to relinquish control. Thus, interpersonal adjustments in the mother-adolescent-father relationships create acute pressures. How well a family system readjusts depends upon the individual adult development of the parents, the development of the couple system, and the history of the parent system.

4. *Disengagement Stage*: This stage lasts from late adolescence through the grandparenting stage.

When the child completes high school and goes off to college, military service, or work, the separation that occurs is more than physical. The parents must reinvest in the couple system or find some other outlet for the physical and emotional energy that they have expended on this child. It is often very difficult for parents and children to "let go" and still retain a healthy emotional tie. Battles are often manufactured to allow the disengagement to occur under the guise of angry rebellion.

The parent relationship with the child is always a psychological bond, regardless of the age of the child. The interpersonal relationship between parents and an adult child needs to be carefully and consciously renegotiated so that boundaries are respected and adult ways of relating are established. If the adult child has met the expectations of the parents, the renegotiation of the relationship is easier than if the adult child chooses a lifestyle that is incompatible with that of the parents. After the child marries, a major issue for the parents may be how they handle the inclusion of in-laws (outsiders) in the family system. After the children have left the home, the couple system is often renewed vigorously and satisfyingly. Sometimes, however, it is dissolved, having been held together by the presence of children.

Grandparenting can produce its own set of stresses and strains. The grandparents and parents may relive some of their own unresolved parent system conflicts, resulting in triangulation of the grandchildren. Grandparents often feel the need to indulge and nurture their grandchildren, and this may conflict with the parents' needs to control and determine their own style of parenting. On the other hand, grandparents who do *not* become involved with their grandchildren because of absorption in their own interests may also create conflict by failing to meet their children's expectations of them as grandparents. Cultural changes can be yet another source of conflict in the grandparenting stage. Whether they actually do create conflict depends on whether the grandparents become wiser and more mellow and tolerant of generational changes or more rigid and intolerant.

Thus, in this stage of parenting the couple must make interpersonal adjustments that involve children, grandchildren, and in-laws, as well as societal and cultural changes.

System Overview.   If, for a moment, we return to the plateau stage and think in terms of David Kantor's model of closed, open, and random types of family systems, we may find some developmental trends. During the infancy, toddler, preschool, and school-age phases, families may appear to be closer to the closed end of the continuum, with the parents assuming control for discipline, allocating resources, and determining the dimensions of time, energy, and space.

At the preadolescent stage, as children begin to question established roles and rules and the family finds that it must begin renegotiation of these areas, a more random type of family system may emerge. As children enter adolescence and adulthood, parents find that they must (willingly or not so willingly) relinquish more control, and at this time a more open type of system may emerge. Children are now "old enough" to have internalized controls and to participate in the decision-making process.

Families who are not able to change and develop usually run into difficulty and seek help somewhere during the later phases of the plateau stage. For example, the parents of fourteen-year-old Barry Pepper presented themselves and Barry for counseling with the complaint that Barry was "uncontrollable," "untrustworthy," and "on the verge of getting into serious trouble." His parents described him as being a "model child" until entering high school earlier that year. The only boy, the oldest of three children, Barry had been obedient, helped around the house, never talked back, and always made his family his top priority. Suddenly, a few months ago, he began refusing to go to church with them, neglecting his chores, and trying in every way to avoid being with his family while spending increasing amounts of time with his friends. Mr. and Mrs. Pepper responded to Barry's behavior by increasing their commands and demands, which were met either with outright refusal or sullen compliance. Barry was very angry and Mr. and Mrs. Pepper genuinely confused.

It quickly became apparent that Barry resented the kinds of chores that were demanded of him and the way in which they were demanded. He felt that his parents were treating him inappropriately for his age and that he was not given enough time for himself and his friends. His acting out was a way of expressing his resentment. Mr. and Mrs. Pepper were so accustomed to giving their orders autocratically and expecting them to be followed automatically that it had never occurred to them that this process needed adjusting as their son grew older. They had become locked into a power struggle in which no matter what position they took or what request they made, Barry opposed it. Furthermore, they did not have an appropriate concept of communication patterns and tasks for a fourteen-year-old boy.

Several sessions were devoted to teaching negotiation and conflict-resolution skills so that this family could learn to relate to each other without combat, to negotiate their conflicts rather than be frozen in polarities. At the same time, the parents were educated about the developmental stage of adolescence and its inherent tasks and problems and helped to look at their own individual and marital developmental stages with their concomitant expectations and needs. Thus, the goals of therapy were to help create a space wherein Barry could begin to differentiate and the parents could aid, rather than hinder, this differentiation.

Thus, the issues and tasks of parenthood depend upon the developmental stage of the parent system. Let us now proceed to our study of the practice and process of working with the parent system.

Working with the Parent System

Because the issues confronting the parent system differ according to the developmental stage of parenting, we will first discuss work with the parents of younger children and then consider work with the parents of adolescents. In each discussion, we will focus on the issues, intervention approaches, and special considerations for the family therapist.

Issues in Parent Systems with Younger Children

As we mentioned before, many writers believe that having children can cause a severe crisis in the marital system and that many marital systems do not survive this crisis. Certainly, the addition of children to the family system presents problems. We have already considered some of these, namely, the planning and distribution of responsibilities and the changes in interactions that the birth of a child entails. Perhaps we should emphasize that women, in particular, have felt the need to make adjustments because of the societal expectation that mothers assume more of the parenthood burdens.

As LeMasters (1978) points out, women who become mothers frequently have to give up their occupations or make drastic occupational adjustments, and many women feel completely unprepared to assume the role of mother. Fathers also feel unprepared and often experience new economic pressures because of increased expenses and their wives' retirements or reductions in salary. New fathers also often claim that their wives' sexual desire and response have decreased and that their fatigue and irritability have increased. The child also interferes with the couple's social life and other activities that they enjoyed previously. Whatever the stress, the dyad is now a triad, and this forces a reorganization of life patterns and styles. Another factor to consider is that the birth of a child seems to constitute a rite of passage: the couple are now, for better or worse, accepted as full-fledged members of adult society.

When children are referred for help, the problem usually concerns their lack of achievement or their interactive behavior at home or at school. Basically, the child is not meeting the expectations of some significant adult—a parent, teacher, or counselor. Somehow the child is deviating from the norms of a particular situation. It is essential that the professional helper be able to differentiate developmental problems from pathological problems.

Interventions with Families of Younger Children

All the interventions that we will explore are based on the premise that it is not desirable to view a child's problem outside the context of the child's interactions within the family and other networks. Therefore, these interventions share the ideology that change can be best realized and maintained if modification of the beliefs, attitudes, and behaviors of significant persons or institutions occurs simultaneously with modification of the beliefs, attitudes, and behaviors of the so-called problem child.

This does not mean, however, that individual child therapy can never be effective. Taking into consideration the age of the child, the conditions of the referral, and the willingness of the family to own the problem as a family problem, the family worker must decide how best to gain access into the family or school system. This access might be through individual work with the child, conjoint family therapy, work with the parents alone, or consultation with school personnel. If the orientation and focus of treatment is on the parent system, the unit of treatment is not critical.

We emphasize this point because we strongly believe that it is possible to change the parent system even in individual child therapy. Montalvo and Haley (1973) defend the practice of individual child therapy by pointing out that spontaneous change can occur as a result of the parents' concern about the child's confidential interviews with an outsider, the therapist. This concern can create a healthy competition between the parents and the therapist. For example, the more permissive the child therapist is in the office, the more the child will act out at home, and the more the parents will be provoked into providing discipline at home. The consultations that the child therapist has with the parents as advisor or child-guidance expert can be very effective in producing change. In addition, the therapist can intervene in the marital system by replacing the father as the person to whom the mother talks about the children.

Thus, the child therapist can effect change in the parent system through work with the child and consultation with the parents. This change probably occurs more slowly and is more serendipitous than it would be if the therapist were able to intervene more directly in the parent system. However, while less efficient than family therapy, it is more useful than individual therapy with the child without any access whatsoever to the parent system.

The major approaches to intervention with parent systems of younger children are: (1) social learning, including the operant-conditioning and Adlerian approaches; (2) client-centered approaches, including parent effectiveness training and experiential approaches; and (3) the communication and structural approaches based on systems theory. Let us see how these approaches apply to the parent system with younger children.

Social Learning Approaches.   The term *social learning* is used loosely to refer to the interactional modification between the client and the client's networks that can effect behavioral and attitudinal change. Social learning techniques can be useful in working with family systems in which some distance or differentiation between parent and child is a goal of therapy. These techniques tend to defuse a tense emotional system by their focus on concrete behaviors. Before turning our attention to operant conditioning, let us first consider the Adlerian approach to working with children and their families.

1. *Adlerian Approach*: In chapter 2 we noted that Alfred Adler was the first of the psychoanalytic pioneers to focus on the social milieu of the patient and the drive for power (as opposed to the sex drive) as the basic motivator of human behavior. Adler coined the term *inferiority complex*. The concept of an inferiority complex led to the belief that a misbehaving child is a discouraged child. All misbehavior, as Adlerians see it, is the result of a child's mistaken assumption about the way to find a place and gain status. The Adlerians postulate four mistaken goals that a child's misbehavior might have:

1. *Attention*: Rewards include positive as well as negative responses. The child who misbehaves and is punished is being rewarded by attention.
2. *Power*: The child wants to be boss. The child who misbehaves for this reason receives payoffs when someone engages in a power struggle or pities or otherwise reinforces the power struggle.
3. *Power with revenge*: The child misbehaves to get even. The payoffs include a parent's expression of guilt or an escalation of conflict.
4. *Inadequacy*: The child misbehaves in order to appear disabled. The rewards include overprotection and a decrease in demands.

Regardless of which of the four goals a child is pursuing, the child's major purpose is to create certain attitudes, to obtain certain responses from parents or teachers that will reward and reinforce the child's misbehavior. When this behavior is reinforced, when the child is allowed to get away with misbehavior at home and in school, the child learns an inappropriate way of dealing with the outside world.

The Adlerians teach parents to block the child's misguided efforts, while simultaneously encouraging cooperation, responsible behavior, and a healthy respect for order and the rights of individuals. For example, Johnny continually engages his mother in debates over minor issues. Mother always gets trapped in the debate and ends up feeling irritated and annoyed. When Mother learns to recognize that the purpose of Johnny's strategies is to gain attention, she is able to ignore him when he begins to "debate" with her and to leave the room, refusing to participate in the debate. She also learns to schedule positive time with Johnny when he is behaving constructively, so that she can meet his need for attention and at the same time teach him how to get attention by behaving constructively, rather than destructively. This helps create some appropriate emotional distance and weakens the enmeshment of Mother and Johnny.

The major tool that Adlerians teach parents and teachers is *encouragement*, allowing the child to feel that he or she can do it. They believe that the child should be provided with many opportunities with reasonable standards to try responsible behavior and that adults should express appreciation for the child's effort.

The disciplinary technique advocated by Adlerians is the use of *natural* and *logical consequences*. They define *natural* consequences as those that follow automatically from the child's behavior without any type of intervention. If a child doesn't put his dirty clothes in the laundry hamper, they don't get washed. If a child gets up late, he or she is late to school. If a child is not ready when the parents leave for the movies, he or she doesn't go. *Logical* consequences are those arranged by the parents when suitable natural consequences either will not occur or would be dangerous. For example, if a child continuously leaves a bike outside in the rain, he or she will have to clean off the rust or pay the bicycle shop to fix it, rather than the parent's doing those things for the child.

The Adlerians advocate the use of *family councils,* where family members come together on a regularly scheduled basis to discuss concerns and issues. The model is that of a democracy in which each person has a say and each individual respects the rights of others and in turn receives respect. In this way, the family members take responsibility for reorienting and reeducating themselves as they apply the Adlerian techniques. The effectiveness of these techniques depends upon a calm, sincere emotional relationship between parents and children, one in which the parents apply the techniques without sarcasm, ridicule, humiliation, or vengefulness. Whenever possible, children are urged to participate in determining logical consequences. The goal for the Adlerian family counselor is to teach the family to use these techniques for evaluating and dealing with themselves and others, to help the clients to develop self-esteem and appropriate social interest. When this goal is achieved, the family system becomes a more open system with a more democratic distribution of power and influence.

2. *Operant Conditioning:* The principles of reinforcement and contingency contracting that we described in chapter 6 in reference to couple systems apply particularly well to parent systems with younger children. Their applicability is a result of the parents' ability to control environmental contingencies and to learn to manage effective reward systems. Parents are taught to define behaviors precisely and then are taught the behavioral principles of learning. The definition of a problem in behavioral terms is most difficult for parents; a typical complaint is that a child is "always fresh." When that complaint is broken down and analyzed behaviorally, it may turn out that the child said no once in two weeks. After defining the problem behaviorally, the parents are asked to record the frequency of the problem behavior and to identify the antecedent and consequent conditions. What happens typically before this behavior occurs and what happens when it does occur? Often, merely by taking the time and effort to record the frequency and intensity of Johnny's temper tantrums, Mom is too busy to attend to it, thereby negatively reinforcing it. Behavior that is ignored tends to be extinguished. The behaviorally oriented therapist uses family sessions to identify behaviors and to help parents respond to these behaviors, rather than to their attitudes about the behaviors.

Parents are taught to identify reinforcements within their family system, to focus on the positive rather than the negative (by telling child what to do, rather than what not to do), to shape behavior by rewarding successive approximations of the desired behavior, and to practice contingency contracting. The philosophy is that rewards and punishments operate implicitly in any system and that when they are made explicit, the child has the choice of determining the outcomes.

The behaviorally oriented therapist helps teach the parents these learning principles and helps them to design and implement programs and to evaluate the outcomes. Often, when symptomatic behavior is relieved, other issues within the family system can be addressed. Remember that operant conditioning has the attribute of circular feedback, that when the child's behavior improves, the parent feels better about the child and, in turn, the child feels better about the parent.

Some families are taught to establish token economies, where all the duties and responsibilities are charted and each member receives points for fulfilling these duties and responsibilities. These points are later translated into some type of privilege, such as a spending allowance. Needless to say, the understanding and application of systematic reinforcement and punishment, when the conditions are explicitly clear, improves the functioning of any organizational system.

Let us consider an example of the utilization of operant conditioning. Mr. and Mrs. Bradford came for counseling because of their distress over their eight-year-old son's academic difficulties, the result of his refusal to do his homework. In talking to the parents, it became clear that there was no systematic application of discipline at home, that, in fact, the Bradford home had what Kantor would call a random style. Eric came home from school every day, helped himself to a snack, and then watched television until dinner. After dinner, he was allowed to watch television until bedtime. He always claimed that he had done his homework, and because Mrs. Bradford did not want to put any pressure on him, she allowed him to do what he wished. The Bradfords were shocked when informed that Eric was falling behind in school, was acting disruptively in the classroom, and was in danger of repeating the third grade. The Bradfords were afraid that Eric would not like them if they said "no" to him, and they were careful to let him do what he pleased so that he could develop his "creativity."

Since homework was the primary presenting issue, a contract between Eric, his teacher, and his parents was worked out. It was agreed that Eric could automatically watch two hours of television per day. To obtain a third hour, he had to bring home a card from his teacher that he had handed in satisfactory homework assignments on that day. After this contract was successfully completed, the Bradfords arranged another contract that allowed Eric the privilege of taking a walk alone with his father (the more noninvolved parent) after dinner every day that his card from his teacher reported positive interactions with other students. Not only did Eric's school behavior (both academic and social) improve, but at the same time Mr. and Mrs. Bradford also learned some effective techniques of behavioral management at home.

Most families are surprised to learn that negative reinforcement systems have been maintaining problem behaviors. Exposure to these concepts and principles provides parents with tools for managing behavior within their family systems without getting sidetracked by emotional hassles.

Client-centered Approaches.   These approaches include the teaching of communication skills and experiential approaches. Thomas Gordon's Parent Effectiveness Training program (PET) borrows the techniques of responsive listening from Carl Rogers, Robert Carkhuff, and Alan Ivey and adds a no-lose problem-solving method which has been utilized by family workers. These approaches seem to help reduce distance in family systems, bringing parent and child closer together and clarifying communication patterns.

Used either in parent education groups or family therapy sessions, the PET method rejects the use of power in the no-lose method of conflict resolution. The first step is the definition of the problem and determination of whose problem it is. This is done by assessing whether the problem behavior is acceptable to the parent. If it is, then either the child "owns" the problem or there is no problem. If it is not, the parent "owns" the problem. The person who owns the problem is the one who feels upset about it, the one whose needs are being frustrated. For example, if a child comes to the table for dinner with dirty hands, it is the parent who is upset and concerned about it, not the child. Therefore, it is the parent's problem.

Gordon (1970) teaches three basic techniques:

1. *Active Listening.* With this technique, the parent learns to send a type of message that helps the child understand, accept, and deal with his or her feelings. For example, if a child comes home from school and says that his teacher was mean to him, the parent would decode that message to identify the underlying feeling and would respond, "You *feel* angry at Ms. Smith today *because* she made you stay after school *when* other children who were misbehaving didn't have to stay." This message keeps the door for communication open so that both parent and child can explore the problem. The effectiveness of active listening depends on the absence of judging, moralizing, lecturing,

questioning, ridiculing, and other types of communicative behavior that tend to increase defensiveness and close doors to further exploration.

2. *Sending "I-messages."* This technique teaches the parent how to express his or her frustrations without giving the child "you're-not-OK" messages. When a father comes home tired from the office and finds his newspaper strewn all over the living room and the children playing noisily around his chair, he can say, "Hey, kids, I'm really wiped out right now and I need some time to relax and unwind. How about letting me have my chair and newspaper for a while and then you can come back and play in here after dinner?" That message is vastly different from telling children how inconsiderate and messy they are. When the parent has just cleaned the kitchen floor and Johnny tracks mud through it, the parent can say, "I'm so frustrated. . . . I just finished cleaning the floor and now it is all messed up again."

3. *No-lose method of problem solving.* There are six steps to this method: identifying and defining the conflict; generating possible alternative solutions (brainstorming); evaluating alternative solutions (screening out those unacceptable to either party); deciding on the best acceptable solution; working out ways of implementing the solution; and following up to evaluate how it worked.

The first two techniques require extensive skill training. The speaker needs to learn to identify feelings precisely and to express them assertively. One unlearns communicative behaviors, such as criticism, judging, moralizing, and questioning, that cause defensiveness and close the doors to communication. The purpose of these techniques is to define the problem accurately and to foster self-esteem.

Often, these two communication techniques solve the problem. For example, if Mother says to Danny, "I really get sick when I have to eat dinner with someone with such dirty hands," the chances are that if they have a good relationship, Danny will respond with, "I'm sorry, I forgot. I'll go wash my hands now." But let us assume that there is some kind of power struggle going on between Mother and Danny. Then the no-lose problem solving method can be used.

Using that method, Mother may say to Danny, "What can we do about it? Let's consider all the possibilities." Together, they list different ways that the problem might be solved. They may ask anyone at the table to participate by offering suggestions. The list of possible solutions might include eating dinner with dirty hands, not eating dinner, eating dinner after the family does, eating dinner in a separate place, washing hands, wearing gloves, and so forth. Mother and Danny then calmly decide which of these alternatives they can both live with, and when and how they will implement it. They then act on their decision. If neither of them can find a solution that satisfies both of them, they have to try again. Neither is allowed to back down or impose his or her solution on the other.

Thus, PET teaches negotiation and conflict-resolution skills without the use of power. An important part of this method is the focus on problem definition before generating solutions. Family systems often focus on solutions before clarifying the nature of the problem that requires solution, with the result that the solutions themselves give rise to arguments. For example, Mrs. Stryker complained about her fourteen-year-old daughter's "lack of responsibility." According to the mother, Betsy was irresponsible because she telephoned her piano teacher to tell him that she was not going to continue her piano lessons, rather than going to the lesson and telling him in person that this would be the last lesson. This particular issue generated a lot of anger and conflict between parent and child. In discussing the issue, the therapist helped the parent to reframe the situation, to see that the real problem was the daughter's taking responsibility for terminating the lessons (rather than the mother doing so), not the mother's disapproval of the particular solution that the daughter chose. The mother was able to recognize that she usually did not allow Betsy to generate her own solutions, that she expected Betsy to adopt parental solutions, and that this was where their conflict lay.

Other client-centered approaches include play therapy and Rogerian and other existential approaches. The *existential* approaches focus on the current interactions of parents and children to heighten the family's awareness of their patterns of interaction. The major goal is to develop both emotional and intellectual awareness of family interactions.

By modeling and teaching responsive listening and encouraging the family members to feel and understand their interactions in family therapy sessions, the therapist helps them experience new feelings and patterns of interaction that influence their behaviors outside of the therapy sessions. They learn new ways of communicating and achieve new heights of emotional understanding and expression. This learning, which increases the family's ability to relate and function, is irreversible.

In the existential approach, the therapist as a person is a potent model for the family. However, it is an indirective type of modeling in that the existential counselor does not coach the parents on parent management or problem solving, but helps family members to experience the here-and-now of what is going on in the family. It is a skills-oriented communicational approach.

Communication and Structural Approaches. The way that Jackson, Satir, and Haley work with the parent system is similar to the way they work with other family subsystems. They focus on the digital and analogic levels of communication to model and teach all the family members to articulate their expectations and rules, to be clear about power struggles and role conflicts. To help clients increase their differentiation, Satir concentrates on teaching them how to send "I-messages."

In helping the family to set rules and controls, Jackson, Satir, and Haley serve as advisors and "traffic cops" (Safer 1966). They teach family members to express both positive and negative emotions and point out inconsistencies between verbal perceptions and expectations and behaviors. Basically, they see the therapist's role as modeling their interpretation of parental rules, encouraging direct verbal and nonverbal expressions of feeling, and educating parents about effective discipline and areas of responsibility. In addition to using operant conditioning techniques, they interrupt repetitive, unrewarding parent-child conflict patterns, support the parents in more adequately structuring and enforcing major rules at home, encourage self-reliant social behavior by the child, and increase positive socialization between negatively involved parents and youngsters.

Haley, more than Satir, uses behavioral techniques, in addition to paradoxical interventions, to teach effective problem solving and parent management. He advocates coaching parents in effective home discipline and spelling out the specific steps the parent must take to win the power struggle with the child and/or modify the structure of the family relationships.

Whereas the communication theorists assess the family system by means of the communication patterns and teach more effective communications to all family members, the structural therapists focus on change through reorganizing coalitions and renegotiating boundaries. They may teach family members new roles in order to form new coalitions and break up dysfunctional coalitions.

The structuralists find that many of the presenting problems are resolved as new boundaries are formed. The types of techniques they use include the assignment of structured family interactional tasks, such as (1) having each member of the family create a living, spatial, relational tableau of the family (a family sculpture), which reveals family relationships in terms of space, attitudes, alliances, and underlying feelings; (2) asking a family to discuss the meaning of a particular proverb and then teach it to the children, which reveals family styles and coalitions (Watzlawick 1966); (3) asking family members to work out a menu with their favorite foods or come to some agreement on how to spend ten dollars (Minuchin et al. 1967); (4) having a family paint a family portrait together; (5) asking the family to play together; and (6) asking each member to select a puppet and make up a story.

These techniques enable the therapist to map out the structure of the family and then assign tasks and roles that will change the existing tableau, resulting in a structural systems change. For example, after all members of the family have had the opportunity to sculpt the family as they currently experience it, the therapist can then ask them to sculpt it as they would like it to be. After they have processed and discussed their perceptions and feelings about each sculpture, the therapist can help them decide what changes they want to make and how they can accomplish those changes.

Another tactic of structural therapists is the use of different subsystems as consultants. For example, the structural therapist may meet with the sibling system alone and coach that system on how to impact on the parent system. In such a way, members of the sibling system can learn to form a coalition in dealing with the parents, can rebalance the power, can mediate for each other, and can translate the parents' behavior for each other. Or the structural therapist may choose to deal with only parts of a system—for example, meeting with a noninvolved parent and the problem child and omitting the over-involved parent in order to establish a necessary link between the child and the parent who is not involved.

If family interactions include a "go-between" process (Zuk 1966), the therapist can use that process to help shift power relations. For example, in a family with whom one of us was recently working, the father and daughter engaged in constant arguing. Every time they did this, the mother became upset and interfered, claiming that she could not stand the arguing and had to protect her daughter from her "critical" husband. In this way, the mother set herself up as a benevolent go-between and became a principal in the conflict. After we pointed out to the mother that she was really interfering in the only relationship that existed between the father and daughter, the mother was encouraged to go and talk to her other daughter every time the father and daughter began to fight. Eventually, the father and daughter learned to relate to each other without arguing. In addition, mother established a differ-ent relationship with her other daughter. For as long as mother was "reinforcing" the father-daughter argument by her benevolent media-tion, the arguments persisted. Once that reinforcement was removed, the behaviors changed.

Issues in Parent Systems with Adolescents

Obviously, the issues of adolescence differ from those of childhood. The rapid social, physical, psychological, and emotional changes of adolescents are manifested in increased uncontrolled emotionalism, self-consciousness, and egocentrism, or narcissism. These manifestations can place such stress on the entire family system that it is difficult for the needs of the adolescent to be accommodated within the system.

Parents are often confused and threatened when their children enter adolescence. The child must deal with his or her burgeoning sexuality, which may cause parents' unresolved fears to resurface. Adolescents appear to be adults one moment and infants the next. Reason and emotion, rationality and irrationality are constantly juxtaposed. The parents' confusion manifests itself in an unclear and inconsistent setting of limits, in withdrawal of physical affection, in confusing, unclear expectations and demands.

Adolescent problems are particularly apt to be manifested in families with unresolved conflicts. Typical manifestations of adolescent problems include drug or alcohol abuse, destructive sexual acting out, alienation, academic failure, career planning failure, some form of delinquency, cognitive disorders, and psychosomatic complaints.

The issues of separation, independence, and freedom from restraint become more critical as the child passes through adolescence. Many families need to be taught how to facilitate the individuation and separation of the adolescent and to alter expectations and demands that are no longer appropriate. Paradoxically, the adolescent's problem usually serves to enmesh him or her in the family, rather than to separate. For example, a family who is concerned about an adolescent's use of drugs is more likely to sniff around and pry in order to monitor the behavior than to allow the adolescent freedom to come and go without a barrage of questions and demands.

Control and power are major concerns of families of adolescents. Whereas explicit control that demands compliance may work as an influence system with younger children, it is likely to fail with adolescents, who are more able to assert their developmental need for independence. Adolescents can obtain approval from their peer group, can work to obtain financial resources, and are usually "too big and strong to spank." The typical six-year-old child lives primarily in two systems: the family and the first grade classroom. His or her "problem" is usually manifest in, has meaning for, and is treated within one or both of those contexts. The typical sixteen-year-old, on the other hand, may (with the rate of current divorces and remarriages) have two family systems, seven different school classes composed of different class-mates, a school lunch peer group, a neighborhood peer group, and so on, adding up to ten or more different contexts in which "problem" behavior may have its etiology and sustaining reinforcers.

Their inability to control all the resources can be very frightening for parents who have not encouraged their children to internalize influence processes—that is, to establish *implicit* control by internalizing parental values. The adolescent who has established inner regulatory controls can now begin to practice self-discipline.

It is at the time of adolescence that the family experiences the most violent clash of values and attitudes. It is difficult for many parents to recognize that they no longer have the power to demand what they want from their children, that their children are separate individuals. Many parents feel cheated if their expectations have not been met and, in addition to blaming the youngster, they blame the schools and other institutions of society.

Interventions with Families of Adolescents

Family therapy involving adolescents differs from therapy with families of younger children in that the issues of conflict resolution and sharing require greater active participation of the adolescents. Adolescents are more likely to be included in the therapy sessions, and the language and strategies of the therapist are likely to be more adult-oriented. In addition, school and peer systems may be included in the therapy; they are certainly viewed as significant resources.

The objective of work with families of adolescents is to improve the family functioning so that the adolescent can make a smooth transition into adulthood and the parents can begin learning how to disengage from the plateau stage of parenting. Obviously, this objective must take into consideration the parents' own stages of adult development —where they are occupationally, what their current relationships and responsibilities to their own parents are, how they intend to disengage from active parenting, and what they intend to do with the time and energy that until now has been committed to parenting. Much attention is focused on the individuation of the family members, on verbal problem solving, and on reequilibration of the family system.

The first major task of the therapist, regardless of his or her theoretical orientation, is to determine whether the adolescent's prob-lem is a family problem. Consider the following case:

Mr. and Mrs. Trent and their daughter Maureen, aged fifteen, came to therapy at the suggestion of Maureen's school psychologist. Maureen had been referred to the school psychologist by her teachers, who were concerned about her lack of friends, her inability to relate to classmates or teachers, and her reluctance to take risks in any of her academic work. Maureen had always been a superior student, and her IQ tests placed her in the superior range. She was to enter a large metropolitan high school in the fall, and her teachers were concerned about how she would make the social and academic adjustment.

Mr. and Mrs. Trent reluctantly attended the first session, not understanding why they should be there since Maureen was the problem, the one who needed "to be fixed." During this first session, the therapist observed that Mrs. Trent sat between father and daughter and did most of the talking to and for them and that communication among the three was controlled and sparse. Mrs. Trent related that Maureen had never had friends, that she had been scapegoated throughout elementary school, and that the family had even moved to another community when Maureen was in sixth grade so that "she could begin all over again." The parents expressed concern and dismay. Their older two children were grown, and they had focused all their energies on Maureen, giving her every conceivable type of specialized lessons and help. Mrs. Trent picked her up at school daily so she wouldn't have to carry heavy books. At home she and Maureen watched television together for six to eight hours each day. Maureen had no interests, was constantly bored, and had no understanding whatsoever of why she was brought to therapy, what the problem was, or how her teachers could be upset about her.

As it began to emerge that Maureen was the focus of the marital interaction, the therapist perceived that Maureen's depression was an intensification of the depression of the entire family system. It took several sessions before the family could understand this and own the problem as a family problem. Therapy with Maureen individually was not successful, as she was resistant and did not perceive any problem. However, when the whole family became engaged in therapy and accepted Maureen's issues as symptoms of family problems, it was possible to effect some changes.

It is important to note that it may take a long while to help the members of the total family system understand the dynamics of a family problem. Many parents bring children or adolescents for therapy with the attitude that the therapist should "fix" them. We believe that in such cases, it is helpful to form an alliance with the offspring and to intervene with the parents however and whenever feasible, always in a supportive, constructive manner. By coaching parents and prescribing interventions, one is usually able to effect some systems change. If, on the other hand, the therapist criticizes the parents and blames them for the youngster's problem, the parents are likely to take their youngster and never return, and the opportunity for change is lost.

The approaches to working with adolescents and their families are similar to those used in working with younger children and their families—namely, approaches based on social learning theory, client-centered approaches, and communication and structural approaches based on systems theory.

Social Learning Approaches.   It is important that adolescents take active part in designing contingency contracts, in learning to provide covert reinforcement, and in arranging logical consequences. Teenagers like to manage their own contracts and have proven to be expert monitors. The more responsibility given to the teenager for behavioral change, the more successful the strategy is likely to be. This type of responsibility not only helps the teenager to act more autonomously within the family system, but also promotes the development of internalized controls. The focus of treatment can be on modifying the family context of the adolescent's behavior. When all family members learn to exchange and administer positive reinforcement, parental behavior changes, as does the behavior of the adolescent.

The techniques of covert sensitization and covert reinforcement can be useful with teenagers. If weight control is the goal for behavioral change, covert sensitization can be used to teach a teenager to imagine clearly and in detail feeling nauseous every time he or she makes a move to snack between meals. As the snacking decreases, there is likely to be weight loss; since weight loss bolsters the adolescent's self-esteem, it is reinforcing in itself. In covert reinforcement, the teenager manages and controls a behavioral contract without involving anyone else, and the technique itself provides for reinforcement. For example, when teenagers manage their own contracts to lose weight by assuming responsibility for preparing their own meals, the autonomy that they express in doing so provides them with meaningful reinforcement. Because the contract involves no one but the teenager, it also eliminates the possibility of power struggles and game playing with parents or siblings. With these techniques, the other family members are encouraged to allow the teenager to own the problem and to remain disengaged and uninvolved with the teenager's attempts at managing it.

Client-centered Approaches. The PET approach would recommend that parents and adolescents not engage in power struggles and that parents avoid such struggles by letting adolescents handle their own problems. This approach may cause some value conflicts. Parents who object strongly to certain adolescent behaviors may find that impasses are unavoidable. If approaches similar to the PET no-lose method of problem solving have not been used during childhood, adolescence is a hard time to begin. Patterns and resistances have already formed, and adolescents are more likely to be influenced by models and systems other than their own family system, particularly if previous conflicts have not been resolved. In other words, the PET approach is only likely to be effective with adolescents if they have been encouraged to internalize their own inner controls and if the parents are ready and able to relinquish control.

Kempler (1968) outlines a gestalt, experiential procedure involving the therapist as a total person who serves to catalyze negotiation among family members. The therapist becomes a member of the family system and behaves spontaneously, expressing his or her gut reactions. In short, the therapist does not act as a powerful expert, does not use techniques, does not hide behind a title, but instead brings his or her total personality and life experiences to family encounters. The therapist's uniqueness in the family system and willingness to engage fully with the family members are the most valuable therapeutic techniques. Gestalt therapists use role playing, videotape recorders, and other strategies to help family members communicate more accurately, to understand each other, and to move toward an increased openness and a greater sharing of feedback with one another. This type of active intervention can clear up distorted communications and improve troubled relationships. The therapist as a person becomes a power-ful model for the adolescent and other family members. This type of therapy has proven popular, as well as effective, with families of adolescents.

Communication and Structural Approaches. Both communication therapists and structural therapists attempt to recalibrate the family system by changing rigidities, improving communications, and promot-ing differentiation. Like the other approaches that we have described, these approaches focus on goal-oriented, problem-solving interven-tions. The only difference between their treatment of adolescents and their treatment of younger children is that their interventions with adolescents are more sophisticated and require more input from the adolescent. Thus, the adolescent is helped to identify double binds and to develop higher self-esteem, a clearer sense of identity, social responsibility, and coping and mastery skills.

Parent Education

When working with the parent system, the family worker is as much a teacher and educator as an agent of change. Most parents do not know much about child and adolescent development and are confused by the expectations and demands placed upon them, as well as by their own needs.

As a teacher, the family worker can correct faulty ideas and perceptions by providing parents with pertinent reading material so that they can educate themselves about constructive alternatives. In addition, the family worker can recommend parent groups, in which parents can develop networks for support and the exchange of ideas. Such groups are helpful in enabling parents to modify their perspectives about problems and issues.

It is often necessary to help parents work through some unfinished business from their own childhoods. For example, a mother who feels that too much household work was demanded from her when she was a child may react by not demanding any household work from her child. At the same time, she may resent the burdens of all the household responsibilities and may be concerned about her daughter's "irresponsibility." If this parent learns to understand the connection between her past and current feelings and beliefs, she will be able to respond, rather than react.

Parents are commonly concerned about problems that are developmental and that will take care of themselves with time. If made too much of, however, these problems can generate other, more serious problems. For example, Mrs. King continuously engaged in a power struggle with her four-year-old child at dinner time. Tim could not sit quietly for the forty-five minutes it took the Kings to dine, and dinner time always ended unhappily. Mrs. King was surprised when the therapist suggested that she ask ten mothers whom she knew how long each of them felt a child could be expected to sit quietly. Her friends' responses, which ranged from eight to fourteen minutes, helped Mrs. King to readjust her expectations and to smooth troubled dinner times.

Family workers need to be aware of current community resources for parent education groups and familiar with appropriate reading materials. Parent education is a powerful adjunct to family therapy and should be utilized as much as possible.

Role of the Therapist

In working with parent systems, counselors and therapists must know how to assess underlying issues and problems, the roles and interactions of the various family members, and the rules of the family system. This can be done by observing interaction, structuring inter-action, gathering information, interpreting and confronting the behav-iors that are observed, joining coalitions, and providing different types of support.

Thus, the therapist is an observer, an interactor, a teacher, a model, and a mediator, regardless of his or her particular theoretical orientation. To work effectively with parent systems, the therapist has to have worked through feelings about his or her own parents. If this has not occurred, the therapist is likely to take sides, to judge, and to project some of his or her own issues on to the family.

For example, several years ago a supervisee reported having difficulty with a family he was treating. He felt that he was at an impasse because he identified with the son and could not get past his angry feelings at the father. The supervisor requested that the supervisee diagram what had occurred at the last session. Figure 7–1 shows his diagram. When the supervisee had finished the diagram, he looked at it and realized that he had become the "son" and was feeling anger toward his own father. In subsequent sessions, he moved his seat behind the father's (to help restructure the system and to empathize with the father) and actively coached the father on effective communications and reinforcements. Once over that hurdle, the supervisee felt differently about the family and was able to move on with treatment.

The therapist's values and belief system about children and child rearing are important. They can be just as faulty as the parents' and require constant reassessment and clarification. If therapists have not been able to differentiate themselves from their own families of origin, they may have difficulty in helping their clients to differentiate and to accept the other members of their family systems.

Needless to say, the therapist's experience as a child, motivation for having children, and experience as a parent will impact on that therapist's functioning as a family worker. Students always ask whether a counselor or therapist must be a parent in order to be able to work effectively with parent systems. While there are no solid answers to questions like this, we believe that the experience of marriage and

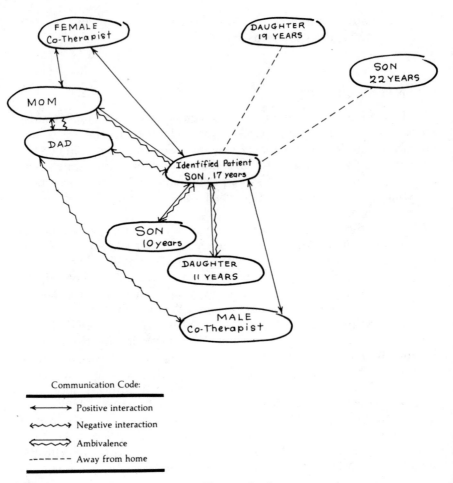

Figure 7–1   *Diagram of Family Therapy Session*

parenthood not only gives credibility to the family worker, but also adds a necessary dimension to his or her understanding of the issues operating within family systems.

Summary

In this chapter, we focused on the parent system, on mother and/or father as they interact with offspring.

As we considered parental attitudes, we noted that the social and emotional well-being of children has only become an important priority of parents in the past century. This priority has resulted in confusion about appropriate modes of parenting. In this century, we have seen the development of two major parenting models: the traditional-restrictive and the rational-permissive. Currently, there appears to be an attempt to integrate these two models, rather than a rigid adherence to either one.

We noted the impact of cultural changes on attitudes toward parenting, on the reasons that people have children, and on their expectations about parenthood. It is too early to assess the long-range effects of voluntary parenthood or voluntary childlessness in our society, but we do know that either choice has a strong impact on the marital system.

When we delineated the stages of parenthood, we were able to consider the different stresses and issues of each stage. When working with parents, it is impossible to ignore the interfacing of each parent's individual development, the stage of the couple system, and the stage of parenthood, as well as the motivation for parenthood. If there is conflict or incongruence between the needs and/or developmental tasks of these different spheres, the result may be dysfunction within the parent system. Helping parents with difficult transitions in their development as individuals or as a couple can, in turn, benefit their functioning as parents.

In discussing work with the parent systems of younger children and adolescents, we considered three major approaches: those based on social learning theory; those based on general systems theory; and client-centered approaches. We have found that a simultaneous focus on the system functions and on improving parent management is very effective in work with parent systems. It is important to remember that one can view and assess the family system from the communication and/or structural viewpoint and yet incorporate strategies from the social learning and client-centered approaches. These strategies can in fact help to achieve system goals. Social learning approaches, for example, often help family members to achieve differentiation and distance from each other within the system. Similarly, client-centered approaches can clarify communications and help family members to relate more honestly and openly.

Because of our belief in the value of parent education and because we are aware that parenting is one major life function for which there is no really adequate preparation, we advocate the use of parent education models as an adjunct to family work. It is impossible for the family worker to separate the roles of teacher, model, and systems interventionist.

In chapter 7 in the manual we have provided some lists of readings for parents and children that you may find very valuable in your work with parent systems. These lists include a bibliography of children's books, each with one annotation for parents and another for children. In that chapter you will also find some exercises in basic parent-training strategies. While familiarizing you with those strategies, the exercises will also increase your understanding of the parenting you yourself received and will help you clarify your attitudes and feelings about parenthood.

We have stressed the normal, developmental issues of parenting in this chapter. In the next chapter we will look at varieties of family experiences, including the experience of single parenthood.

References

Ackerman, N. 1962. "Adolescent Problems: A Symptom of Family Disorder." *Family Process* 1:213.

Fein, R.A. 1976. "Men's Entrance to Parenthood." *Family Coordinator* 25 (4):341–48.

Gesell, A., and F. Ilg. 1943. *Infant and Child in the Culture of Today*. New York: Harper & Row.

Gordon, T. 1970. *Parent Effectiveness Training*. New York: Wyden.

Group for the Advancement of Psychiatry (GAP). 1973. *The Joys and Sorrows of Parenthood*, 8, no. 84. New York: Science House.

Kempler, W. 1968. "Experiential Psychotherapy with Families." *Family Process* 7 (1):88–100.

LeMasters, E.E. 1970. *Parents in Modern Amercia*, rev. ed. Homewood, Ill.: Dorsey Press.

———. 1978. "Parenthood as Crises." In J. De Burger, ed., *Marriage Today*. New York: Wiley.

Masters, W., and V. Johnson. 1970. *Human Sexual Inadequacy*. Boston: Little, Brown.

Minuchin, S., et al. 1967. *Families of the Slums*. New York: Basic Books.

Montalvo, B., and J. Haley. 1973. "In Defense of Child Therapy." *Family Process* 12 (3):227–45.

Moriarty, J. 1970. "The Psychology of Human Reproduction." *Science News* 1:148–49.

Pohlman, E.H. 1969. *Psychology of Birth Planning.* Cambridge, Mass.: Schenkman.

Safer, S. 1966. "Family Therapy for Children with Behavior Disorders." *Family Process* (2):243–56.

Spock, B. 1963. *Baby and Child Care,* Revised Cardinal Giant Edition. New York: Pocket Books.

Watzlawick, P. 1966. "A Structured Family Interview." *Family Process* 5 (2):256–72.

Zuk, G. H. 1966. "The Go Between Process in Family Therapy." *Family Process* 5 (2):162–79.

Nondevelopmental Family Crises

Chapter

8

In the last two chapters we examined some of the challenges that face the marital dyad as spouses and as parents. These challenges have been related to developmental events, such as the birth of the first child or the parenting of an adolescent. Crises that develop from them are experienced by most families within the context of the regular developmental life cycle and, as such, must be seen as *developmental* crises.

This chapter treats some of the many crises that cannot be considered part of normal family development, but that nonetheless appear with considerable frequency in families in our culture. Our intent is not to cover all of the "nondevelopmental" crises, nor is it even to explore in depth the few presented here. Rather, the intent of this chapter is to show how a family systems framework enables one not only to differentiate among nondevelopmental family crises, but also to understand some of the critical ways in which these crises and family systems interact either to sustain disruption or to accept the challenges posed and move on.

We will discuss *voluntary* and *involuntary* crises as separate phenomena, in each case indicating with specific crises the etiology and sustaining dynamics of the crisis, as well as its treatment implications. We will use the crises that stem from family violence and substance abuse to illustrate voluntary crisis development and resolution. To illustrate involuntary crisis development and resolution, we will explore the crises that mental retardation and terminal illness pose for the family. We will then discuss some other common nondevelopmental crises in terms of their implications for family systems work.

Voluntary Family Crises

You will recall from section II, especially from Haley's work on symptom development and Bowen's work on tension resolution, that family system theorists postulate three major strategies that the dysfunctional family uses to manage its tension: (1) diffusing the tension within the couple relationship by open fighting between the spouses; (2) diffusing the tension within the couple relationship through triangulation—that is, through extending the tension to another member of the system, usually a child; and (3) submerging the tension by the development and maintenance of a symptom, which allows the disabled partner to continue the fight covertly and "win by losing" (Haley 1963; Rappaport 1976).

We have chosen family violence and substance abuse as examples of voluntary crises not only because of their prevalence within families in our culture, but also because they illustrate the three disabling strategies of tension resolution mentioned above. Spouse abuse in family violence is an extreme but valid example of the open fight. Child abuse is frequently the unfortunate extension of family triangulation. And chronic alcoholism and other forms of substance abuse are increasingly being understood as examples of the covert family fight in which the drug-disabled member controls the relationship through symptom maintenance.

Let us now explore the dynamics of the interaction between these specific crises and the family system and consider the implications of these dynamics for the family therapist.

Family Violence

Spouse abuse has usually been one of the best-kept family secrets. Professionals, as well, have for decades minimized its prevalence and, when recognizing it at all, have included it under the rubric of more generalized problems, such as marital disharmony and character disorder or other "mental illnesses" (Rounsaville 1978). Child abuse is as old as civilization. It has been practiced in the name of religious beliefs, birth control, and a variety of cultural rituals and social customs. Justice and Justice (1976) point out that in colonial America a father not only had the right to kill his child, but was also allowed to call upon colonial officers to assist him.

The abusing family in our culture is subject to increasing scrutiny, not only by social scientists (Davidson 1978; Gelles 1976; Levine 1975; Rounsaville 1978), but also by feminist publications and other trade media (Martin 1976; Pizzy 1976; Warrior 1976) who take issue with the social service and medical professions' ignoring or underrating the magnitude of the problem.

Theories about Family Violence. The literature abounds with studies of spouse abuse and child abuse that attempt to isolate the etiology of abusive behavior within a particular causal model (Justice and Justice 1976). Let us briefly review these different theoretical viewpoints before applying the systems perspective to the crises associated with family violence.

The *psychodynamic* explanation of family violence is that early childhood intrapsychic determinants come to the fore in later life and create the individual's potential to abuse (Kempe 1971). In other words, unresolved conflicts from childhood result in later frustration, which in turn leads to violent aggression.

The *personality-* or *character-trait* perspective differs from the psychodynamic model primarily in its focus. Rather than focusing on the underlying psychodynamic etiology of behavior, this perspective assumes the underlying etiology and attempts to define the abusive problem in terms of labels that imply styles of behavior, for example, *immature, impulse-ridden, chronically aggressive,* and *highly frustrated* (Spinetta and Rigler 1972; Melnick and Hurley 1972).

The *social-learning* model is based on the assumption that abusive behavior results from failure to learn appropriate relationship skills and from the lack of an adequate reinforcement system. "Fighting is the only way they know how to work it out" and "they expect too much from their kids" are typical explanations of family abuse based on this viewpoint. This perspective would also suggest that abusers have been taught to abuse by inappropriate role models.

The *environmental-stress* theory postulates a variety of social forces as causes of family violence—for example, poverty and poor education and the daily uncertainties and situational stresses that accompany them. This theory implies a larger social responsibility for the abusing family, one that calls for political reform (Gil 1970). However, this perspective fails to account for the reality that some poor, stressed people are abusive while most are no more so than people in any other socioeconomic stratum.

The *social-psychological* model formulated by Gelles (1973) draws together the environmental-stress theory and the trait-factor theory. It postulates that environmental stresses create certain "types" of people with particular traits. Individuals with abusive traits, in the presence of an "immediate precipitating situation," such as a nasty remark or a misbehaving child, resort to physical assault.

The *mental-illness* model might see the abuser as operating within the delusional system of the "paranoid," who retaliates as he would against the rest of the environment that is "persecuting" him. The abuser, perceiving himself or herself as the victim, forestalls being victimized by becoming a persecutor.

Justice and Justice (1976) review each of these models in more detail than is possible here, but even the cursory review that we have presented is sufficient to see that precisely because each of these theoretical models has a germ of truth in it, no one model can fully explain the phenomenon of family violence. Ultimately, the abused spouse or child, along with the abuser, must be seen as symptomatic of more fundamental disturbances within the entire family relation-ship system.

That is not to say that the abusing family is not partially the consequence of mental illness, stress, personality traits, or inadequate social relationship skills, for each of these conditions may exist to some degree. However, the inescapable fact is that while the abuser may be "psychotic" or under "economic stress" or unable to communicate effectively, it is *his* or *her* spouse who receives the abuse, not another adult, and it is *his* or *her* child who is beaten, not the child of another family. Consequently, the etiology of the violence must be found in the particular family relationship between the abused and the abuser as it is supported by the larger family system and the culture and environment with which the family interacts.

Systems Perspective. Let us return to Bowen's notion of the "emotional relationship system" and recall that when marital partners of relatively low levels of self-differentiation develop a relationship, tremendous emotional fusion may exist between the partners. That fusion not only offers the opportunity to make one's self whole by combining with the incomplete self of another, but in times of stress the fusion also threatens loss of one's self to the partner. Understandably, battles of control develop, spoken and unspoken resentments build, overt fighting occurs, and spouse abuse is frequently the eventual and chronic disabling consequence of the individual's attempt at self-preservation (Kantor and Lehr, 1975).

Recall further that a relatively poorly differentiated couple rather than continuing the fight, may triangle a third party, usually a child, into the relationship. From this triangulation, a symbiotic relationship (that is, one meeting mutually shared needs) may develop between one of the adults and the child. Again, as with the couple relationship, the parent-child symbiosis promises wholeness with the two together, but threatens loss of self as the dyad moves toward separation. Similar dependency resentments build, control battles ensue, and, as with the couple relationship, overt fighting between parent and child may eventually lead to child abuse, which thus may be seen as the ironic consequence of the individual's attempt to achieve self-respect and wholeness.

Implications for Treatment. The implications of these theories of family violence for treatment extend to the entire relationship system. Using the systems perspective, one would focus on differentiation and triangulation. Because both spouses participated in the original fusion, both must be helped to achieve higher levels of differentiation, a sense of separateness and of independence. When the abuse involves a child, the child must not only be protected from violence, but he or she, as well as the parents, must also be helped to develop a sense of self and independence. In this way, the child will be less vulnerable to future triangling moves.

A variety of strategies ranging from behavioral interventions and parent effectiveness training to the communication and structural strategies may be highly effective in enabling all family members to take the "I"-position in their family relationships. The choice of intervention must be left to the particular style of the therapist and the special idiosyncrasies and preferences of the family.

Regardless of the treatment modality chosen, family violence must be seen as symptomatic of disturbances in relationships, disturbances that precede the disruption that we call a crisis. These disturbances must be treated in a way that will foster stronger individual selves among family members, as well as more effective communication skills and more stable relationship structures within the entire family system.

Reviewing family violence as an example of a nondevelopmental family crisis, we see that to the extent that family members intended their initial behaviors, even though the eventual outcome was less than desirable, spouse and child abuse are clearly examples of *voluntary* family crises. The initial positive motives for fusion of those involved in the eventual crisis may promise a willingness to learn and to implement more enabling strategies and may point toward a more hopeful prognosis for such families in systems-oriented treatment.

However, spouse abuse and child abuse are voluntary crises that illustrate only two of the disabling strategies that families use to diffuse tension, namely, the open fight and the triangulation of a third member. Let us look now at another type of voluntary family crisis, substance abuse, which illustrates a third type of disabling strategy of tension diffusion, namely, symptom maintenance, the covert struggle.

Substance Abuse

Drinking alcoholic beverages has always been an accepted part of most cultures. In some cultures, before alcohol became popular, other substances—all of which had the ability to produce pleasantly altered states of consciousness—were used as part of religious ceremonies or simply as a regular part of the day's activities.

In the United States today, approximately 70 percent of adult Americans drink, and at least 15 percent of them are heavy drinkers (Unger 1978). A National Institute of Alcohol Abuse and Alcoholism (NIAAA) study estimates that 1.3 million youngsters between the ages of twelve and seventeen have a serious drinking problem. Heroin ranks slightly above alcohol as the most frequently abused drug (see table 8–1). As the dimensions of the problem have expanded, substance abuse in the last quarter century has become a "family affair" (Huberty 1974).

Symposia and surveys on the efficacy of family therapy in treating substance abuse have recently begun to appear (Kupetz et al. 1977; Coleman and Davis 1978). More specific focuses on particular aspects of substance abuse range from behavioral treatment of the alcoholic through in-patient couple therapy (Steinglass 1976) to a school and

Table 8–1 *Primary Drug of Abuse in Rank Order*

Rank	Drug	Mean %
1	Heroin	27.7
2	Alcohol	21.4
3	Marijuana	19.5
4	Barbiturates	8.9
5	Amphetamines	6.9
6	Other sedatives	5.8
7	Hallucinogens	4.9
8	Other opiates	3.9
9	Inhalants	2.6
10	Cocaine	1.7

Source: Reprinted with permission from Coleman, S.B., and D.I. Davis. "Family Therapy and Drug Abuse: A National Survey." *Family Process* 17, no. 1 (1978):21–31.

family-based program for adolescent alcoholics (Unger 1978). Nonalcohol forms of substance abuse have produced research that has focused, for example, on interpersonal perceptions and the particular characteristics of "addict families" (Alexander and Dibb 1977). The literature now yields more speculative papers, such as one that views heroin addiction and death of the addict as part of a savior-martyr script within the family system (Stanton 1977).

Since our purpose here is to view substance abuse as one example of a voluntary family crisis involving symptom maintenance, we will arbitrarily narrow the field of substance abuse to alcohol abuse by the adult male. Certainly alcohol abuse by women and youngsters, as well as other forms of substance abuse, might be equally illustrative, but the scope of this chapter does not permit nor necessitate such a comprehensive explication. Let us look at some of the particular features of alcohol in our culture and see how these features allow it to be abused and then used as a symptom in the couple's relationship strategies.

Alcohol in Our Culture.   Drunken comportment connotes different behavior to different families. For some it means Dad's sitting and drinking in front of the television for hours until he falls asleep. For others, it means the daily or weekend-long vigil to see when or whether Dad will return home safely, only to stagger to bed. For still others, it means verbal and/or physical abuse.

However, the research into the biochemistry of alcohol indicates that there is no pharmacological basis for such varieties of behavior (MacAndrew and Edgerton 1969). Schwartzman (1975) has referred to the "pharmacological fallacy," the assumption that drugs (defined as any chemicals that alter the mind) have certain effects irrespective of the context of the drug use or the characteristics of the user. Most of us have seen people at a party imbibing the same type of drink and then later have seen some of them fall asleep, some become rude and loud, and others become just plain silly. Clearly, the alcohol was not the "cause" of such different behaviors.

Nevertheless, our culture continues to support such explanations as, "I guess the boys were 'feeling good' when they burned the barn down last night," or "your dad didn't mean what he said; he just had too much to drink," or, simply, "he can't help it; he's an alcoholic." Underlying such statements are two basic and now disproven assumptions: (1) alcoholics cannot help taking a drink; and (2) once drunk, alcoholics cannot control their behavior. Alcoholics Anonymous has certainly shown that alcoholics in fact can refuse to drink, and research in the field has clearly shown not only that alcoholics can control their behavior while drinking, but even that they can control the actual amount they drink (Steinglass 1976) and can learn to drink moderately.

The popular mythology, however, gives alcohol abusers a powerful tool for use in interpersonal relationships. As long as their families underwrite the "pharmacological fallacy," alcohol abusers can control and, in fact, dominate their relationships with family members and, at the same time, avoid responsibility for doing so. Thus, the alcoholic is able to claim, "Because I'm drunk, I decide what goes on here; and because I'm drunk, I'm not responsible for the consequences of my decisions."

Let us now look at the third of the three disabling strategies for tension resolution, symptom maintenance, and see how chronic alcoholism allows for such a strategy.

Symptom Maintenance.   Some families are unable to diffuse tension through triangulation and open fighting because there is no third member who is emotionally vulnerable to triangling, and because, at the same time, one spouse refuses to take responsibility for continuing an open battle with the other spouse. If the spouse who refuses to take responsibility for open fighting has a history of drunken comportment, or develops a chronic drinking pattern, he or she can continue the battle with the spouse, dominate the couple relationship, and at the same time avoid responsibility by attributing his or her behavior to the "drinking problem," the "disease," the symptom. You will recall from chapter 4 that Haley defines a symptom as having two characteristics: it has an overwhelming effect on the individual and/or others; and it is something for which the individual cannot be held responsible. In our culture, alcoholism clearly meets these criteria.

An interactional study of sixty-nine families (Rappaport 1976) has shown that regardless of demographic variables, male alcoholics are: (1) more willing to engage in control battles with their wives than with their children, and more willing than their control counterparts to do so; and (2) more willing to choose strategies that avoid responsibility than to engage in open conflict. These two tendencies are certainly congruous with the type of person who would prefer the couple fight rather than triangulation and who would at the same time prefer symptom maintenance rather than open battle as a strategy. An interesting and unexpected outcome of the study was that the wives of alcoholics, although nondrinkers themselves, were also more willing to choose strategies that avoided responsibility as they battled with their husbands. Thus it would seem that other members of the alcoholic's family accept strategies that avoid responsibility as valid ones. (Such strategies obviously include the symptom maintenance of the alcoholic.)

Implications for Treatment. Treatment of chronic alcoholism, like treatment of other types of substance abuse, must begin with an accurate assessment of what the behavior associated with the substance abuse means for the abuser. As an example, imagine a chronic drinker whose drunken behavior at the corner bar allows him the following: (1) a regular peer group, his drinking buddies; (2) relative ease of entry to this social network, accomplished simply by taking a seat at the bar and ordering "a draft"; and (3) the ability to feel comfortable with sharing affect and being close (after several drinks, he may put his arm around his buddy and tell him a tale of sadness, a prerogative accorded few males in our machismo-dominated culture). Imagine further that he is thirty-six years old and that he has used drunken comportment for the last twenty years to facilitate such peer relationships. The probability is small that he has developed alternative ways of establishing and maintaining such interpersonal connections. Even if he were to stop drinking immediately, how long would it take him to find another peer group? And how much longer would it take him to develop the types of behavioral, communicational, and relationship skills that would enable him to perceive himself as viable in another social environment? The only nonalcoholic-assisted skills he currently has are probably those of his clumsy middle-adolescent years, hardly acceptable as he moves toward forty. It would be foolish to expect him to easily abandon the drunken comportment that provides him such social viability. Moreover, even if he were involved in a fused family relationship, it would be folly to focus on treatment of the family system without integrating the dynamics that sustain his problem outside of the family system.

However, suppose that the sustaining variables are not external to the family system, that he does his drinking at home, and that his alcoholism serves primarily to allow him to dominate his marital relationship while avoiding responsibility for the conflict. Treatment would then appropriately focus on the marital relationship and on relationships within the larger family system. In this case, chronic substance abuse, like spouse and child abuse, would have to be seen as symptomatic of a more fundamental problem whose etiology is in the fusion of relatively poorly differentiated individuals and in the disturbed relationship between them. Again, *both* spouses would have to be helped to achieve higher levels of differentiation of self, as each participated in the original fusion. As with spouse and child abuse, a variety of interventions can be effective in fostering this kind of growth; but regardless of the type of intervention used, the chronic substance abuse—the symptom that precipitated the crisis—must be seen as having its etiology and sustaining dynamics in fundamental relationship disturbances, not in the temporary crisis.

Reviewing substance abuse as an example of nondevelopmental family crisis, we see that substance abuse is pharmacologically a matter of choice and that it serves as a strategy, albeit a disabling one, within the family system. Thus, substance abuse, like family violence, must be correctly viewed as a *voluntary* family crisis—that is, a crisis of choice. Even though substance abuse and family violence are eventually disabling, they are strategies paradoxically employed by family members to reduce tension and protect against the threat of loss of self that an intense symbiotic relationship holds. They are essentially voluntary disruptions of the normal developmental cycle of the family.

Let us look now at some family crises that are also nondevelopmental, but that clearly cannot be considered voluntary: mental retardation, and terminal illness and death.

Involuntary Family Crises

The etiology of an involuntary family crisis, such as mental retardation or terminal illness and death, cannot in any sense be found in a strategy (enabling or disabling) on the part of a family member (or members) to influence the homeostasis of the system. Nevertheless, such events, initially manifested in physical consequences for a family member, quite quickly impact on the emotions and interactive prerogatives of all family members. Consequently, these involuntary crises may ultimately have the same disabling effects on communication patterns and structural dynamics as do some of the voluntary crises.

We have chosen mental retardation as an example of an involuntary family crisis for three reasons: (1) At least 6 million Americans are mentally retarded; only four disabling conditions have a higher incidence, cancer, arthritis, cardiac disease, and mental illness (Price-Bonham and Addison 1978). (2) Because mental retardation is an early and unexpected occurrence in the family life cycle, it is representative of a number of other involuntary crises that beset the young developing family. (3) Mental retardation is an involuntary crisis that may exist for the entire life cycle of the family; roughly 59 percent of all mentally retarded Americans are over the age of twenty (Goodman 1978).

We have chosen terminal illness and death as another example of involuntary crisis for two reasons: (1) Terminal illness and death touch an increasing number of families in this country. (2) The emotional process of terminal illness and death has finally reached a stage of public awareness at which it is appropriate to consider the implications of those conditions for the family systems to which the terminally ill, dying, or dead persons belong (Kubler-Ross 1969).

Let us look now at these examples of involuntary family crises in terms of their impact on the family system and the implications of that impact for the family therapist.

Mental Retardation

Mental retardation has been defined as a "significantly sub . . . intellectual functioning existing concurrently with deficits in adaptive behavior . . . manifested during the developmental period" (Stigen 1976). Difficulty in learning as a result of less than normal intellectual ability is thus only one aspect of mental retardation. Differences in the functioning of the mentally retarded are great, ranging from the total helplessness of profoundly retarded individuals with IQs of 10, who require constant and complete care, to the ability of mildly retarded children with IQs of 70 to attend public schools in regular classes and to go on to lead fairly independent lives. With about three-fifths of our mentally retarded over the age of twenty, the condition obviously exists in adulthood, but it is usually diagnosed in childhood and initially impacts on the family then.

Research on how parents are informed that their youngster is mentally retarded indicates substantial mishandling of this procedure. The consequences have considerable impact on how the parents and family adjust to and accept the retarded child (Price-Bonham and Addison 1978). The later the parents are told, the more likely they are to be resentful of the way in which they were told (Jenson 1960; Thurston 1963). The most appreciative parents are those who are told soon after the child's birth (Drillian and Wolkinson 1964). In one study of mongoloid children, 62 percent of the parents were either told nothing or were told that their child was normal, even though 35 percent of the physicians admitted knowing that the child was mentally retarded (Kramm 1963). Clearly, although physicians may now be less hesitant in their communications with families than they once were, telling parents that their child is mentally retarded will always be a difficult task. We focus on this beginning awareness of the problem because it is the first disruption to the family system homeostasis and because it sets the stage for the process of family reaction, which, of course, will determine the impact on the system.

Stages of Reactions.   Parents' responses to the knowledge that their child is mentally retarded range from ambivalence to denial, guilt, grief, shame, self-pity, sorrow, depression, and even a wish for the child's death (Price-Bonham and Addison 1978). Guilt is the most frequently reported response (Zuk 1962), but it is most probably related to specific incidents, such as previous unsuccessful attempts at abortion (Bryant and Herschberg 1961; Wortis 1965).

Mothers and fathers tend to respond differently to learning that their child is mentally retarded. Mothers initially exhibit more emotional reactions than do fathers, sensing the expressive crisis (Gunz and Gubrium 1972). Fathers tend to show more concern about the long-term financial and social implications, sensing the instrumental crisis (Love 1973).

For both parents, however, there generally emerges a pattern of stages of reaction to the news. Gearheart and Litten (1975) divide the responses as follows: (1) awareness; (2) denial; (3) recognition; (4) search for a cause; (5) search for a cure; and, finally, (6) acceptance. However, this pattern is not necessarily completed by all individuals. Kanner (1953), for example, found three types of ultimate responses: (1) a mature acknowledgment of the actuality of retardation and the ultimate acceptance of the child as he or she is (following through all of Gearheart and Litten's stages); (2) "disguise of reality" in which the child is seen as handicapped, but the handicap is ascribed to some ultimately correctable circumstance; and (3) a complete inability to face the reality and the dimensions of the problem.

In most cases, regardless of the response pattern, the impact on the family system is profound. Individual lives, the parents' marriage, sibling relationships, and relationships with extended family and the larger community—all diverge from normal developmental schemes. Stress in the marriage is estimated to be three times that of normal families (Love 1973). The desertion rate of fathers is also disproportionately high (Reed and Reed 1965), and the suicide rate for these family systems is twice the national average (Love 1973).

Obviously, in families with a retarded member, integration is weaker, financial expenses are higher, and many family activities are curtailed. For most families, the need to meet the retardate's demands seriously thwarts the gratifications that the family would otherwise enjoy (Koch and Dobson 1971). Whereas in normal families there is constant role redefinition throughout the life cycle, in the retardate's family, parental roles are fairly constant, which not only slows or arrests the parents' own development, but also that of the other family members (Farber 1959).

A veil of confusion, despair, and disappointment may descend over the family. Olshansky has described a condition, which he calls *chronic sorrow*. It is not a stage, nor does he see it as something that can be treated. Rather, he sees it as "an understandable, non-neurotic response to a tragic fact. The sorrow is chronic and lasts as long as the child lives" (Olshansky 1966, p. 22). Considering that the parental responsibility for a child may last fifty years or more, the meaning of *chronic* takes on a new dimension.

The paucity of social science literature dealing with the mentally retarded throughout the entire family life cycle is paralleled by the naiveté and lack of information and sophistication on the part of parents (Legeay and Keogh 1966). The literature reveals a variety of traditional attempts at individual and group treatment. Recent legislation has resulted in increased awareness of community services and increased coordination of those services.

Implications for Treatment. The major goals in the treatment of families with retarded members seem to be to help the family members move through stages, such as those postulated by Gearheart and Litten, toward acceptance and to help the parents to shift from short-term preoccupation with the crisis to long-term planning.

Treatment must also focus on integrating both the immediate and developmental needs of other family members with those of the retarded child. This focus places the therapist in the role of long-term consultant, as a variety of crises present themselves over the decades. These crises include the *instrumental crises*, precipitated by the increase in financial and social demands that the presence of a mentally retarded child creates; the *role organization crises*, which occur as other family members attempt to move through normal developmental stages while the retarded child may not; and the *expressive crises*, the ever-present emotional challenges and the "chronic sorrow" that may arise again and again.

We have found parent groups and sibling groups helpful in enabling families to cope with these crises. A supportive network can be developed in a group setting, which, when combined with the expertise of a family therapist, can prove therapeutically beneficial.

Thus, mental retardation not only constitutes an *involuntary* crisis for the family, but it is also one that may begin with the early life of the family and continue throughout the family life cycle. The experience of a family whose first child is retarded will differ from that of a family whose last child (perhaps the fourth or fifth) is retarded. One of the variables will be the developmental stage of the couple system while another will be that of the parent system, to say nothing of the individual developmental stages of the parents. Thus, the way in which a family system copes with an involuntary crisis necessarily reflects an interfacing of the developmental stages of the individual family members and the family subsystems.

Let us turn now to a different type of involuntary crisis—terminal illness and death. This involuntary crisis may be of relatively shorter duration than mental retardation and may occur during any developmental stage of the family life cycle. Certainly, it is a crisis that impacts heavily upon all family members.

Terminal Illness and Death

In an age in which science has given a touch of reality to youngsters' dreams of going to the moon, more people are living, and more of them are living longer. As the advances of medical technology have increased the life spans of persons suffering from terminal cancer, cardiac disease, and other life-sapping illnesses, more and more families are finding themselves affected in some way by terminal illness.

Although the subject of death has been taboo until very recently, it is now increasingly recognized that the dying individual continues to have an active intrapsychic life. And however long the terminal stage of illness, the family system must continue to live on a day-to-day basis and to cope with normal developmental tasks and issues, as well as with the implications of a terminal illness.

The way in which the knowledge of a terminal illness is initially presented has a considerable impact upon the way the family system adjusts to this involuntary crisis. Let us briefly review the pioneering work of Elisabeth Kubler-Ross (1969) in identifying the stages of the dying process.

Stages of Reaction.   Out of more than two hundred interviews with dying individuals, Kubler-Ross identified five stages in the dying process: denial and isolation, anger, bargaining, depression, and acceptance. Although these stages may not build on each other in the true sense of developmental stages (an individual, for example, might experience all of them in a few hours in a variety of sequences), most dying individuals do seem to experience the majority of these reactions. While death may obviate the necessity of the terminal patient's completing all of the stages, the family may be stuck on one stage (denial for months, or depression for decades) to the detriment of the normal growth and development of the surviving family members.

Let us look at each of Kubler-Ross's stages in terms of the complex interactions between dying individuals and their families, as well as in terms of the challenges that this crisis poses to the family members who must live through the experience of loss and who must survive.

Stage 1. *Denial and Isolation*: The story is told of three patients on a hospital ward. Each was given a terminal diagnosis by the physician. They were each given one last request. The first asked for some religious counseling; the second to see his family for the last time; and the third asked for another physician. Needless to say, the third patient was experiencing denial, a refusal to hear the diagnosis. Denial is usually preceded by shock, the jolt that one feels when first being hit with totally unacceptable news. Denial is a form of protection, a defense mechanism, and a natural reaction to cushion the initial shock.

Hope is a key emotion throughout the dying process and, while denial is a healthy way of initially maintaining hope, it is interesting to note that only three of the more than two hundred patients whom Kubler-Ross interviewed maintained denial up to the time of their deaths.

Denial may also be a healthy way for the family to cope initially with the news of a terminal illness in one of its members. However, when the dying individual has moved considerably past denial and is prepared to accept death, and one or several family members are still at the denial stage, family system complications can easily arise. Kubler-Ross cites the case of a woman whose husband, still denying his wife's terminal condition and her acceptance of it, arranged for her to have "one last operation." The woman managed to avoid it only by having a gross psychotic episode in the operating room. The next day she asked the doctor to talk to her husband and help him to understand.

Stage 2. *Anger*: Once the individual has begun to accept the terminal illness, the statement shifts from "it *isn't* happening to me" to "*why* is it happening to me?" Families frequently have trouble understanding the tremendous anger of the terminal individual, which may be vented over trivia on objects or individuals. Kubler-Ross suggests not taking the anger personally, but rather hearing it as the statement that it is ("I'm still here, don't you see?") and responding to the individual with respect and understanding for who he or she still is, not because of the anger.

Stage 3. *Bargaining*: Just as some people believe that you "catch more flies with honey than with vinegar," some terminally ill individuals never take up anger (some have never allowed themselves to feel and express anger). Many others eventually pass through the stage of anger and turn then to "asking nicely," either from God, the hospital staff, or even the illness itself. The tacit deal might be: "If I do everything the doctors and nurses tell me to and I am very good, I will get better," or "Please, God, if you make me better, I'll never do another mean thing ever." Bargaining, as another style of coping, can be encouraged, although unfortunately the nature of most terminal illnesses shows through most "bargains" fairly quickly. Many individuals apparently do not bargain, or do so personally and quietly, and so it may go unnoticed by the family. Nevertheless, even as a brief siege, bargaining is helpful to some people. For example, many people survive until after a particular event or holiday: "I want to live until John's wedding and then I'll go quietly."

Stage 4. *Depression*: Kubler-Ross has divided this stage into two separate phases: reactive depression, and preparatory depression.

Reactive depression is a response to an actual loss, such as the amputation of a leg or a breast, which may be experienced with guilt and/or shame. In certain instances, family members may appropriately respond to this type of depression with attempts to "cheer up" the individual and to restore his or her self-esteem.

Preparatory depression, on the other hand, moving toward giving up everyone and everything the individual loves, including life itself, is "necessary and beneficial if the patient is to die in a stage of acceptance and peace" (Kubler-Ross 1969). Allowing the dying person this experience, just sitting and being with the patient, can be very supportive during this stage of tremendous loss.

Stage 5. *Acceptance*: For Kubler-Ross, this is the last stage, reached after having successfully moved through the other four stages. It is not clear whether the individual is finally tired and weak only from the progress of the illness, or whether some of the quietness and void of feelings comes from the actual acceptance of the coming end. One of Kubler-Ross's patients described it as "the final rest before the long journey."

Although the terminally ill individual may have death obviate the necessity of reaching this stage, the family who remains has no such "pardon," and a substantial amount of family treatment may take place after the death of the family member.

We wish to reiterate that these stages suggest a general model of grieving and mourning. Naturally there are variables that affect whether and how one passes through these stages. Some of these variables are the nature of the illness (how much pain and discomfort is experienced); ethnic and cultural variables about expression of emotion and attitudes toward illness and death; and whether one is hospitalized or at home.

Implications for Treatment. Let us look now at some of the adaptive challenges that terminal illness and death pose directly to the family. Kubler-Ross emphasizes the importance of open communication among the hospital staff, the dying individual, and the family as much as she emphasizes her delineation of the stages in the dying process. Open communication depends upon the ability to tolerate the tremendous feelings of anger, resentment, guilt, sadness, and loneliness that accompany the experience of terminal illness. Kubler-Ross points out that when the family is able to tolerate these feelings, open communication may not only fulfill the dying individual's need to say farewell and to finish unfinished business, but may also fulfill the family's need as well.

In earlier chapters we saw that much of how communication is handled within the family system is determined by the family's pattern of functioning, definition of roles, assignment of tasks, developmental stage of family life, and actual communication styles. A study by Cohen, Dizenhuz, and Wingate (1977) found that while family communication styles seemed to have little effect on how a family utilizes external support systems (schools, agencies, friends, clergy, and so on), the degree of free flow of communication within the family did correlate positively with the utilization of internal support systems. This finding has definite implications for the family in the case of the death of a parent, especially the mother. Since in our culture, the female has generally been the expressive leader and has been responsible for the integrative role in the family system (Parson and Bales 1955), it is not surprising to find that families in which the mother has died were rated significantly lower in communication patterns than those in which the father had died. Professionals working with families facing the death of one of their members certainly need to be cognizant of whether the dying person (mother, father, or whoever) has played an expressive and integrative role; and if that person has, the professional must then help the family transfer that function to someone else within the family system.

Within the family's experience of death and dying, there seem to be particular times of stress when intervention is more welcome. These times include the period of the initial diagnosis (when it is learned that the individual is terminally ill), the actual death, and the period after death. Most families report the most difficulty during the period of learning about the terminal nature of the illness and the actual death (Cohen, Dizenhuz, and Wingate 1977).

Grief and mourning normally last for a year or two, during which individuals pass through several stages. Bowlby (1960) has identified the characteristics of these stages: (1) thought and behavior directed toward the lost loved object; (2) hostility toward the lost loved object or others; (3) appeals for help and support from others; (4) despair, withdrawal, regression, and disorganization; and (5) reorganization of behavior directed toward a new love object. Bowlby points out that passage through these phases is not steady; periods of regression frequently occur during the first year or two.

The therapist usually functions more as a consultant during the grieving and mourning process, seeing family members less often on a regular basis and more frequently in times of specific need. The therapist must be aware of the number of years it may take for all family members to resolve the loss fully and must provide support to them throughout their slow struggle. The therapist also watches for a variety of pitfalls that may await family members. These include a "pseudoreorganization" that usually proves insufficient to meet the emotional demands of the person's life (Paul 1969); promiscuity on the part of young adults seeking a new love object (Kimmel 1974); and a general but subtle impairment of the ability to function. During this period, there seems to be an increase in acting-out behavior, fatal illnesses, accidents, and suicides among the immediate family members of the deceased (Hinton 1967; Rees and Lutkins 1967).

The individual mourner has three tasks: (1) to experience and reflect upon feelings toward the lost object during life and the feelings evoked by death; (2) to review the history of the attachment; and (3) to examine personal wounds and confront the task of continuing to live without the lost object (Cassem 1978). Family therapists have found it possible to help the mourning family with these three tasks by working with the family members as a system unit and/or by seeing individual members. The therapist allows the bereaved to express feelings and helps them to understand the mourning process so that they can accept their feelings as normal reactions rather than view them as pathological disturbances. It is important for therapists to be able to tolerate reversals and to be comfortable with violent expression of emotion (such as weeping, bitterness, and anger). It is also important that therapists encourage family members to share memories, to return to activity, and to recall past strengths and coping mechanisms when dealing with loss.

Although research on terminal illness and dying has generally focused on the death of an adult family member, slightly different patterns and problems among families dealing with childhood terminal illness are increasingly being noted. Our focus here on presenting terminal illness and death as an example of involuntary family crisis precludes an extensive examination of the problems facing the family of the pediatric terminal patient. However, two major areas, which may become increasingly evident as research and medical progress continue, are worth noting briefly. The first area concerns those special problems facing the parents: the initial emotional strain of the "tragic crisis"; the logistical and psychological difficulties in their personal outpatient management of their dying child (explaining amputations, encouraging return to school during remission, helping a youngster come to terms with a "passage" that they may not have accepted themselves); and the management of the psychosomatic symptoms and phobias that develop in siblings in half of the families in which a child has died (Binger et al. 1969).

The second major area of problems facing the family of the terminally ill child are the problems created when the child does not die, but recovers. Modern medical techniques have made this an increasingly frequent occurrence. Studies have shown that the child involved may make good medical recovery while the family suffers marked adjustment problems. The sudden onset of the illness and then the equally sudden recovery can leave parents feeling inadequate to evaluate situations involving their children. Depression and preoccupation may set in, and incomplete mourning may be the result of a process unexpectedly interrupted. Also, there may be a generalized lack of control of family dynamics compounded by the child's manifesting irritability, mild hyperactivity, and changes in affective style (Benjamin 1978). Clearly such an event can create a period of family turmoil in which the family may benefit from prompt and supportive intervention.

We have looked now at mental retardation and terminal illness and death as two examples of involuntary family crises. Adding them to our two earlier examples of voluntary family crisis—family violence and substance abuse—let us review some characteristics of nondevelopmental family crises.

In chapters 6 and 7, we examined many of the family crises that confront the spouse subsystem and the parent subsystem. The crises facing the couple most usually grow out of the developmental issues facing the family. Although the crises discussed in this chapter are not considered "developmental," they nonetheless complicate and delay the growth of individual family members, of family subsystems, and of the family system itself. In many families, these nondevelopmental crises permanently arrest some members' growth and development. The characteristics of nondevelopmental family crises that we wish to emphasize are: (1) that they add additional stresses and strains to the family system even if they facilitate avoidance of developmental tasks; (2) that they impact upon the entire family system, disrupting the existing homeostasis; (3) that they usually require immediate, active, supportive crisis intervention; and (4) that recalibration of the homeostasis is a necessary part of the recovery process.

Other Nondevelopmental Crises

There are many other nondevelopmental crises facing the family in our culture. These range from the crises presented by sudden single parenthood and other increasingly acceptable alternate styles of living to what are still the more taboo crises, such as multiple overt incest as a defense against family loss (Gutheil and

Avery 1977). Although we have not included these crises in our discussion, we in no way mean to minimize the profound ways in which they may impact on family systems. Rather, the examples of nondevelopmental crises that we have presented are meant to show how all nondevelopmental crises impact upon the family system and how the etiology of the crisis may be within the dynamics of the family itself.

However, we do want to include a cursory discussion of one additional nondevelopmental issue in family systems, that of the single-parent family. We are singling out this phenomenon for attention because of its increasing frequency in our culture and because of the implications that it has for family systems. Single parenthood may be classified as either a voluntary or an involuntary crisis. It would be considered voluntary when it is the result of divorce or of having a child outside of marriage, and involuntary when the result of death or some type of involuntary incarceration. The voluntary or involuntary nature of single parenthood effects differences in the experiences of family systems. For example, a widowed parent, who is likely to receive more support and understanding from the community than a divorced parent, feels differently about the state of single parenthood than a divorced parent. Let us now consider the impact of single parenthood on family systems.

Single Parenthood

In their review of the literature on the effects of the absence of parent on children, Marino and McCowan (1976) point out that although much research has been done in this area, it is fraught with methodological weaknesses, simplistic definitions, and oversimplified generalizations. They note some of the obvious differences between one-parent and two-parent homes: (1) the single parent generally assumes the roles and responsibilities of both mother and father, which may result in some emotional and intellectual neglect; (2) immediate financial stress may detract from the time and energy that a single parent can devote to the child; (3) since the single parent most often has to work, the child often must assume increased responsibilities at home; and (4) outside child-care services for the child of the single-parent home are often necessary.

These differences can affect the sex-role development, the intellectual development, the academic achievement, and the social development of the children. Although many studies refer to the relationship between single parenthood and these effects, the studies themselves contain so many contradictions and oversimplified statements of results that it is impossible to claim an adequate theoretical base for such hypotheses.

The advent of single parenthood has a dramatic impact on the family system. Although differences exist between voluntary and involuntary single parenthood, let us briefly mention some of the common effects that the loss of a parent, whether from divorce or death, has on the family system.

First of all, the change in status to single parenthood alters communication patterns. If, for example, the lost parent was the expressive parent, then new expressive patterns must be established if the system is to be maintained. If, on the other hand, the lost parent was more of what Satir and Kantor refer to as a "bystander," the adjustment may be different. In any case, the roles need to be reshuffled, and the rules of the system need to be renegotiated.

One of the major concerns that arises in newly formed single-parent families is the issue of power. The absence of one parent requires immediate restructuring of the power system, and the remaining parent is often overwhelmed with the sudden impact of total responsibility.

Many adjustment problems result from the single parent's attempt to integrate parental and adult roles and responsibilities. It is difficult for the single parent, regardless of sex, to reorganize his or her adult life as an individual and, at the same time, deal with increased parental responsibilities, which require additional expenditures of time and energy. These difficulties naturally affect the adjustment of the children to their suddenly reorganized family system. Confusion and turmoil are often part of the mourning and grieving process.

Implications for Treatment.   Many families are referred to family therapy at the onset of the crisis of single parenthood, regardless of whether it is caused by death or divorce. In these cases, the first task of the therapist is to help the family members deal with the loss by facilitating their passage through the various stages of grief and mourning.

When the "recalibration" or "reorganization" stage is reached, the family therapist provides supportive and educational services to the family, teaching the parent new ways of parenting and helping the members of the family system to form a newly calibrated homeostasis and to renegotiate and restructure their interactions. The family therapist does not assume the role of the departed parent. Rather, he or she becomes more of a consultant as the family system begins to gain strength as a new family system, which, in fact, it must become. We are emphasizing Bowen's focus on differentiation; it is important that the family therapist *not* become triangulated into the system to replace the lost parent.

Many therapists find that individual sessions with the single parent to work on individual adjustment issues are a necessary component of the family work. Some suggest that the parent join a group of single parents to gain a new support network and to benefit from constructive modeling experiences. Some school counselors have established groups for children from single-parent families. The point is that families who have recently lost a parent need to develop new support networks and that peer groups that provide such networks can be an invaluable supplement to family systems work.

While the literature suggests that two-parent families result in fewer adjustment problems for children than one-parent families, there really are no substantial data to support that claim. One can find evidence to support whatever claim one wants to make. We would all agree that a stormy, violent two-parent family can be more destructive than a calm, stable one-parent family. Since our culture persists in perpetuating the myths that "two-parent families are superior to one-parent families" and that "natural mothers are better parents than natural fathers," the family worker takes on the task of disputing and questioning the validity of these myths, which are almost always on the minds of new single parents.

Summary

In this chapter we looked at nondevelopmental crises in the family life cycle as either voluntary or involuntary and selected two of each to illustrate the impact of nondevelopmental crises on family systems. The two voluntary crises that we examined were family violence and substance abuse; the two involuntary crises were mental retardation and terminal illness and death. In addition, we briefly looked at the issue of single parenthood, pointing out that it could be either voluntary or involuntary.

These nondevelopmental crises occur in addition to the normal developmental tasks and issues that we discussed in chapters 6 and 7. They may result in the delay of normal individual and/or family development or in the forced acceleration of some of the developmental passages. Much depends upon the particular developmental stages of the family system and the couple and the parent subsystems at the onset of the crisis.

We discussed the nature of the crisis, its cultural implications, and the types of impact that it can have on the family system. We then discussed the implications for treatment of the family system and pointed out the commonalities and differences between the voluntary and involuntary natures of the crises. Much of what we know about crisis intervention techniques and strategies can be applied to family systems at the onset of a crisis. It is often during this period of crisis that radical and rapid system changes can be affected. Further supportive work is usually necessary to maintain the system change and to help the family continue to develop within the confines of the crisis.

Because nondevelopmental crises occur with less frequency than developmental crises, the issues inherent in these crises may be less familiar to you. The purpose of the exercises in chapter 8 in the manual is to increase your familiarity and comfort with such issues and thus to enable you to work more effectively with a broader range of family problems. In that chapter you will also find suggested readings pertaining to single parenting and the effects of marital disruption on children.

We have now examined patterns of developmental and nondevelopmental crises and the issues that they raise. They challenge not only the communications styles and structures of the family system, but also the resources of the clinicians attempting to facilitate their resolution. Let us look now at the research and professional issues involved in such a complex endeavor.

References

Alexander, B., and G. Dibb. 1977. "Interpersonal Perception in Addict Families." *Family Process* 16 (1):17–29.

Benjamin, P. 1978. "Psychological Problems following Recovery from Acute Life-Threatening Illness." *American Journal of Orthopsychiatry* 48 (2):284–90.

Binger, C., et al. 1969. "Childhood Leukemia: Emotional Impact on Patient and Family." *New England Journal of Medicine* 280 (8).

Bowlby, J. 1960. "Grief and Mourning in Infancy and Early Childhood." *Psychoanalytic Study of the Child* 15:9–52.

Bryant, K. N., and J. C. Herschberg. 1961. "Helping the Parents of a Retarded Child." *American Journal of Disabled Children* 102:52–66.

Cassem, N. 1978. "Treating the Person Confronting Death." In A. M. Nicoli, Jr., ed., *The Harvard Guide to Modern Psychiatry.* Cambridge, Mass.: Harvard University Press.

Cohen, P., I. Dizenhuz, and C. Wingate. 1977. "Family Adaptation to Terminal Illness and Death of a Parent." *Social Casework* 58 (4):223–28.

Coleman, S., and D.I. Davis. 1978. "Family Therapy and Drug Abuse: A National Survey." *Family Process* 17 (1):21–31.

Davidson, T. 1978. *Conjugal Crime: Understanding and Changing the Wifebeating Pattern.* New York: Hawthorn Books.

Drillian, C. M., and E. M. Wolkinson. 1964. "Mongolism: When Should Parents Be Told?" Washington, D.C.: U.S. Government Printing Office.

Farber, B. 1959. "Effects of a Severely Retarded Child on Family Integration." *Monograph of the Society for Research in Child Development* 24:5–81.

Gearheart, B., and F. Litten. 1975. *The Trainable Retarded: A Foundations Approach.* St. Louis: Mosby.

Gelles, R. J. 1973. "Child Abuse as Psychopathology: A Sociological Critique and Reformulation." *American Journal of Orthopsychiatry* 43:611–21.

———. 1976. "Demythologizing Child Abuse." *Family Coordinator* 25 (2):135–42.

Gil, D. G. 1970. *Violence against Children.* Cambridge, Mass.: Harvard University Press.

Goodman, D. 1978. "Parenting an Adult Mentally Retarded Offspring." *Smith College Students in Social Work* 48 (3):209–34.

Gunz, E. J., and J. F. Gubrium. 1972. "Comparative Parental Perceptions of a Mentally Retarded Child." *American Journal of Mental Deficiency* 77:175–80.

Gutheil, T. G., and N. C. Avery. 1977. "Multiple Overt Incest as Family Defense against Loss." *Family Process* 16 (1):105–17.

Haley, J. 1963. *Strategies of Psychotherapy.* New York: Grune & Stratton.

Hinton, J. 1967. *Dying.* Baltimore: Penguin Books.

Huberty, D. 1974. "Treating the Adolescent Drug Abuser: A Family Affair." Paper presented at the North American Congress on Alcohol and Drug Problems, San Francisco (December 1974).

Jenson, R. A. 1960. "The Clinical Management of the Mentally Retarded Child and the Parents." *American Journal of Mental Deficiency* 106:830–33.

Justice, B., and R. Justice. 1976. *The Abusing Family.* New York: Human Services Press.

Kanner, L. 1953. "Parents' Feelings about Retarded Children." *American Journal of Mental Deficiency* 57:375–82.

Kantor, D., and W. Lehr. 1975. *Inside the Family.* San Francisco: Jossey-Bass.

Kempe, C. H. 1971. "Pediatric Implications of the Battered Baby Syndrome." *Archives of Disease in Childhood* 28 (28):28–37.

Kimmel, D. 1974. *Adulthood and Aging.* New York: Wiley.

Koch, R., and T. Dobson. 1971. *The Mentally Retarded Child and His Family: A Multidisciplinary Handbook.* New York: Brunner/Mazel.

Kramm, E. R. 1963. "Families of Mongoloid Children." Washington, D.C.: U.S. Government Printing Office.

Kubler-Ross, E. 1969. *On Death and Dying.* New York: Macmillan.

Kupetz, K., et al. 1977. "The Family and Drug Abuse Symposium." *Family Process* 16 (2):141–90.

Legeay, C., and B. Keogh. 1966. "Impact of Mental Retardation on Family Life." *American Journal of Nursing* 66:1062–65.

Levine, M. 1975. "Intramarital Violence and Its Effect on Children: A Study of 50 Families in General Practice." *Medical Science Law* 15:172–76.

Love, H. 1973. *The Mentally Retarded Child and His Family.* Springfield, Ill.: Thomas.

MacAndrew, C., and R.B. Edgerton. 1969. *Drunken Comportment.* Chicago: Aldine.

Marino, C., and Richard McCowan. 1976. "The Effects of Parent Absence on Children." *Child Study Journal* 6 (3).

Martin, D. 1976. *Battered Wives.* San Francisco: Glide.

Melnick, B., and J. R. Hurley. 1972. "Distinctive Personality Attributes of Child Abusing Mothers." *Journal of Consulting and Clinical Psychology.* 33:746–49.

Olshansky, S. 1966. "Parent Responses to a Mentally Defective Child." *Mental Retardation* 4:21–23.

Parsons, T., and R. Bales. 1955. *Family Socialization and Interaction Process.* Glencoe, Ill.: Free Press.

Paul, N. 1969. "Psychiatry: Its Role in the Resolution of Grief." In Austin H. Kutscher, ed., *Death and Bereavement.* Springfield, Ill.: Thomas.

Pizzy, E. 1976. *Scream Quietly or the Neighbors Will Hear.* London: Penguin Books.

Price-Bonham, S., and S. Addison. 1978. "Families and Mentally Retarded Children: Emphasis on the Father." *Family Coordinator* 27 (3):221–30.

Rappaport, Louis J. 1976. "Role and Context Interaction in Families of Alcoholics." Ph.D. dissertation. Boston College.

Reed, E.W., and S.C. Reed. 1965. *Mental Retardation: A Family Study.* Philadelphia: Saunders.

Rees, W. D., and S. G. Lutkins. 1967. "Mortality and Bereavement." *British Medical Journal* 4:13–16.

Rounsaville, B.T. 1978. "Battered Wives: Barriers to Identification and Treatment." *American Journal of Orthopsychiatry* 48 (3):487–94.

Schwartzman, T. 1975. "The Addict, Abstinence and the Family." *American Journal of Psychiatry* 132:154–57.

Spinetta, J. J., and D. Rigler. 1972. "The Child Abusing Parent: A Psychological Review." *Psychological Bulletin* 77:296–304.

Stanton, M.D. 1977. "The Addict as Savior: Heroin, Death and the Family." *Family Process* 16 (2):191–99.

Steinglass, P. 1976. "Experimenting with Family Treatment Approaches to Alcoholism." *Family Process* 15:97–123.

Stigen, G. 1976. *Heartaches and Hanidcaps.* Palo Alto, Calif.: Science & Behavior Books.

Thurston, T. R. 1963. "Counseling the Parents of Mentally Retarded Children." *Training School Bulletin* 60:113–17.

Unger, R. A. 1978. "The Treatment of Adolescent Alcoholism." *Social Casework* 59 (1):27–35.

Warrior, B. 1976. Mimeographed pamphlet from National Organization of Women, Task Force on Wife Abuse.

Wortis, T. 1965. "Prevention of Mental Retardation." *American Journal of Orthopsychiatry* 35:886–95.

Zuk, G. H. 1962. "Cultural Dilemma and Spiritual Crisis of the Family with a Handicapped Child." *Exceptional Children* 28:405–08.

IV

Future Directions

This section deals with the professional concerns common to any helping profession. In chapter 9, rather than reviewing the abundant research that has been conducted to date, we focus on the major issues affecting contemporary research. These issues include methodology, validity, and research ethics. In this chapter we also cite some of the more significant research models for evaluating family treatment and explore criteria for use in evaluating future research.

In chapter 10 we discuss the issues of training, licensing, and professional ethics as they apply to the field of family therapy. It is our hope that our presentation of theory and practice will have made these topics more meaningful. We deal only with those issues pertaining to the specialty of family therapy, leaving the more general professional issues of the mental health field to other texts.

If we are to develop and further refine our conceptual understanding of family dynamics and appropriate intervention strategies, cooperation between researchers and practitioners is essential. The provision of effective preventive and curative services depends on that cooperation. As trainers and practitioners, we are deeply concerned with providing top quality services to our students and clients; we look to concerned researchers and practitioners to help us develop appropriate criteria for evaluation and further development of training and delivery programs.

Research in Family Therapy

Chapter 9

You will recall from chapter 2 that the field of family therapy emerged from research on communications in the early 1950s. Since then, the literature on the research and practice of family therapy has been steadily growing. It had its first major growth spurt in the 1960s and has expanded exponentially since the early 1970s.

There are several excellent reviews of the literature. For example, Riskin and Faunce (1972) provide a necessarily narrowed review that evaluates only quantifiable family interaction studies published since 1960. In it they cite 286 references and offer a comprehensive glossary that explicates, with references to the citations, 157 key terms in the literature. In a more recent study, Wells and Dezen (1978) survey research in family therapy from 1971 through 1976. This study points out the significant single-group and comparison research that has contributed substantially toward establishing family treatment as a legitimate therapeutic intervention.

As one reviews the literature, one finds diverse research interests. They include such topics as husband-wife dominance; family decision making; the family's contribution to the etiology of schizophrenia; conflict resolution; effects of maternal employment, divorce, single parenthood, and death on family systems; and comparison of specific experimental techniques.

It is obviously beyond the scope of this chapter to begin to undertake even a superficial review of the research literature. Rather, our intent here is to focus on methodological issues, validity and ethics, and suggestions and implications for future research. In doing so, we will offer some criteria for use in sorting among the tremendous output of excellent, mediocre, and weak studies now in the literature. We hope that these criteria will also serve to stimulate the interest of the beginning family therapy researcher.

We wish to underscore the imperative need for qualitative and quantitative research both on family system dynamics and on strategies and techniques of intervention. Without a solid integration of research, theory, and practice, the field of family therapy cannot grow and develop to its full potential.

Methodological Issues

Let us begin our discussion of methodological issues by looking at the very real difficulty of finding research subjects and engaging their cooperation. We will then examine strategies for obtaining valid and reliable data.

Finding Subjects and Engaging Cooperation

Whether in an apartment complex, a suburban home, or a rural farmhouse, effecting even a purely social interface with a family system is quite a challenge. Recall from chapter 5 Kantor's levels: family-unit space, interpersonal space, and personal space. In one's first contact with a family system, one usually experiences, to varying degrees, the family-unit space, an amalgam of how the family "really" is and how, in public, the family thinks it ought to be. The family researcher who has the disadvantage of the family's knowing that they are being studied, can expect no different amalgam on first contact. And even if the family members should present themselves as they "really are," remember that one must still ascertain whether they are presenting their family-unit, interpersonal, or personal selves.

Beyond this, the fundamental nature of the family stands in the way of research. To study fighting, one might appropriately observe the maneuvers of an army battalion, for it is actually designed as a fighting unit and is open to "inspection." The family, on the other hand, is designed for privacy and intimacy. While what it may *do* is fight, what it will *show* you may be quite something else. And, quite simply, although researchers can survey reports of child beating, it is very improbable that they would be able to schedule the observation of such beating, or that ethics would allow observation rather than intervention even if the family consented to "a showing."

A variety of methods must be employed in researching such sensitive family issues, and the careful research reviewer will note whether the study indicates the methods used and which methods have been employed. In a recent review, Gelles (1978) has cited some of the more common methods currently found in family research. Let us examine each of them to familiarize ourselves with their advantages and liabilities.

Sampling. Although inferring general population behavior from a "representative" sample is a quite acceptable procedure in the social sciences, the nature of many sensitive family issues is such t at the sample size needed to achieve usual statistical significance is prohibitively large and difficult to find. For example, Gelles points out that "if one were to attempt a study of the incidence of child abuse (assuming a base rate of .005) and wanted a confidence level of 95%, the needed sample size would be 76,448 people. At $40 per interview, the cost of the study would exceed three million dollars!" (Gelles 1978, p. 411).

The four kinds of sampling that Gelles discusses are: group sampling, snowball sampling, neighbor-informant sampling, and family-informant sampling.

1. *Group Sampling*: This type of sampling is applicable to specialized problems. For example, to survey child abuse, one might find families by contacting members of Parents Anonymous, and to survey problem drinkers one might contact Alcoholics Anonymous. The obvious advantage in contacting these groups of special populations is the high probability of finding subjects within the designated group.

The problem, however, is whether these people are representative of the child abuser or chronic drinker in general, and not just representative of child abusers or problem drinkers who join groups. Consequently, when the study reads, "The sample consisted of sixty-three chronic substance abusers . . .," the research reviewer must carefully scan to see whether group sampling was the method of initially contacting the subjects.

2. *Snowball Sampling*: This type of sampling proceeds just as its name implies. The researcher interviewing one homosexual father, for example, may learn that the subject knows other homosexual fathers, who, in turn, know others, and so the sample expands geometrically. When the family issues being researched mitigate against close social networks, or when social isolation is an underlying cause of the issue, snowballing obviously is diminished in effectiveness.

3. *Neighbor-Informant Sampling*: This method is valuable in family situations in which the probability of the family's self-report is low, such as in instances of deviant or illegal behavior. However, the neighbor usually has access only to surface dynamics. Furthermore, the neighbor can rarely provide the demographic data required for standard research procedures.

4. *Family-Informant Sampling*: Using this method, Straus (1974) studied family violence by interviewing college students about the interaction in their homes. Family-informant sampling has the advantage of providing a rich access to data without requiring actual intervention in the family system. On the other hand, family informants not only filter the family dynamics through their own subjective perspectives, but also may have been denied full access to the family experience under study, either because they were too young to comprehend the experience when it initially took place, or because other members of the system shielded them from topics that were considered taboo.

5. *Other Sources of Sampling*: Other possible sources for sampling are police records (and now, with CB radio, monitoring of police calls), newspapers (which publish police activities for the week, divorce settlement data, numbers of restraining orders, and so on), and private agencies. In using the private agency, the researcher would, as Gelles (1978) did, first let the agency know what type of family problem is being researched. If willing to cooperate, the agency would then search its files, contact appropriate subjects, in confidence, and determine whether they would be willing to participate, thus obviating the need for any initial contact and invasion of privacy by the researcher.

A final resource is the advertisement in the newspaper, professional journal, supermarket bulletin board, church newsletter, radio, television, or other media. Although the subjects obtained in this manner may be comparable to the subjects obtained through any of the other methods we have described, the representativeness of a sample found through advertising still may be questioned.

Obviously, one needs to consider the motivation of families who agree to participate in research. One must also consider the impact on the family system of the agreement to participate, as well as the impact of the way that that agreement is formulated. The issue of sampling seemed far less complicated back in the 1950s when the MRI group and Bowen, Lidz, and Wynne used hospitalized schizophrenic patients and their families as the sample.

Strategies for Obtaining Data

Once the subjects have been obtained, by whatever method, the researcher is then confronted with a plethora of techniques for obtaining data. Let us consider some of the major strategies that have been used in research studies of the past two decades.

Interviews.   Interviews that ultimately must deal with sensitive topics (for example, "Do you and your spouse engage in anal intercourse?" or "Have you ever molested your child?") may be extremely difficult. Gelles (1974) describes a "funneling technique," whereby the initial aspects of the interview focus on the family's neighbors and friends, and conflicts and problems in the neighbors' and friends' families, eventually moving closer to the sensitive topic. General questions about conflict are followed by questions about family fights, ultimately leading to a discussion of the family's own violent interactions.

Collaborative and conjoint interviews have been used in an attempt to counteract a deficiency in most interviewing research—that is, that the family data are reported by only one family member, or separately by different family members. What one family member considers child abuse, based on his own reluctance to employ corporal punishment, may be viewed by the spouse who administered the spanking as good, healthy discipline, based on her perception of the spankings she experienced as a child. Laslett and Rapoport (1975) found that by conducting repeated interviews with several family members and by using more than one interviewer, they increased the internal validity of the data. Trained family interviewers know how to elicit process data by focusing on the family interactions and metacom-munications, rather than focusing on the cognitive content of the communications.

The disadvantage of the collaborative or conjoint interview is inherent not so much in the process of the interview, but in the dy-namics of the family being interviewed. Gelles (1974) found that con-joint interviews used while studying intrafamilial violence frequently produced open conflict between the subjects during the interview as they disagreed about "correct" answers. This conflict, stimulated by the initial experience at the interview, may have spilled over to vio-lence at home.

Conflict Resolution Technique. An alternative to interviewing is Straus's "conflict resolution technique" (Straus 1974, 1976). This tech-nique structures a list of methods for resolving conflict that range, for example, from discussing an issue calmly to using a knife. This technique is similar to the therapeutic techniques that we described in section III, which give the family a problem to solve or a conflict to resolve at the outset of treatment as an assessment strategy. The advantage of this technique for obtaining data rests on the supposition that in progressing through the list of issues, the family subjects become increasingly desensitized to a previously taboo subject.

Observation. Direct observations, as we mentioned earlier, can be limited by the family's need for privacy and intimacy, as well as by an observer's lack of clarity about the level at which the interface is being made (Kantor and Lehr 1975). In other words, the process of observation can affect the data collection itself. Moreover, because the sample size in direct observation is frequently small, the validity of extending the data to families in general may be tenuous at best.

Focused observation (for example, an observation intended to examine a particular type of interaction in the home) may prove quite fruitful. Bossard (1966) and Gelles (1974) found that family meals tended to crystallize family dynamics and frequently produced conflicts, arguments, and other behaviors typical of the family system, which might not be present in the laboratory setting.

Laboratory Interaction. The laboratory setting, through the skillful choice of interactional tasks that are analogous to actual private family interaction, may provide quite reliable and valid data. The mid-1960s saw a flourish of creativity in the design of family interaction analogues. A notable example is Ravich, Deutsch, and Brown's (1966), train-racing game for couples. Riskin and Faunce (1972) describe many of these designs in their excellent review, as does Framo in the now classic *Family Interaction: A Dialogue between Family Researchers and Family Therapists* (1972). More recently, laboratory interactional tasks have been used to study a variety of family dynamics—for example, simulation and game playing to highlight power relationships, affect relationships, and specific communication styles.

Although experimental design may not always be appropriate for the study of sensitive issues, such techniques as the "simulated family," or SIMFAM, (Straus and Tallman 1970) do create laboratory-induced stress and crisis and enable the researcher to observe firsthand, albeit in a laboratory setting, the resolution of family conflict.

The methodological issues we have discussed here relate primarily to studies of family interaction and the testing of hypotheses about the etiology and sustaining dynamics of family dysfunction. However, they also apply to studies about family therapy intervention. Regardless of the method used to obtain data from the therapist and/or family members, the impact of the study on the process of therapy and the motivation of the therapist and client family to participate in the research can affect the results of the study.

Now let us take a look at the validity of the data collected and the research ethics involved.

Validity, Research Ethics, and Current Models

When all the subjects have been obtained and all the various studies have been completed, analyzed, and disseminated, questions remain. They include: "How do you know the family really behaves that way at home?" "How do you know they told the truth?" "How can you relate this game to real life, and how can you project from this small sample to the population at large?" In the case of a study of family therapy, questions would include: "How do you know he or she would do this if unobserved?" "What is a result of therapeutic intervention (technique or strategy) and what is a result of the therapist's charisma?"

Many researchers assume that families would not behave in dysfunctional, "inappropriate" ways during experiments if they did not normally do so at home. For example, family members would not admit to spouse abuse if that were not the case. However, with regard to the individuals who contend that they are not abusive, or the family who is "well behaved" at the experimental session, the question remains: "Is this how they really are at home, or are we sampling covertly deviant family systems?" Humphreys (1970) has suggested that covertly deviant family members will not only answer in socially desirable ways, but may also wear the "breastplate of righteousness" and adopt a "holier-than-thou" posture. One of us, in conducting our own research, observed that subjects who presented themselves as complete "teetotalers" had many of the interactional characteristics of chronic alcohol abusers (Rappaport 1976). Nevertheless, while a "holier-than-thou" attitude often *may be* a signal of covert deviance, let us not forget that there still exist people who actually *are* "holier than we."

Kinsey and his associates (Kinsey, Wardell, and Martin 1948) pioneered the "direct-approach interview" in an attempt to cut through the tendency on the part of subjects to respond in socially desirable ways. Kinsey researchers, to encourage honesty and present an accepting context for the subjects' behaviors, assumed the position that all types of sexual activity had in fact happened. Rather than asking, "Do you ever masturbate?", they asked, "When did you last masturbate?" This approach leaves the burden of denial with the subject.

Despite more than three decades having passed since the Kinsey technique was pioneered and the many studies that have been conducted in the meantime, validation studies of the actual techniques used in family research are still rare (Gelles 1978). To complicate the question of validity further, even if the methodological issues were completely resolved, the particular nature of family research creates special "validity issues."

Validity issues are of particular concern when the study is a longitudinal one or when it involves a large number of families. For example, when a research project is surveying seventy to one hundred families or undertaking a longitudinal study that may extend over a decade or two, the need to employ many staff members for major aspects of the research or part-time help for minor but exacting portions of the work (running experiments, typing transcripts, coding subject responses, and so on) may create certain problems. These problems might include "faked" observations; collaborations among coders to make results similar; interview schedules completed by the interviewers themselves; and a general lack of investment in the purity of the research on the part of "hired hands" (Roth 1966, p. 193). Also, there may be decreasing staff morale on extended projects which can endanger the reliability as well as the validity of the study. Although projects of shorter duration and smaller scope reduce the probability of these problems occurring, they at the same time sacrifice the comprehensiveness of data that permits generalization.

These issues of validity are also obviously ethical issues. Of course, one of the major ethical issues involved in any research with human beings pertains to the welfare of the research subject. When intervention is necessary, it must take precedence over observation. Family researchers must be certain to provide follow-up services for participating families in case of difficulties uncovered by the actual study. They must ensure that no lasting harm can result from their methods. The subject families must have the right to refuse or withdraw from participation. Most codes of ethics prescribe that the welfare of the subjects surpasses the intent of the research.

In addition, researchers must consider the issue of confidentiality and must respect their subjects' feelings about this matter. The purpose of the research and the proposed utilization of the results must be available to research subjects, and the researcher has the ethical responsibility to be honest and clear about his or her intentions. Recent litigation proves that ethical issues in research continue to be a major concern of the social sciences.

Keeping these criteria in mind, let us examine the research models used in recent studies on the outcomes of family therapy. These studies not only tend to legitimize family therapy as a therapeutic intervention, but also point to specific focuses for its application, especially with populations formerly considered "untreatable," or at best "unpromising."

Single-Group and Comparison Studies

Wells and Dezen (1978) cite three broad levels in the methodology of outcome research: (1) uncontrolled, single-group studies of the effects of family therapy intervention; (2) comparisons between family therapy as an intervention and no formal treatment; and (3) comparisons between family therapy as an intervention and an alternative treatment modality.

Obviously, in the first model, a study with no *control* cannot validate family therapy as the "treatment of choice." However, if such a study seems to indicate that there is a *relationship* between family therapy and a change in the treatment population, the effect is at least to recommend such a treatment for further research. For this reason, we will review several such studies here.

In the second model, the research attempts to determine whether family therapy produces any greater measurable positive change in the treatment population than the change occurring without any formal treatment. Although this research model may validate family therapy as a therapeutic intervention, it still does not indicate whether it is more or less effective than other therapeutic interventions. Nevertheless, studies based on this model have demonstrated the superiority of family therapy over no formal treatment and have thus established family therapy as a legitimate mode of helping. We will discuss several such studies.

Finally, several excellent studies have used the third methodological model, comparing family therapy with other treatment alternatives in an attempt to answer the question: "Which of treatments x and y produces the greater positive change in population z?" The answers to emerge from this model of research are the most important. As Wells and Dezen (1978) point out, with family therapy often a highly complex treatment to administer, "Why should a practitioner employ family therapy if a less complicated treatment is just as effective?" Let us now look at examples of each research model.

Uncontrolled Single-Group Studies.   The majority of uncontrolled single-group studies of family therapy intervention suffer either from inadequate outcome criteria or from contamination by simultaneous exposure of the treatment group to other interventions.

A number of these studies (Gartner et al. 1975; Golner 1971; Meeks and Kelly 1970; and Weakland et al. 1974) use the therapist's personal rating of improvement as the criterion of success. Although family therapists' ratings of the efficacy of their treatment in these studies do not differ substantially from the ratings of therapists using other methods (Wells and Dezen 1978), this can hardly be construed as a validation of the intervention.

An interesting series of studies (Liebman, Minuchin, and Baker 1974a, 1974b; Minuchin 1974; Minuchin et al. 1975; Rosman et al. 1976; and Minuchin 1978) has focused on psychosomatic reactions in children and adolescents. In citing success with anorexia nervosa and intractable asthma, the studies have seemed to validate Minuchin's "structural family therapy." Closer examination reveals that the structural family therapy was paired with learning theory and the specific application of behavior modification techniques. Wells and Dezen (1978) point out that although the behavioral component is fully described by Liebman, Minuchin, and Baker (1974b), it is hardly mentioned by Minuchin (1974), and it is even discounted by Rosman et al. (1976). Thus, these studies' apparent validation of structural family therapy might be more correctly viewed as a strong argument for "structural family *analysis*" as an aid to determining the most appropriate use of a combination of structural therapy and behavior modification techniques. This powerful treatment effect certainly merits further exploration.

Comparions between Family Therapy and No Formal Therapy. Perhaps one of the better series of studies to date is the one that has been conducted by Guerney and his associates (Guerney 1964; Guerney, Guerney, and Andronico 1966; Stover and Guerney 1967; Guerney and Stover 1971; Oxman 1972; and Guerney 1976). Evolving out of a filial therapy program, Parent-Adolescent Relationship Development (PARD) became a structured training program using the principles of multiple family therapy to develop and strengthen communication patterns within the parent-adolescent dyad.

Ginsberg (1971) found that PARD groups benefited from their treatment more than control groups in a preventive mental health program. Coufal (1975) and Vogelsong (1976) studied both PARD and general discussion groups to determine whether these groups would enhance the communication patterns in mother-daughter dyads more than no treatment whatsoever. They found that both interventions produced outcomes that were superior to the outcomes of the control group who received no treatment; in addition they found PARD's outcomes superior to those of the general discussion groups.

The major criticism of these studies is that the treatment population may not be typical of clinical populations since the subjects were usually recruited through the media. Guerney and Stover (1971) argue that the treatment group clearly represented a disturbed population. However, even if the gains were demonstrated with a "normal" population, they do validate the superiority of a family systems approach over no treatment whatsoever.

Comparisons between Family Therapy and Alternative Treatments. There are several methodologically adequate studies that compare family therapy with other treatments (Wells and Dezen 1978). Love, Kaswan, and Bugental (1972) compared the effects of individual child psychotherapy, parent counseling, and information feedback on children with social and behavioral problems. They found each one of the treatments effective in reducing problem behavior in school and in raising school grades. Parent counseling was the most effective of the three (Wells and Dezen 1978) in that it was equal to or better than the other two treatments on outcome measures; took less time; could be utilized by less "highly trained" personnel; and was effective with socioeconomically disadvantaged populations.

In looking beyond the statistical significance of the study, however, Wells and Dezen (1978) argue quite cogently that we must be careful not to equate statistical significance with practical significance. For example, the parent counseling did produce higher achievement and conduct scores for children than did individual therapy; however, a statistically significant difference between a "C" and a "C-minus" may have had little real value in those children's lives.

Stanton and his research group (Stanton and Todd 1976; Stanton 1977), utilizing Minuchin's structural family therapy model, appear to have demonstrated significant statistical success, as well as "real-world" success. Working with heroin addicts (a characteristically difficult treatment population) in a Veterans Administration outpatient center, they examined the outcomes of the standard drug counseling. They then compared those outcomes with the outcomes of (1) that same standard treatment combined with an attention placebo; (2) the standard treatment plus unpaid family therapy; and (3) the standard treatment plus paid family therapy. Outcome measures included percentage of drug-free urines, reduction of methadone usage, and return to school or part-time or full-time employment. A six-month follow-up found the standard treatment with unpaid family therapy more effective than both the standard treatment alone and the standard treatment with the attention placebo. Standard treatment with paid family therapy was superior to any of the other combinations. Researchers may argue that the extraordinary effort required on the part of the family therapists (a median of twenty-one pretreatment phone calls, interviews, or home visits) detracts from the results. However, clinicians in this field may counter this argument with the knowledge that "pretherapy" contact is indeed part of the treatment.

Suggestions for Future Family Research

Each of the studies that we have discussed illustrates one of the three research models currently appearing in the literature on family therapy. The future of family research may be less dependent on the development of new research models and may be better served by replications of important studies already in the literature. Certainly family research would be more enhanced by a search for new targets of study to which the current methodology could be applied than by a search for new methodology with which to approach the same targets.

As we enter the 1980s, we note that there are still very few replication studies in the family field. Researchers either move on to newer, more exciting challenges or conduct validation studies with minor, although significant, changes in the study design (Riskin and Faunce 1972). Therefore, many "landmark" studies remain landmarks not because they have been replicated and validated, but simply because they are "there." Thus, there is a need to replicate and revalidate some of the significant early research.

Among those few studies that have been replicated and validated, much of the focus is on pathology and family dysfunction. Studies in general have paid too little attention to the more holistic issues of general coping and functioning, to family growth and development, and to the most significant issue of how the family accomplishes its major function—that is, how it nurtures and educates its young so they are able to grow, leave, and have lives of their own. We need more data on the differences between functioning and nonfunctioning families, healthy and unhealthy family systems.

Another direction for future research concerns the interface between the family as a system and school systems, hospital systems, and systems of other social institutions. If, as Bowen suggests, the system attributes of family systems and larger social systems are similar, then we need to determine access interventions to improve the interfacing of these systems. How can the family system work more effectively with larger social systems to the benefit of all participating systems? A common problem is that of the school system blaming its difficulties with students on the family and the family system blaming its difficulties with youngsters on the school. Is there any validity in either of these claims, and how can we learn to recognize these systems problems and deal with them?

Another dimension for future research is in the relationship between family interaction and the biological and biochemical aspects of our lives. Although systems theory posits many cases of dysfunction in individuals as having their etiology within the communication patterns and structures of the family system, the fact remains that we are also biological beings. Are there biological factors, for example, that can account for some differences between family systems?

Obviously, we need much more research on different styles of family functioning, such as the effect of maternal employment on family systems, the effect of day care, and so on. These topics become popular, are researched for a time, and then are dropped in favor of a newer and more popular current social issue. Thus, we lack substantive research, which often leaves social policy undefined.

Research is also needed on the practice of family therapy. We need to know what interventions work best in what cases; whether or not co-therapy is more effective and, if so, when; what kinds of training result in more effective therapy; and so forth.

On a more idealistic level, family researchers need to experience each others' research directly. Clearly the logistics of finances and personal time involved in firsthand sampling of other studies are considerable. Gelles (1978) has pointed out "one cannot gain in a few hours of personal discussion a reasonable grasp of other researchers' work." Nevertheless, such "researching the researchers" is not only desirable for the cross-fertilization that it can produce, but also necessary. Reading about research in the hope of "knowing it" is no more realistic than reading about a family in the hope of really knowing them.

There needs to be an integration of theory, research, and practice. This is a problem that applies to the entire mental health profession. Does the researcher understand the practice of therapy, and does the therapist understand the research? If there is not collaboration or cross-fertilization between researchers and practitioners, the practitioner will find the research results useless. Particularly with family research, the ability of skilled practitioners in obtaining data and the expertise of trained researchers in designing studies and interpreting results can, in combination, be extremely fruitful.

Summary

In this chapter, we attempted to provide the reader with some general guidelines for considering the tremendous output of literature in the research and practice of family therapy. To do so, we focused on the methodological issues and difficulties of research, on validity and ethical issues, and finally on suggestions for future research.

We noted that the family's need for privacy and intimacy initially shield it from the scrutiny of the researcher. We explored techniques of sampling—group, snowball, neighbor-informant, and family-informant sampling—as well as the alternative method of obtaining subjects through advertisement. We reviewed strategies of securing actual data through interviews, observations, and structured experiments.

We explored some of the issues of validity and research ethics. These issues concern the intent of the researcher, the welfare of the client system, and the true meaning of the data collected. The system attributes of the family make research with families more complex and complicated than research that focuses on individual dynamics. Thus, if research on individual therapy is fraught with difficulties, research about family therapy is complicated exponentially.

We cited studies illustrative of different methodological models. These models include both single-group and comparison studies. This discussion led to the more general consideration of areas for future research. We particularly emphasized the need for collaboration between researchers and practitioners if research studies are to be improved and the results of research fully utilized.

To increase your familiarity with research issues and methodology, we refer you to the activities and reading lists in chapter 9 in the manual.

References

Bossard, J. 1966. *The Sociology of Child Development.* New York: Harper & Row.

Coufal, J. D. 1975. "Preventive-Therapeutic Programs for Mothers and Adolescent Daughters: Skills Training versus Discussion Methods." Ph.D. dissertation. Pennsylvania State University.

Framo, J., ed. 1972. *Family Interaction: A Dialogue Between Family Researchers and Family Therapists.* New York: Springer.

Gartner, R., et al. 1975. "A Retrospective Study of the Effects of Family Constellation on the Course of Family Therapy." Paper read at the Society for Psychotherapy Research, Boston.

Gelles, R. 1974. *The Violent Home: A Study of Physical Aggression between Husbands and Wives.* Beverly Hills, Calif.: Sage.

———. 1978. "Methods for Studying Sensitive Family Topics." *American Journal of Orthopsychiatry* 48 (3):408–24.

Ginsberg, B.G. 1971. "Parent-Adolescent Relationship Development: A Therapeutic and Preventative Mental Health Program." Ph.D. dissertation. Pennsylvania State University.

Golner, J.H. 1971. "Home Family Counseling." *Social Work* 16 (4):63–71.

Guerney, Jr., B.G. 1964. "Filial Therapy: Description and Rationale." *Journal of Consulting Psychology* 28:304–10.

Guerney, Jr., B.G., L. Guerney, and M. Andronico. 1966. "Filial Therapy." *Yale Scientific Magazine* 40:6–14.

Guerney, Jr., B.G., and L. Stover. 1971. "Final Report on Filial Therapy for Grant MH182–64–01." National Institute of Mental Health.

Guerney, L. 1976. "Filial Therapy Program." In D. Olson, ed., *Treating Relationships*. Lake Mills, Iowa: Graphic.

Humphreys, L. 1970. *Tearoom Trade: Impersonal Sex in Public Places*. Chicago: Aldine.

Kantor, D., and W. Lehr. 1975. *Inside the Family*. San Francisco: Jossey-Bass.

Kinsey, A., B. Wardell, and C. Martin. 1948. *Sexual Behavior in the Human Male*. Philadelphia: Saunders.

Laslett, B., and T. Rapoport. 1975. "Collaborative Interviewing and Interactive Research." *Journal of Marriage and the Family* 37:968–77.

Liebman, R., S. Minuchin, and L. Baker. 1974a. "An Integrated Treatment Program for Anorexia Nervosa." *American Journal of Psychiatry* 131:432–36.

———. 1974b. "The Use of Structural Family Therapy in the Treatment of Intractable Asthma." *American Journal of Psychiatry* 131:535–40.

Love, L.R., J. Kaswan, and D.E. Bugental. 1972. "Differential Effectiveness of Three Clinical Interventions for Different Socioeconomic Groupings." *Journal of Consulting & Clinical Psychology* 39:347–60.

Meeks, D., and C. Kelly. 1970. "Family Therapy with the Families of Recovering Alcoholics." *Quarterly Journal of Studies on Alcoholism* 31:399–413.

Minuchin, S. 1974. *Families and Family Therapy*. Cambridge, Mass.: Harvard University Press.

Minuchin, S., et al. 1975. "A Conceptual Model of Psychosomatic Illness in Children." Archives of General Psychiatry 32:1031–38.

Minuchin, S., L. Baker, and B. Rosman. 1978. *Psychosomatic Families: Anorexia Nervosa in Context*. Cambridge, Mass.: Harvard University Press.

Oxman, L.K. 1972. "The Effectiveness of Filial Therapy: A Controlled Study." *Dissertation Abstracts International* 32:6656.

Rappaport, Louis J. 1976. "Role and Context Interaction in Families of Alcoholics." Ph.D. dissertation. Boston College.

Ravich, R.A., M. Deutsch, and B. Brown. 1966. "An Experimental Study of Marital Discord and Decision Making." *Psychiatric Research Reports* 20: 91–94.

Riskin, J., and E. E. Faunce. 1972. "An Evaluative Review of Family Interaction Research." *Family Process* 11 (4):365–455.

Rosman, B., et al. 1976. "Impact and Outcome of Family Therapy in Anorexia Nervosa." Unpublished manuscript.

Roth, J. 1966. "Hired Hand Research." *American Sociologist* 1:190–96.

Stanton, M. D. 1977. "Some Outcome Results and Aspects of Structural Family Therapy with Drug Addicts." Paper read at the National Drug Abuse Conference, San Francisco (May 1977).

Stanton, M. D., and T. C. Todd. 1976. "Structural Family Therapy with Heroin Addicts: Some Outcome Data." Paper presented at the Society of Psychotherapy Research, San Diego (June 1976).

Straus, M. 1974. "Leveling, Civility and Violence in the Family." *Journal of Marriage and the Family* 34:13–30.

————. 1976. "Cultural and Social Organizational Influences on Violence between Family Members." In R. Prince and D. Barrier, eds., *Configurations: Biological and Cultural Factors in Sexuality and Family Life.* Lexington, Mass.: Heath.

Straus, M. A., and I. Tallman. 1970. "SIMFAM: A Technique for Observational Measurement and Experimental Study of Families." Unpublished manuscript.

Stover, L., and B.G. Guerney, Jr. 1967. "The Efficacy of Training Procedures for Mothers in Filial Therapy." *Psychotherapy: Theory, Research, Practice* 4:110–15.

Vogelsong, E.L. 1976. "Preventive-Therapeutic Programs for Mothers and Adolescent Daughters: A Follow-Up of Relationship Enhancement versus Discussion and Booster versus No-Booster Methods." *Dissertation Abstracts International* 36:7677a.

Weakland, J., et al. 1974. "Brief Therapy: Problem-Focused Resolution." *Family Process* 13:141–68.

Wells, R. A., and A. E. Dezen. 1978. "The Results of Family Therapy Revisited: The Nonbehavioral Methods." *Family Process* 17 (3).

Contemporary Professional Issues

Chapter 10

No presentation of theory and practice would be complete without discussion of current and emerging professional issues. Although we will limit our discussion to issues peculiar to the practice of family therapy, we do want to acknowledge that there are also important social issues to be considered. For example, society's attitudes toward housing, day care, welfare, abortion, euthanasia, divorce, and custody—all affect the functioning of families and the availability of services to families before, during, and after crises. For the purposes of this book, however, we will focus on the licensing, training, and ethics of family therapists and counselors.

As the practice of family therapy continues to expand, new questions and problems arise. Any young profession is vulnerable to demands that it "prove" itself, and the credentials of its practitioners are subject to comparison with those of other, established professionals. However, because of the rapid growth of family therapy practice and the wide diversity of practitioners in terms of their training and background, these demands and comparisons sometimes take on threatening proportions. The unfortunate result has been defensive claims that family therapy is a panacea for all ills and the only effective form of treatment in the area of mental health.

We want to reaffirm our contention that family therapy is a viewpoint and that regardless of the treatment unit, this viewpoint permeates different types and forms of therapy.

In chapter 9 we noted that to date there has been no substantive research that indicates that family therapy is any more efficacious than any other treatment modality. Remember that the entire mental health profession is still in the stage of "proving" itself and is still regarded with suspicion in many parts of the country. As one of the youngest and newest offshoots of the psychotherapy profession, family therapy has a long way to develop before it gains widespread acceptance and credibility.

Because professional training reflects the need to meet certain criteria for licensing, the issues of licensing and training are tightly interwoven. We will look first at the issues of licensing and accreditation and then at the concerns of training. Finally, we will explore ethical issues in family therapy and the emerging concerns of this new field.

Licensing

Until quite recently, the only mental health workers who were able to be licensed were medical doctors. You may wonder why nonmedical therapists have been so eager to obtain licensing. Briefly, licensing legitimizes a profession and provides certain benefits. Among those benefits are third-party payment for services, use of certain mental health institutions, legal protection of the right to practice, and favorable malpractice insurance premiums. While licensing makes therapists eligible for third-party payments, it also makes families eligible for family therapy by trained professionals. In the past, families could not afford therapy except with psychiatrists who were eligible for third-party payments. Many of these psychiatrists were not trained in family work. The point is that licensure means that more people can receive help from properly trained professionals.

Many nonmedical therapists feel that their clinical training is at least equal to that of medical therapists and that they ought to be able to practice the same therapy with the same clientele. It is important to note that any physician can call himself or herself a psychiatrist, that neither board certification nor an approved residency is required for use of this title. Of course, the ability to claim board certification is an asset since it implies certain rigorous training and residence achievements.

In recent years, psychologists and social workers have been receiving licensing in an increasing number of states. As a result, they have become as eligible for third-party payments as physicians. Because of increased costs and extended insurance coverage, counselors and school psychologists are working earnestly to obtain licensure so that they too can receive third-party payments and make their services available to more needy clients. In fact, licensing has become the single biggest professional issue among nonmedical mental health practitioners. One need only review professional journals and the proceedings of conferences and conventions to note the amount of time and energy devoted to this issue. The emotional dimension of the issue is legitimacy—who is a "real" therapist and who is not.

Thus, the major differentiation in licensing has been between medical and nonmedical mental health professionals. Those who have embraced the medical model have received the benefits of immediate licensing while those who have embraced the nonmedical model have had to struggle to earn the right to practice therapy. There is currently no way of evaluating whether one type of orientation and training is more effective therapeutically than another. Until such data is forthcoming, it is likely that the old rivalries and competitiveness will continue.

As a subspecialty of psychotherapy, family therapy presents two major licensing questions: (1) Should marriage and family therapists be eligible for third-party payments? (2) Should licensed psychologists and psychiatrists be allowed to practice marriage and family counseling *without* specialized training in these areas?

In response to the first question, we wonder how marital and family dysfunctions can be segregated from mental health dysfunctions. Perhaps we need to redefine normality and pathology so that we can gain a better understanding of the relationship between individual pathology and family dysfunction. If a therapist accepts family therapy as a viewpoint, then it stands to reason that he or she will include that viewpoint as part of any treatment package. We would like to point out that the state of Massachusetts does have a family therapy intervention code that provides for third-party payment for family therapy treatment if performed by a licensed psychologist. What we are arguing for is acceptance of the viewpoint that marital and family functioning are inextricably intertwined with one's mental health and that if mental health treatment is eligible for insurance reimbursement, any subspecialty within the field ought to be eligible for the same benefits.

The issue of whether or not a license to practice psychotherapy entitles one to practice any area or subspecialty of psychotherapy is indeed controversial. It relates to the whole professional licensing issue of continuing education and the updating of skills and conceptual knowledge. It is ludicrous to think that a general practitioner trained in the 1930s could practice intricate open heart surgery in the 1980s without further training. Likewise, a psychologist or psychiatrist who was licensed fifteen years ago would need to have some additional training and supervision in systems theory, sex therapy, and family dynamics in order to claim competence as a family therapist today.

Most professional codes of ethics forbid a practitioner from claiming expertise without appropriate training and credentials. To deal with rapidly changing knowledge and technology, many professional associations (such as the American Medical Association, the American Bar Association, the American Psychological Association, the American Nurse's Association, and the National Association of Social Workers) provide for continuing education training and credits. Many state legislatures are beginning to consider criteria for renewal of licenses that would require evidence of such continuing education and/or reexamination. These requirements are also aimed at practitioners who receive licensing under "grandfather" clauses in licensing bills and whose training may not be comparable to that of newer graduates. The Association of Counselor Educators and Supervisors (ACES, a division of the American Personnel and Guidance Association) is recommending that its accreditation and licensure program require ongoing professional development of counselor educators and supervisors (Hart 1978).

The issue of accountability is emerging as one of the most dynamic professional concerns today. As malpractice suits increase, insurance companies and state legislatures are forced to become more responsive to consumers' needs and demands for quality treatment. The professional associations are attempting to devise their own criteria for competence before state legislatures impose their politically designed plans. The established professional associations that we mentioned above have divisions that focus on marital and family issues. In addition, there are currently two national professional associations concerned with family and sex therapy. They are the American Association for Marriage and Family Therapy (AAMFT) and the American Association of Sex Educators, Counselors, and Therapists (AASECT). A third association, the American Family Therapy Association (AFTA), has recently been formed.

Professional Associations

Founded in 1942, the American Association for Marriage and Family Therapy (formerly known as AAMFC, the American Association of Marriage and Family Counselors) includes over sixty-five hundred psychologists, psychiatrists, social workers, ministers, physicians, sociologists, attorneys, and educators who have met certain professional standards (including both academic training and supervised professional experience) in the practice of marriage and family counseling. Most of the members are master's level professionals. Although AAMFT certification has no legal status, it is a credential that is recognized and respected within the mental health profession as denoting reputable standards of academic course work, clinical work, and approved supervision.

Early in 1978, the Department of Health, Education, and Welfare (HEW) granted AAMFT formal recognition as the national accrediting body for graduate and clinical training programs in marriage and family therapy. How this association proceeds in this area and what impact it will have on training programs are yet to be seen. Much will undoubtedly depend on its budgetary support and how successful it is in getting individual states to extend their licensing requirements, thus increasing third-party insurance coverage for marriage and family therapy services.

A continuing professional issue is whether marriage and family therapy is a field unto itself or a specialization of psychotherapy. It is noteworthy that the American Psychological Association and the National Association of Social Workers opposed HEW's recognition of AAMFT on the basis that marriage and family therapy is but a subspecialty of psychotherapy.

The American Association of Sex Educators, Counselors, and Therapists (AASECT) began a nationwide voluntary certification program in 1974. Like AAMFT's certification program, this program requires academic course work, approved supervision, and clinical experience. Whether specialized training in sex therapy should be in lieu of or in addition to training in psychotherapy and what the ethical and training standards of sex therapy should be are issues that this association is currently arguing. Membership is increasing as this relatively new professional association attempts to provide quality services and accountability to consumers.

The newest professional association to appear is the American Family Therapy Association (AFTA), under the leadership of Murray Bowen. Many see AFTA and AAMFT as competitive, rival groups, with the former oriented to systems theory and research and the latter more oriented to a psychodynamic approach to marriage and family therapy. AFTA, for example, believes that marriage counseling and family therapy are two separate areas in mental health care and that professionals certified as marital counselors are not necessarily equipped to handle family therapy casework. The next few years will allow us to see whether these differences are reconcilable.

Current State Legislation

As of this writing, there are six states who license family therapists. In California since 1 January 1978, to receive licensure or renew licensure as a physician, psychologist, social worker, or marriage, family, and child counselor, one has even been required to present evidence of training in human sexuality. Some other states are considering such licensure, and proposals are in various states of readiness. The problem could become thorny in that one must differentiate between so many kinds of mental health professionals that the differences can become arbitrary, and too many narrow specializations can occur. Even if we have different licensing regulations and different standards and criteria for family therapists, marriage counselors, sex counselors, school counselors, mental health counselors, social workers, psychologists, psychiatrists, and pastoral counselors, can we specifically say that their functions differ? How do they differ? Or do they practice the same type of therapy, coming to their practice via different training and philosophical routes? Who should go to whom for what? The proliferation of specializations could create a situation analogous to the one that now exists in the practice of medicine: one might have a specific complaint and waste valuable time trying to ascertain which type of specialist to consult! Likewise, training programs could become so bogged down in attempting to obtain various accreditations that they could end up with superficial packages of courses or too narrow a focus.

We cannot leave the discussion of licensure without mentioning the likelihood of national health insurance in the United States. Anxiety about which health professions will be eligible for reimbursement under a national health insurance system has resulted in intensified attempts to obtain state licensure. In other words, if reimbursement for mental health services becomes nationally available, it stands to reason that those practitioners who are now eligible under state licensure to receive reimbursement will have a decided advantage over those who are not. Hence, the intense lobbying in Washington and at the state level to settle these issues before the advent of national health insurance.

There is definitely a political aspect involved in the issue of licensure, both at the state and federal levels. Whom does licensure protect and how? Gross (1978) defies the notion that licensing protects service consumers against charlatans and incompetents. In fact, he claims that licensing maintains a structure that is in the self-interest of the service provider and in opposition to the public consumer. In other words, licensing does not improve accountability to the public and may, in fact, serve the purposes of a particular professional association over another professional association.

Training

Closely related to the standards for training and accreditation are questions about who provides the training and what type of training is the most effective for family therapy. If professional associations participate in setting the standards for licensing, they may also be obliged to set accreditation criteria and procedures for training programs. If the professional associations then attempt to provide the training themselves, they may find themselves engaged in a conflict of interest. Many professional associations solve this problem by accrediting established programs that fully meet the state licensing criteria.

There is a growing number of institutes throughout the country that offer training in family therapy to professional, paraprofessional, and lay mental health workers. Each institute has its own defined orientation, methods, and an ever-increasing array of techniques. The training models and treatment modalities differ from institute to institute. Because most of these institutes are not accredited, their quality varies. Some provide training that is obviously superior to that of the more traditionally recognized and established programs (such as university and hospital programs); some do not. Many offer innovative learning models that use both didactic and experiential opportunities to teach one how to do family therapy, how to teach family therapy, and how to consult with organizations about family therapy.

The piece of paper that one receives upon completion of such an institute program has no accreditation status and does not entitle one to licensure or any other professional recognition. In fact, a person with a doctorate in psychology and not one course in family therapy could more easily claim to be a family therapist than one who has a master's degree in a human service field and who has completed an institute training program in family therapy.

Some universities are beginning to design and implement graduate-level training programs in family therapy. AAMFT conducted a survey of 2,700 schools and colleges in 1977. Of the 1,700 respondents, 7 listed doctoral programs and 24 listed master's level programs in marriage and family therapy. Another 33 departments might fall into this category (*APA Monitor* December 1978). As higher education faces its own economic and attrition problems, some schools are attempting to cope by having neighboring family therapy institutes provide students with supervision and specialized training in conjunction with the regular academic program. As the demand for services increases, the demand for specialized training is increasing, and many universities that cannot afford to add permanent staff find that the use of adjunct staff in a particular specialty provides the necessary expertise. Evaluation of current training programs is still in the developmental stage, and it will be some time before accurate criteria can be refined for such evaluation.

Problems that arise in training programs include the selection and assessment of trainees, curriculum, and supervision.

Selection and Assessment of Trainees

Many of the family therapy training institutes are not affiliated with accredited institutions of learning and thus are not allowed to confer recognized academic degrees, which are, of course, required for certification or licensure. Without the necessary credentials, it is difficult for one to obtain a job today in any type of clinical setting, regardless of the type and extent of institute training. Therefore, many of the training institutes are having difficulty in recruiting the type of student they originally intended to train. And because economic factors are very real and tuition must be obtained in order to survive, many institutes find that they have to be "flexible" in their standards for admission to their programs. This kind of policy can result in the admission of anyone with the necessary tuition and in the subsequent dilution of training, as the training group becomes quite heterogeneous in terms of background, training, experience, and aptitude for training.

The training institutes are in an odd position. Most of them began centered around the work of one of the early pioneers of family therapy. With the passage of time and an increase in competition, their need for survival has become as important as their desire to offer top quality training. Therefore, many find themselves caught in a bind. Likewise, the consumer student is in a bind, wanting specialized training in family therapy and also wanting the credentials to gain an entry-level position in the practice of family therapy. It may be that the training institutes are best suited to those professionals already holding credentials, those who wish to continue their professional growth and education.

The Minuchin group in Philadelphia was the first to attempt the training of lay people. This program was in addition to the Minuchin group's regular training program for professionals with substantial backgrounds and experience. The training program for lay persons proved successful during the years that funding was easily obtained, but became more and more impractical as the market for lay mental health therapists began to shrink. However, this experience does have implications for the training of nurses and teachers and other human service professionals who do not have direct training and counseling. The implications are that some exposure to family therapy training can be of enormous help to these professionals in their understanding and treatment of the populations with whom they work. Thus, it would be an extremely valuable service if school systems and other human service institutions were to encourage their personnel to obtain this type of training as part of their continuing education.

The thorny issue that still remains is whether or not one can be an effective family therapist without training as a general psychotherapist. Does a student of family therapy need previous experience or academic training in counseling, clinical psychotherapy, or social work? Is the family systems perspective dependent upon knowledge of developmental theory and psychodynamic theory, or is it sufficient in and of itself? Remember that most of the family systems therapists today have had training and experience as general psychotherapists. It is too early to discern whether the new generation of trainees can provide effective family therapy with training only in systems theory and practice. There are so many legal, political, and educational implications in these loaded issues that we feel that the data are not sufficient to attempt to answer this question.

Assessment of trainees is another issue. In most training programs supervision is mandatory and includes assessment of the trainee on the basis of some kind of competency standards. All mental health professional training programs, whether sponsored by universities, hospitals, or institutes, have difficulty with the evaluation of trainees, with measuring how well they integrate theory and practice. This difficulty is due, in part, to the difference in what we actually do, how we perceive our behavior in therapy, and how we report it. It is possible, for example, for an individual to perform outstandingly well in either the experiential or cognitive learning mode but not in the other. Does this make for a competent family therapist? Do we know how to compensate for learning deficits by designing appropriate learning experiences? Is assessment continuous and on going or does it come at the end of the program, when it is really too late to correct deficiencies? More importantly, are our methods and process of assessment valid? It is hoped that these questions will be answered as more and more attention is devoted to the issue of training and assessment.

One of the issues that always arises in terms of selection and assessment of mental health trainees is that of the mental health and actual life experience of the trainee. Many family therapists believe that one of the important ingredients of training is to work through one's own issues with one's family of origin, so that one has not only the benefit of that experience, but also the opportunity to develop a personal theory of family. In addition, this process helps one to become more aware of how one's own family can influence one's practice of family therapy. Some trainees who enter the field for "personal therapy" can emerge into sensitive, competent helpers after working through their own issues. Others who are unable to resolve personal issues may need to remove themselves from training in order to gain a helpful perspective on their motivations and issues.

Another issue previously mentioned is that of the trainee's personal experience with marriage, parenthood, and, of course, sexuality. Certainly, in selecting trainees, one must also consider their attitudes and values, regardless of what their life experiences may be. However, aside from some basic and subjective criteria, such as "flexibility," "sensitivity," an "open-mindedness," we really do not know what the appropriate criteria are.

As you can see, there are no concrete answers to these issues of selection and assessment. Scores, grades, and other concrete data appear to be quite arbitrary. Intensive interviewing and personal assessment do not necessarily result in better selection. Perhaps the answer is to create options by being flexible in admissions and by providing competency assessment along the route of training. In this way administrators and supervisors might be able to make appropriate decisions about accelerating or slowing the rate of training and about encouraging students to remain in training or to change their career paths. However, this process could be hampered if the program depended economically upon retaining a certain number of trainees.

Curriculum

Although most training programs claim to offer experiential and didactic learning modes, there seems to be some imbalance and inconsistency among the curricula of existing training programs. Some are strictly didactic and some strictly experiential. Perhaps this is due to the inconsistencies between the theories that we use and the theories that we espouse.

Some programs focus more on skills and techniques than on underlying theoretical knowledge. Certainly it seems that we need some comprehensive theory building and conceptualization to deal with the existing theoretical inconsistencies and divergent theories about human behavior and how these relate to family process. In addition to basic theory dealing with family systems, personality, developmental, and learning theory can help us understand individual human behavior within the family system. Again, we refer to the need to redefine normality and pathology, to move away from the traditional medical model of illness, and to focus on family strengths and the nonpathological process in families.

Another curricular issue concerns therapeutic methods and diagnosis. It has been suggested that today's family therapy is too pragmatic and problem-oriented, and not enough concerned with scientific methodology. Some professionals have raised the possibility that training in individual therapy is an important prerequisite for family therapy. Others refute this by saying that one has too much to unlearn if one is first trained in individual theory and practice. We need research to answer these questions, some of which we hope will be answered in the near future.

The issue of dogmatism versus eclecticism is another curricular issue. If a therapist is trained in just one treatment modality, he or she may not be able to change or modify the treatment approach and strategies appropriately. Commitment to just one treatment modality may result in an attempt to fit all clients into that one framework, which will undoubtedly be insufficient to accommodate them all. If family therapy is seen as a philosophical viewpoint, then the treatment approaches and strategies can be flexible and eclectic.

Another criticism of the curricula of current training programs is that they pay inadequate attention to ethnic, subcultural, economic, and social issues. If one views working with families as preventive and educational as well as curative, sensitivity to and understanding of these variables are imperative. Heterogeneous training groups consisting of members of diverse ethnic and socioeconomic groups can probably do as much to further cross-cultural understanding as a formal course. However, we must also consider the theories and material available to us from such fields as anthropology and sociology.

Thus, it seems to us that the ideal curriculum would include instruction in family systems theory; child, adolescent, and adult development; personality development; learning (including the psychology of the exceptional child and learning disabilities); psychopathology, psychophysiology; treatment strategies and techniques, including the indications and counterindications for family therapy, as well as transference effects and other side effects of family therapy, sex therapy, and divorce therapy; and philosophical, social, and ethical concerns, including school issues and community resources.

We recognize how difficult it is to design a program that includes all the courses that the practitioner might possibly need. As those of us involved with the training of mental health professionals well know, designing the ideal program can become a futile task as there are just so many hours and so many units of training that can be accommodated in any one program. Therefore, one needs to cut here and there, always reassessing and revising. Our viewpoint is that the family therapist is the "general practitioner" of mental health and must have a broad base of knowledge and skills in order to meet the family's needs, including its needs for educational and preventive services, as well as its needs in time of crisis. We envision the family therapist as serving a consultative role whenever necessary throughout the family life cycle; there may be long periods without contact, but follow-up and check-up sessions should be always available.

Supervision

The issue of providing quality supervision to mental health professionals becomes intensified when the professionals involved are working with families. Traditional methods of discussing process notes and listening to audiotapes do not suffice for supervision of family therapy. As we noted earlier, much is missed when we depend on one family member's account of what is happening within the family system; just as much is missed when the conventional format of discussing the supervisee's report of a session is the only modality of supervision. Some of the most innovative strategies of supervision have emerged as the result of attempts to find effective ways of supervising family therapy trainees. Among these are the use of co-therapists, videotape, and the "bug-in-the-ear," which allows the supervisor to become an active consultant and participant. Naturally, supervisory relationships will be affected by the nature of family therapy and its special needs.

The use of *co-therapists* in family therapy stems from a strategy of marriage counseling in which the co-therapists model appropriate couple and sex-role behaviors. Co-therapy by supervisor and supervisee has proved very effective as a form of supervision. It allows the supervisee the latitude to take risks and to see the supervisor practice what he or she preaches. In addition, it enables the supervisor to have immediate feedback. Many family and sex therapists view co-therapy itself as an unnecessary luxury or as a cop-out from taking control of the therapeutic situation, but few would eliminate it as a supervisory strategy. There are, needless to say, pitfalls involved in co-therapy if there is not a trusting, healthy relationship between the two therapists and if they are not both equally committed to processing and working through their own relationship difficulties as they arise.

Videotape provides an accurate feedback of the counseling process, illuminating both verbal and nonverbal interactions. It allows the supervisor and trainee to process the session thoroughly and at leisure. One can always run through a segment again or stop the videotape to concentrate on particular segments. Reviewing the videotape allows the supervisor and trainee to integrate the actual process with the theoretical conceptualization of what is going on. The trainee receives objective feedback that, although painful at times, leaves no doubt as to its accuracy. Many therapists who have been trained by videotape use it as a therapeutic technique, insisting that the family watch themselves to learn about their interactional processes.

The use of the *bug-in-the-ear* is a technique whereby the trainee is connected to the supervisor by microphone and the supervisor, observing the therapy session through a one-way mirror, intercepts with suggestions and criticisms. A variation of this occurs when the supervisor enters the therapy session or calls the trainee out of the room to receive instruction. The problem with this method of training is that it can communicate to clients some disturbing messages about the therapist's capabilities and methods. Thus, although the bug-in-the-ear may provide good training for the supervisee, it may not always provide the best therapy for the client family. In addition, negative inputs during a session may interfere in the therapy by creating doubts in the trainees themselves about their own abilities.

The supervisee's personal development as a therapist is a major concern in the supervisory process. It is thus impossible to separate arbitrarily the supervisee's personal and professional lives. The supervisor usually attempts to point out inconsistencies between the supervisee's espoused theory and theory of use. Most supervisors find that their processing of the supervisory relationship is a useful and important part of the supervisory relationship. In this way, issues of independence and dependence, submission and dominance, distance and intimacy can be recognized and worked through.

For modeling to be effective and for effective processing to occur, an open, trusting relationship between supervisor and supervisee is obviously necessary. Although supervisors are certainly not personal therapists for trainees, an important supervisory task is helping trainees recognize and cope with their own families' influences on their perceptions and practice of therapy.

Ethics

We do not intend to recapitulate the customary ethical issues affecting the practice of therapy and counseling. Not that they are not important, but for that discussion we refer you to the many excellent texts on the practice and theory of counseling and psychotherapy (Combs, Avila, and Purkey 1978; Hansen, Stevic, and Warner 1977; Egan 1975; Okun 1976). Our focus here will be on the new ethical issues that the practice of family therapy has presented. These are chiefly issues of values, confidentiality within a system, advocacy, and manipulation.

Values

Obviously, the therapist's personal motivation, attitudes, and values will affect the way in which he or she conducts therapy and teaches skills. These factors will also determine the behaviors that the therapist models and reinforces. In family therapy, the therapist's attitudes toward marriage, sex, parenting, divorce, and other family issues can raise or lower the expectations of clients and can result in increased satisfaction or dissatisfaction.

The reason it is so important for family therapists to be aware of their own values is so that they can identify their biases as biases and not as dicta for others. There is no way that individual preferences and values cannot influence, to a degree, the family models deemed most appropriate. They determine the questions asked, the answers perceived, and the strategies selected for treatment. However, with experience and training, the therapist can learn to recognize and acknowledge his or her own values and biases and work to ensure that they do not contaminate therapy.

Whether or not family therapists openly acknowledge their own values and biases to clients depends upon the circumstances. There are times when family therapists feel a need not to work with families, such as when they are experiencing crisis within their own family systems. For example, family therapists who have just lost a spouse or child may find it difficult to work effectively with intact families until after they have worked through their own grief. A frequent guideline is that when one's own pain or value system is interfering with the therapy, that fact must be acknowledged. The point is that discussion of the therapist's values and biases can be helpful when presented for the clients' needs, not for the therapist's.

Indications that the therapist's own issues are operating are: (1) overidentification with a particular family member; and (2) failure to appreciate, understand, and empathize with individuals in a particular family role. In these instances, the family therapist needs to focus on his or her involvement with the family. A co-therapist, colleague, or supervisor can be helpful in this process.

Since there is no such thing as value-free therapy, it is important for training programs to allow time for consciousness raising, clarification of values, and open discussion of how values can affect therapy. Family therapists can then become educators for client families, helping them to clarify their values and to choose what they consider to be .ethical mores.

Confidentiality

If the family therapist is to maintain an effective therapeutic relationship with the family system, he or she must be sensitive to the individual needs of family members vis-à-vis the family system needs. Sometimes, for example, one family member will request an individual session and ask that certain information not be revealed to other members of the family. If the therapist feels that he or she has a contract of complete openness with the system, the therapist must inform that individual that the confidence cannot be maintained and that the individual would be better off keeping the material confidential until he or she is willing to share it with other family members.

It is important that the therapist have a clear ethical code established before getting into a tight spot. In other words, the therapist has to be on guard against becoming triangulated into an issue of confidentiality. For example, a woman recently consulted one of us about her husband's sudden and abrupt desire to end their marriage. He had left their home, refusing to discuss the matter or to explain his feelings. The husband agreed to therapy if he could first have an individual session. During this individual session, it came out that he was having a clandestine affair and did not want to tell his wife that the affair was the reason for his sudden request for a divorce. Being unable to reveal the confidence, the therapist urged the client to tell his wife what was going on so that she could understand what precipitated his abrupt departure from their home. There were several conjoint sessions during which the husband was obviously waiting to see if the therapist would let this knowledge slip, while the wife pleaded with her husband for the reasons behind his leaving. Although the therapist indeed felt frustrated, there was nothing to do but wait it out until the husband felt enough trust in the therapeutic process to begin leveling with his wife. It was then that the two of them could get down to the business of understanding and working through their difficulties.

Another issue of confidentiality involves record keeping. Many family therapists use audiotapes and videotapes. Obviously, if these tapes are going to be used as teaching or conference presentations, the therapist needs to obtain a release from the client family. What happens if some of the family members agree and some do not? Do the adults have the final say? How is this determined? The increased possibility of litigation and the legal right of patients to examine their own case records can create dilemmas in the area of record keeping.

When divorce and custody disagreements occur, the therapist may find himself or herself in a peculiar position. Sometimes the therapist has knowledge that could affect the custody decision. To whom is the therapist responsible—the children, the parents, or the parent who initiated treatment? There are other times when the therapist is in a quandry, having knowledge of physical or emotional abuse within family systems. Again, at what point does the therapist break confidentiality in order to provide protection to a particularly vulnerable member of the system? These issues lead us into our next ethical issue, that of advocacy.

Advocacy

If there is a custody fight, who is the therapist's client? Does the therapist have the right to act for the child? If information obtained in a family therapy session before divorce or custody issues became paramount might influence the custody decision, what is the appropriate role for the therapist? There are no clear-cut answers to these questions, other than the desire of most family workers to help create a constructive climate for negotiation and to keep in mind the welfare of all the family members. It has been our experience that in cases of bitter disagreement, we can serve a useful function by becoming advocates for the children within the framework of therapy sessions. We can appeal to the parents' better instincts and help them see the need to protect their children. Whether or not therapists can serve such a function in cases in which they are required to appear in court depends on the local judiciary process. If called upon to testify, most therapists do not have the right to privileged information and may well have to testify. Some states do grant licensed psychologists the right to privileged information, but these laws are not uniformly applied.

Other family system issues require that the family therapist take an advocacy position *within* the family system. Sometimes the goal of maximizing growth of family members means that certain members will gain more than others. For example, to insure that each family member realizes his or her inherent potential, the therapist may choose to support a move for a particular individual, thereby incurring the discomfort of another family member. The skilled systems therapist knows how to assume an advocacy position within the system and simultaneously apply strategies that provide relief, rather than heightened tension, for the rest of the system.

In other forms of advocacy, family therapists must contend with societal institutions, such as welfare departments, schools, and medical and legal services. Family therapists must determine when they will step in to obtain legal protection for abused children or spouses, when they will help families find adequate housing and foster placements, and when they will help families cut through the bureaucratic red tape of obtaining necessary services.

In short, family therapists must determine what types of system interventions they are willing to practice as change agents. These interventions may involve actively seeking legislation and funds for day care, foster placement, relevant educational placement, and so forth. This type of intervention requires far more involvement and energy than the traditional medical model of therapy.

Manipulation

When we refer to *manipulation*, we must consider whether the ends of treatment justify the means. For example, is a family therapist justified in giving people paradoxical, intentionally distorted instructions in the hope that these instructions will help in the long run? Is it ethical to encourage people to fight, to prescribe the symptom? Are the gimmicks and tricks that some family therapists teach, use, and prescribe ethical? Hines and Hare-Mustin (1978) suggest that the family therapist cannot assume that all members of the family will benefit from the disruption caused by the direct expression of anger. In addition, it may violate an individual's right *not* to be treated when a family therapist insists that all family members attend the sessions. Client welfare can become confusing in family therapy. How does an individual's welfare conflict with the system's welfare? Is this clarified at the outset of therapy? We are suggesting that the family therapist has the ethical responsibility to explain the nature and limits of family therapy to the family members at the beginning of treatment and to clarify any misunderstanding clients may have regarding the role of the therapist.

Other questions of ethics concern the responsibility of teachers and supervisors to trainees as opposed to their responsibility to client families. How ethical is it to use real families to train family therapists? What kind of back-up services do we provide, and what type of accountability is insured? In other words, which has top priority—the training of the family therapist or the welfare of the client family?

Another ethical issue involves the use of client families at conventions and conferences for demonstrations. The therapist who presents the case sees the family once, in a public demonstration. Should issues emerge from this session, the therapist is no longer there to deal with them. Often, the person presenting is so anxious to "do his stuff" that the demonstration assumes greater priority than the welfare of the client family. Is merely consulting with the family or ensuring that they are in regular therapy sufficient?

In the area of sex therapy, more specific ethical issues arise. Is it ethical to conduct sexological examinations? What about the use of surrogate partners? What about the issue of sex between therapist and client? What is the ethical and professional responsibility of a therapist if a new client reveals sexual relations with a previous therapist?

These are the kinds of issues that have emerged with the practice of family therapy. Existing professional codes of ethics may provide some guidelines, but we need to develop specific guidelines relevant to family systems. Systems ethics differ from individual ethics, and these differences need to be explored and further defined.

Emerging Concerns

As family therapy becomes more of a recognized specialty, the issues that we have just discussed are likely to assume even greater proportions. The concerns that we believe require future study involve the varieties of family systems we see increasing today. By this, we mean reconstituted families, homosexual families, families with prolonged terminal patients. How the theory and strategies developed to date apply to these variations is really unknown. What particular types of knowledge and training may be required is equally unknown.

In addition, as medical technology continues to prolong life, we will have to consider intergenerational family systems, regardless of geographical distances between generations. This issue will undoubtedly be affected by the growing tendency of two-career families to postpone having children until parents are well into their thirties.

We cannot predict how federal and state governments will intervene in family life. There has been much talk in Washington about providing support for nuclear families, the mainstay of American life. What types of programs and ideology might emerge from this talk remains to be seen.

In any case, we hope that the development of theory and practice will take these important issues into consideration and that the next decade will see a ripening and maturity of the field of family therapy.

Summary

In this chapter, we considered significant professional issues that affect family therapists. In particular, we discussed matters of licensing, training, and ethics. These three categories are intertwined: the standards for licensing are reflected in training programs, and ethical issues involve training, as well as practice and research.

We discussed the benefits of licensing for nonmedical therapists, emphasizing the need for broader delivery of services to needy families. We then focused on the issues of accountability and continuing education, citing the roles of existing professional associations.

With regard to training, we pointed out some of the common problems facing the institutes, universities, and hospitals that train family therapists. We focused on selection and assessment of trainees and the issues that plague curriculum design and implementation. Of particular concern is the need to find a moderately reasonable way of integrating didactic and experiential learning, theoretical and process knowledge. We suggested that an ideal training model blends didactic and experiential learning and includes instruction in family systems theory, developmental theory, treatment strategies and approaches, and philosophical, social, and ethical issues. We returned to the issue of the personal and professional requisites of the family therapist and pointed out the complexities of supervising family therapy trainees vis-à-vis individual therapy trainees. We mentioned specific innovative supervisory tactics and emphasized the need for an open, trusting relationship between supervisor and supervisee.

The ethical issues that we emphasized are of special concern in the practice of family therapy. Confidentiality takes on new dimensions when dealing with family systems and can provide moral dilemmas for the therapist. Confidentiality led us to the issue of advocacy. The therapist, privy to much primary data, must decide whether or not to intervene actively with outside systems and issues affecting the client family. We also dealt with the issue of manipulation as a training and therapeutic matter and posed questions about the ethics of some current practices.

In the exercises in chapter 10 in the manual, you will confront some ethical and legal issues that you may well encounter in your family therapy practice. That chapter, which includes lists of family therapy training institutes and academic programs, is also designed to acquaint you with matters pertaining to training and licensure.

We obviously raised many more questions in this chapter than we answered. While we do not have definitive answers, we do endorse an advocacy position for family therapists and urge all those committed to this field to consider active involvement as change agents as part of their professional identities.

References

APA Monitor. December 1978.

Combs, A.W., D.L. Avila, and W.W. Purkey. 1978. *Helping Relationships*, 2nd ed. Boston: Allyn & Bacon.

Egan, G. 1975. *The Skilled Helper*. Monterey, Calif.: Brooks/Cole.

Gross, S. J. 1978. "The Myth of Professional Licensing." *American Psychologist* 33 (11):1009–17.

Hansen, J.C., R.R. Stevic, and R.W. Warner. 1977. *Counseling Theory and Process*, 2nd ed. Boston: Allyn & Bacon.

Hart, G. 1978. "Continuing Professional Development: Outlook for Counselor Educators and Supervisors." *Counselor Education and Supervision* 18 (2):116–26.

Hines, P.M., and R.T. Hare-Mustin. 1978. "Ethical Concerns in Family Therapy." *Professional Psychology* 9:165–71.

Okun, B.F. 1976. *Effective Helping*. North Scituate, Mass.: Duxbury Press.

Index